Fahrenheit	Celsius
Zone 1	below -50°	below -46°
Zone 2	-50° to -40°	-46° to -40°
Zone 3	-40° to -30°	-40° to -34°
Zone 4	-30° to -20°	-34° to -29°
Zone 5	-20° to -10°	-29° to -23°
Zone 6	-10° to 0°	-23° to -18°
Zone 7	0° to 10°	-18° to -12°
Zone 8	10° to 20°	-12° to -7°
Zone 9	20° to 30°	-7° to -1°
Zone 10	30° to 40°	-1° to 4°
Zone 11	above 40°	above 4°

Hardiness Across America

Zones in the United States are based on average minimum temperatures, with Zone 11 rated warmest, and Zone 1 coldest. Plants in this book are rated according to the coldest temperatures they survive. Summer heat and humidity, and lack of winter chilling in warmer climates, may limit the ability of some plants to thrive. Because of this, and the fact that within each Zone are micro-climates that can be colder or warmer, we suggest that you use the Zones as a guide—but feel free to experiment with plants rated marginally hardy.

Organic
GARDENING
FOR THE 21st CENTURY

Organic
GARDENING
FOR THE 21st CENTURY

JOHN FEDOR

Consultant: Bob Sherman of the HDRA

Photography by Steven Wooster

The Reader's Digest Association, Inc.
Pleasantville, New York/Montreal

A READER'S DIGEST BOOK
ORGANIC GARDENING FOR
THE 21ST CENTURY

DEDICATION
For David and my mother,
who are always there when I need them,
and for Babcia,
who inspired me to garden.

© Frances Lincoln Ltd 2001
Text © John Fedor 2001
Photography © Steven Wooster
Illustrations Sarah John and
Kate Simunek © Frances Lincoln Ltd 2001

Designed and edited by **PAGE***One*,
for Frances Lincoln Ltd
Printed in Hong Kong

READER'S DIGEST PROJECT STAFF
Editorial Director Fred DuBose
Senior Design Director Elizabeth L. Tunnicliffe
Editorial Manager Christine R. Guido
Consultant Fiona Gilsenan

READER'S DIGEST
ILLUSTRATED REFERENCE BOOKS
Editor-in-Chief Christopher Cavanaugh
Art Director Joan Mazzeo
Director, Trade Publishing Christopher T. Reggio
Editorial Director, Trade Susan Randol

Library of Congress Cataloging in Publication Data
Fedor, John.
Organic gardening for the 21st century / John Fedor;
consultant, Bob Sherman of HDRA; photography by
Steven Wooster.
p. cm.
ISBN 0-7621-0296-9
1. Organic gardening. I. Title: Organic gardening for
the twenty-first century. II. Reader's Digest Association.
III. Title.

SB453.5 .F43 2001
635'.0484—dc21

00-062692

CONTENTS

INTRODUCTION
A PERSONAL VIEW

When I was a very young child and learning to garden at my grandparents' home, I had no idea what the term "organic gardening" meant. It was not a term my grandparents used, but it was how they gardened. And the way I garden now was passed down to me from them, who learned it from their parents. They reared a large family during difficult economic times and gardened primarily to put food on the table. On their plot (see plan, p. 108) they produced all the food a family of nine needed.

The techniques they used were rather simple, virtually the same as those used for hundreds of years. They turned the soil by hand (and occasionally had a nearby farmer plow their vegetable plots), made compost and incorporated it along with manure into the garden. I sometimes helped with the weeding and often picked produce right off the plant to eat immediately. When picking blackberries, I had a rule: for every two in the mouth – one in the basket. And I was often given the chore of taking the bowl of kitchen scraps out to dump in the "gnuj" box, or compost bin.

Their composting method was a simple two-bin cool-pile system (see pp. 44–5). Kitchen scraps and garden debris were added to one box, while the other contained compost ready for use in the garden. They alternated which bin refuse was added to yearly. Red worms loved living in these bins and often my grandfather would collect some to use when taking us children fishing. My grandparents generated almost no trash or refuse to be hauled away. Practically everything was recycled. Garden debris, leaves, and kitchen scraps were composted. Papers, cardboard, and useless wood were converted into heat in the wood stove (paper recycling did not exist then). They rarely bought things that came in plastic packaging or in cans. And glass bottles for milk were returned to the dairy. Canning jars were reused over and over again to preserve the harvest in the fall.

One of the most notable things about the way my grandparents gardened was that it was not a great chore, but simply a part of daily life, like so many people today go to the store for produce. The perfectly natural thing to do was to take a stroll outside before supper to pull some weeds and collect a basket of vegetables for the meal. My grandmother would also throw the poultry some grain and collect some eggs for the next morning's breakfast. Putting up produce for the winter was a pleasant part of many fall evenings.

Colorful harvest
Nothing looks or tastes as good as your own home-grown organic produce harvested freshly for the kitchen table.

When I went away for college, I had my first garden of my own. I lived in a city and did not know where to get manure to work into my newly dug bed. I remember stopping at a nursery to ask for well-rotted manure. They laughed at me! They had no idea where to get it either and brought me over to their bags of chemically enhanced soils. I had never seen or heard of such things before and the smell of the chemicals was overwhelming. They expounded the benefits of their products, but somehow it was the odor that kept me from buying them. It just seemed wrong to add something so toxic smelling to the area that I would use to grow vegetables to eat. It really made me start to think about how food is grown, the environment, and health and nutrition.

Since that time, I have experimented with different techniques. I have used inorganic fertilizers on a bed to see if they made a difference. And I have tried a weekly watering program with a liquid inorganic feed. The results showed me that inorganic fertilizers do not produce a greater harvest than organic methods. And I even found that occasionally plants were more susceptible to pests. (Studies now show that excessive nitrogen causes an imbalance that can encourage pests.) The claims about inorganic fertilizers seemed to be false, and fertile organic beds produced an equally abundant crop.

I have also learned that organically grown vegetables consistently test higher in vitamins and minerals than those grown with inorganic fertilizers.

Labor of love
Organic gardening embraces the gardener's deep love for plants and the process of growing, and combines it with a profound respect for the environment.

Health and good nutrition are so very important. I decided that when writing this book, it would be essential to make nutrition a central concept. As you read through the chapters, you will find information on eating well, on health-promoting produce, and on the nutritional value of specific fruits and vegetables, particularly in terms of vitamins, minerals, and beneficial phytochemicals.

As an environmentalist, I am keenly aware of the many sources of pollution that are in our environment. I hope that what I have written about preserving fresh water, and my comments on genetically modified seeds, and environmental damage will be taken to heart. And I hope that you will leave that little plot of land entrusted to you, your garden, in a little better shape than you found it. I hope it will be not only more fertile, but also a place where there is a greater diversity of wildlife.

Human beings are using the Earth's resources at an alarming and unsustainable rate. Because of this, I am experimenting with sustainable technologies on our farm in the hopes of promoting a way for humans to live comfortably without depleting the resources that future generations will need. Growing one's own food organically is an important step in that direction. Though we have only been here at the

Health-giving produce
Asparagus, along with several other vegetables, fruits, and nuts, are high in disease-fighting phytochemicals. Eating fresh, home-grown, nutritious produce is good for your health.

farm (see plan, p. 111) for a short time, many projects in sustainable living have already begun. When renovating the home, we have chosen almost exclusively local materials that have been harvested sustainably. Avoiding toxic finishes and materials is a given. And renewable energy is in the planning stages in the form of micro-, hydro-, and solar-electric generation. Livestock are being raised organically both for their meat and for their manure. And of course there is an organic garden to provide wonderful fresh produce for the table.

I hope you will take one small step by growing your food organically. May you have a bountiful and beautiful garden.

JOHN FEDOR

CHAPTER 1

GARDENING ORGANICALLY

WHY GARDEN ORGANICALLY?

As more people are now discovering, gardening is a fun pastime that takes us away from our hectic duties. With growing concern about manmade chemicals in what we eat, gardening organically offers us the opportunity to produce tasty food that is good for us and for the environment.

GOOD FOOD FOR GOOD HEALTH

Our personal health and diet have assumed growing importance in recent times. Awareness and consideration of the relationship between our health and the food we eat is receiving more attention every day. News stories report that some vegetables have cancer-fighting properties; government campaigns urge us to eat more vegetables and fruits, and to reduce the amount of fat and sugar in our diets.

The welfare of the environment is also a key issue in the 21st century, and has become a common topic in political debates. The effects of global warming are evident in our changed weather patterns. Many of us are concerned about reports of toxic environmental pollutants being spilled or leaked into our rivers and drinking water, especially when these incidents happen uncomfortably close to our homes. The apparent disregard for the environment is putting our health at risk.

WORKING AGAINST NATURE

Most commercial agricultural practices work against nature, which produces some undesirable results: topsoil is lost or is of lower quality; land becomes less fertile; and the excessive use of pesticides results in resistant insects. The natural predators of these pests are often greatly reduced in number by the pesticides, which in turn creates more pests and the need for even stronger pesticides to be produced. The problem has been aggravated by the introduction of non-native pests, for which there are no local predators. As the population of the world grows in size, cities sprawl and the amount of usable farmland decreases. At the same time, the productivity of the existing farmland decreases because of topsoil degradation and loss. To keep productivity levels the same or higher, inorganic fertilizers are often deemed necessary; however, these products create other problems. For example, inorganic fertilizers can kill off soil microorganisms which make nutrients and trace elements available to plants.

WORKING WITH NATURE

Using synthetic chemicals in the garden is not a sustainable method of growing food. Today's organic gardeners are looking to produce fresh, tasty, nutritious food for the table. They wantto enjoy food that is not tainted with chemicals; they also want what is good for the environment.

Many gardeners are choosing to use the environmentally friendly techniques offered by organic gardening. They then no longer have to worry about young children coming into contact with synthetic weedkillers and fertilizers on the lawn and shrubs, or causing unintentional harm to visiting wildlife. With organic gardening, very few commercial products are required. Kitchen and garden waste are recycled into compost, reducing the amount of garbage sent to the incinerator or landfill, while soil fertility is increased by the organic method and helps to reverse environmental damage. Especially in the home garden, organic practices need a minimum of space to grow plants intensively and produce a large crop of vegetables.

FRESH PRODUCE FOR THE KITCHEN

If you garden organically, the food that you grow is picked fresh and used in the kitchen for the next meal or preserved for later in the year. It is also much fresher than store-bought produce. Generally, when fruits and vegetables are harvested, they begin to lose nutrients. Vitamins and enzymes start to break down, and the more time that passes, the less nutritious the food and less delicious the flavor. When you grow vegetables in your garden, you are likely to choose the variety based on flavor, texture, scent, appearance, and nutritional value. In contrast,

A constant harvest Using successional planting, you can ensure a steady supply of lettuces for use in the kitchen from spring through fall.

the varieties grown for commercial production are generally chosen for good looks, the ability to be shipped long distances without spoiling or bruising, and for their ease of cultivation and harvesting.

The most common reason why gardeners choose to practice organic techniques is to provide pesticide- and additive-free, nutritious food for the table; however, there are many other reasons to garden organically. The environment benefits from the reduction in chemical pollution, destruction of the soil, and contamination of drinking water, rivers, lakes, and streams. When trees, shrubs, and flowering plants are grown organically, they provide a healthy habitat for beneficial insects and animals.

DRAWING ON TRADITION

I have been asked many times if beautiful ornamental gardens can really be grown without using synthetic chemicals. The answer is a resounding "Yes." The use of manufactured pesticides and other chemicals in the garden is a recent invention, dating back a little over one hundred years. Long before these chemicals were invented, beautiful gardens existed (although they were more labor-intensive).

Throughout history, people have lived by using the land around their homes to grow food for use in the kitchen. The kitchens were miniature factories where fruits and vegetables were preserved in summer and fall for use throughout the year. Bread was baked, not bought; food was prepared, not taken out of a box and reheated. People were much more self-sufficient than they are today.

By gardening organically and preserving our own food using methods that retain flavor and nutrients, we are learning to become a little more self-sufficient like our forebears, providing better food for ourselves and our families, and helping to save the environment.

What is Organic Gardening?

The definition of organic gardening is quite elusive. It involves a complicated series of rules and regulations drawn up by governments or organic certifying organizations. But generally it boils down to a few key issues that can be explained and understood quite easily.

KEY CONCEPTS OF ORGANIC GARDENING
Organic practices avoid the use of manufactured pesticides, herbicides, and mineral or synthetic fertilizers. The soil is kept healthy, rich with nutrients and, most importantly, it is kept alive with a high content of microorganisms. The essence of all organic techniques is to work with nature, not against it. All refuse produced in the kitchen and garden is recycled back into the soil. Organic gardening is a sustainable activity: the soil is fed by the gardener; the soil feeds the plants; the plants feed the gardener. The plants

Intensive planting By using close spacing when planting crops in beds, you will help to keep weeds at bay and prevent the loss of moisture from the soil.

WORKING WITH THE SOIL

Organic gardeners have a particularly close relationship with the soil. They do not think of soil as a largely inert medium to which mineral fertilizers and nutrients are added. Nor do they think of it as being simply the place where plants' roots reside. Organic gardeners value and respect the soil as a living ecosystem of organisms, minerals, and organic matter. The organisms interact with organic and inorganic materials and water to provide nutrients that the plants need in order to survive. Organic gardeners know that healthy, vital soil is essential to grow flowering plants, shrubs and trees, and vegetables successfully. They need to understand the complexities of the soil's ecosystem in order to develop and maintain optimal conditions for soil health and plant growth.

also provide excess organic matter, which is composted and used to feed the soil. The entire cycle is fueled by sunlight and water. By working with nature, you can control pests in your garden. If you create an inviting habitat for natural predators, they will be drawn to your garden where they will feed on pests. Weeds are removed by hoeing. Plants are spaced closely to conserve water by reducing evaporation from the soil. By shielding the soil from sunlight, the intensive planting helps to prevent weed seeds from germinating and growing. Soils with a high humus content will feed the plants, making them healthy, vigorous, and less prone to damage by pests and diseases.

Organic gardeners rotate crops to discourage pests and diseases – even in small gardens, crop rotation is very beneficial (see pp. 78–81). Choosing resistant varieties of plants is not a requirement of most organic standards; however, by selecting varieties that best suit your region and climate you will greatly reduce pest and disease problems in the garden. Seed-saving (see p. 24), again not a requirement by most organic standards, enables you to select a strain of a variety that particularly suits your garden. In effect, you are producing a site-specific plant variety that will experience fewer problems.

As an organic gardener, you will be rewarded for keeping a close watch over the garden, taking note of birds and other predators, and looking out for pests and weeds. From these observations, you will learn to recognize the delicate balance in nature. For example, the presence of particular weeds in a bed may draw your attention to deficiencies in the soil.

When a problem occurs, you will realize that something is out of balance. The instant "fix" may be an organic remedy, but the long-term solution is to restore the balance in nature. If a plant begins to fail, an application of a high-nitrogen liquid organic feed may provide the immediate cure, while the long-term solution would be to rotate the crop in the following year to a bed where beans or peas – valued for their ability to fix nitrogen in the soil – had grown that year.

Looking after the soil is the organic gardener's number-one task. If the soil is fertile, full of life, and moist (not waterlogged or dry), plants will be healthy and vigorous, bearing an abundant crop with little damage from pests and diseases.

SUSTAINABILITY

Sustainability refers to the ability of a society or an ecosystem to function indefinitely without squandering the resources on which it relies. In terms of the organic garden, it means no net loss of nutrients or topsoil in the garden.

SUSTAINABILITY IN AGRICULTURE

Most common agricultural practices call for the use of large tractors, which consume lots of fuel. Chemicals are brought onto the field by the truckload. Yet more fuel is used when crops are subsequently transported long distances. It is estimated that for every calorie of food produced by this form of agriculture, between three and ten calories are used, mostly in the form of non-renewable fossil fuel. Clearly this type of agriculture is not sustainable indefinitely.

The solution to this problem lies in local food production utilizing organic techniques. While it is sometimes argued that organic practices are not commercially viable, in fact these techniques can cut production costs faced by farmers. Savings on chemicals and fuel more than offset the cost of extra labor demanded by organic methods.

Local food produced using organic techniques offers many benefits for the environment:

- Global warming and pollution are not further increased by burning fossil fuels.
- Groundwater does not become polluted with agricultural chemicals.
- Topsoil is not lost or reduced because of poor soil management.
- Topsoil is created by organic techniques.
- Biological diversity is promoted.
- A natural balance between predator and pest is encouraged.

EDIBLE LANDSCAPING

Planning the landscaping around your home is an important part of organic gardening. By choosing a wide range of trees, bushes, perennials, and annuals, you are encouraging biodiversity – of plant, animal, and insect species – in your garden. Group together plants that have similar cultural needs, and try to provide food for wildlife as well as for people when designing the landscape. The land around your home provides an opportunity not only to grow food but also to plant a variety of flowers and herbs that nourish the soul. In many developed nations around the world, natural habitats are disappearing. Organic gardeners are provided with the opportunity to care for their small plot in a way that protects and sustains wildlife. They are able to leave the land in better ecological shape than when it came under their stewardship.

THE IMPORTANCE OF BIODIVERSITY

What is biodiversity and why is it important? Biodiversity refers to all organisms on Earth, from single-cell bacteria to plants, viruses, and fungi. Biodiversity often refers to the genetic variation between individuals. The evolution of a species is dependent on this genetic variation because conditions may change, making some members unable to survive, while others that have even very slightly different genes may flourish.

Thus, biodiversity takes on three specific meanings:
- Genetic diversity between individuals.
- Diversity of breeds within a species.
- Diversity of species existing in an ecosystem.

Diversity in all three areas is important. As an ecosystem of its own, the garden needs different species. If a single crop were planted, the monoculture could easily result in a crop failure due to pests. By planting a diversity of crops, a wide variety of wildlife can be attracted into the garden. Beneficial insects and other predators will control pests also drawn to the garden.

The diversity of breeds within a species is also vital. In commercial agriculture, either very few varieties or only one of any particular vegetable is grown, such that many varieties are fast being lost (for example, three open-pollinated varieties of corn are now extinct). This results in a reduction of the gene pool for any particular vegetable. When a change in growing conditions or the introduction of a disease affects commonly cultivated varieties, the food supply may be in jeopardy. Less popular varieties are often kept from extinction by home gardeners. On a few occasions these near-extinct varieties have been used to develop new strains after disaster has hit commercial varieties.

Open pollination is a means of growing a seed crop so that it is pollinated only by plants of its

*A **wildlife-friendly habitat** Create informal areas with wild flowers and fruit-bearing shrubs to provide habitats and food for beneficial insects and wildlife.*

own variety. Open-pollinated plants show greater genetic diversity between the individuals of a particular variety than F1 hybrids (see p. 67). This genetic diversity results in some individual seeds producing plants that perform better than others in the growing conditions of a particular garden. If the seed from the better plants is saved and replanted, the beneficial traits can be epeated with a greater portion of the crop raised in the following year.

THE ORGANIC CYCLE

Organic gardening imitates the cycles found in nature, but with the addition of our help, to produce wonderfully nutritious vegetables and fruits for the table. Nothing is wasted here, everything is recycled by making compost and saving seeds. The only deviation from the cycle in nature is the deliberate rotation of crops, in order to discourage pests and diseases. In the organic cycle, the compost feeds the soil; the soil feeds the plants; and the plants feed the people. The plants are used to make the compost; and this year's plants provide next year's seeds.

Saving seed

Making compost

Food to eat

HARVESTING

Harvested food is eaten fresh or stored to ensure a supply of produce throughout the fall and winter. The remains of harvested plants, together with kitchen waste, are added to the compost pile, while seeds for sowing in the following year are saved from varieties that have grown successfully.

DIGGING THE SOIL
In nature, the soil is loosened by earthworms, deep-rooted plant growth, and the freeze–thaw cycle. This process is imitated in the organic garden by double digging new beds to achieve the best possible soil structure.

ADDING COMPOST
Made from garden and kitchen waste, well-rotted compost is worked into the soil to improve soil structure, drainage, and its ability to supply plants with essential minerals.

SOWING SEEDS
Seeds from the previous year's harvest are selected and sown for their suitability to the climate and location of your garden.

WATERING AND WEEDING
As the young plants grow, they need a regular supply of water and frequent weeding to reduce the competition for space and nutrients in the bed.

DIGGING THE SOIL

In nature, the soil is loosened by earthworms, rodents, deep-rooted plant growth, and by the freeze–thaw and drought–rain cycles. Walking through the woods in early spring, the effects of the freeze–thaw cycle can easily be seen. Where water has frozen in the soil, there are mounds of frozen earth loosened and pushed up from the ground. And in an unmowed field, you can see where rodents have been digging the soil.

While these activities help in the organic garden, they are not equal to double digging the soil (see pp. 129–31). This is the way the organic gardener helps and improves on nature. Over time soil can become compacted, which inhibits root growth. By double digging, the soil is loosened quite deeply, promoting good root growth and allowing the plants to access water and nutrients deeper beneath the surface. These healthier plants are less susceptible to diseases, and more likely to recover quickly from pest damage. Digging also improves drainage and allows air to reach the roots of plants. When digging the soil, it is important not to mix the subsoil with the topsoil; however, a small amount of organic matter will work its way down. Ultimately this will increase the depth of the topsoil and improve fertility.

ADDING COMPOST

For the best quality and most nutritious vegetables, adding organic matter to the garden annually is essential. This mimics the cycle in nature, whereby leaves fall to the ground and decompose, animals eat plants and return manure to the soil, the roots of annuals add organic matter deeply to the soil when their season is over, and the bodies of dead animals decompose.

A well-prepared bed
Double dig beds to mimic the natural cycle of loosening and breaking up the soil. Add compost to increase fertility and give plants the best possible start.

All of these become humus and feed the soil. As you weed and harvest your crops, you need to replenish the soil with compost – the organic gardener's fertilizer. Containing manure and decomposing vegetation, compost is very close to nature's fertilizer. Add it to the surface of the garden bed after digging; a light lifting action with a garden fork will incorporate the compost into the top layer of the soil. Using a rake to smooth the bed will further mix the compost into the soil surface.

Compost provides nutrients, which are released very slowly to the plants, without any danger of the benefits being washed away by rain or watering. Compost also builds soil structure: it allows sandy soils to retain water and nutrients, and loosens clay soils so that they drain and permit better root growth.

SOWING SEEDS

In nature there are many ways that seeds are sown. Birds which eat fruit scatter the seeds when they add their manure to the soil elsewhere. Some seeds are sown by the wind, others by gravity. Some seeds have burs and travel long distances on animals. Most of these seeds never germinate because they are not sown under optimal conditions. But the gardener can improve on nature, sowing the seeds at the right times and the right depths, in prepared seedbeds.

Many gardeners regard seed sowing as a spring activity, rather than an ongoing process. While many crops can be sown in late spring, a succession of planting works better. If lettuce is planted out all at once, then it will be ready for harvesting all at once, whereas planting a small amount of fast-maturing crops each week is less work for the gardener and provides an extended harvest throughout the season. When early season crops such as peas are harvested, the site can be replanted with a fall crop such as spinach, or used to raise a green manure, like winter rye.

A sheltered start Seeds sown indoors are given a head start over outdoor seedlings. Sowing indoors protects seedlings from late frosts and temperature variations.

Nature does not plant crops in rows interspersed with walking paths, and neither should the organic gardener. Planting in rows leaves large areas of bare earth for you to walk on, but the soil quickly becomes compacted. Worse still, bare earth is simply an invitation for weeds to grow. A better method is to plant in beds that are narrow enough for you to reach the middle from either side. In this way, the soil that you have spent time and effort digging does not subsequently get trampled underfoot. Within the bed, plant the seeds with equal spacing, but close enough for the mature plants to touch, and leave no bare earth visible. This restricts the light that reaches the soil surface, preventing the soil from drying out and discouraging weed growth.

ROTATING CROPS

Crop rotation is the gardener's best defense against soil-borne pests and diseases. In a small garden, rotating crops from one area to another makes a tremendous difference in productivity and health in the garden. Even with just two crops, such as corn and beans, your plot will benefit from alternating the site on which they are grown each year. Beans add nitrogen to the soil, and corn needs nitrogen to grow – so an annual rotation provides the corn with the nitrogen it needs (see pp. 78–81). Different insects and diseases affect corn and beans, so anything left in the soil will be kept in check.

WATERING AND WEEDING

To grow nutritious vegetables, consistent watering is essential. Nature provides rain, but to produce the best vegetables additional watering is usually necessary. Too much rain floods the garden, and there is little that you can do other than provide good drainage. If there is too little rain, plants will be stunted or die without supplementary water: aim to provide an average of 1in/2.5cm of water per week.

The sky usually clouds over during rain, such that plants are protected from the sun scorching their wet leaves. This is worth bearing in mind when watering. If you water in the midday sun, most of it will evaporate and the wet foliage may be damaged by the sun. To avoid this happening, water the soil at the roots of the plants, and try not to wet the leaves. A good way to accomplish this is with a soaker hose or drip irrigation system (see pp. 144–5). Another way is to apply the water with a hose or watering can only at the roots of plants. Water early in the day, when the sun is still low in the sky; watering in the evening

Beneficial weeds Weeds are not all bad in the garden. For example, nettles attract wildlife and can be made into a mild pesticide and tea (see p. 50).

may encourage molds and fungi to develop as the plants stay moist in cool night air.

Weeding the garden has no equivalent in nature, but it is necessary to reduce competition with the vegetables on your plot. In some cases, the weeds that you have pulled out can be left on the bed as a mulch; however, if the weeds have set seed or are quite large, it is better to add them to the garden compost. By composting the weeds that are "harvested" from the garden, you can recycle their nutrients to enrich the soil.

HARVESTING

In nature, the final crop is not as abundant or large as it is in the garden. This is because of droughts, lack of good soil structure, competition from weeds, and pests. The gardener improves on nature by watering, digging, weeding, and pest control.

When a gardener finds that groundhogs or deer are eating the vegetables, a fence can be erected. If birds are eating the berries, netting can be installed. Nature has methods of pest control too: ladybugs eat aphids; frogs eat slugs; and so on. You, too, can encourage natural predators by providing habitats for them in or near the garden (see pp. 121–5).

When harvesting edible crops, the remainder of the plant should be composted. If the crop was a nitrogen-fixing legume, take care that you cut off the plant at the soil surface in order to leave the fixed nitrogen in the soil to fertilize next year's crop.

If the garden is planted over time with successive sowings, it is possible to harvest fresh vegetables from late spring through to winter. The choice of variety of vegetable sown has a great effect on harvest, too. Some varieties, especially F1 hybrids, are very uniform and mature all at once. This is wonderful for the commercial grower, but not for the home gardener. There are varieties that can be harvested over a long period of time, extending fresh usage for the table. Certain varieties of bean can be picked in different forms. For example, some beans can first be harvested as green string beans, then later as shell beans, and followed by a final harvest of dried beans. Other crops can be buried or placed in cold frames (see pp. 94–5) to produce a harvest in the winter and spring.

SAVING SEEDS

When harvesting crops, let some plants go to seed so that you can save those seeds. They must be harvested properly, cleaned, dried, and stored. There are many important reasons why you should save seed. Old varieties with unique qualities are being lost at an alarming rate, and preserving this biodiversity is important. Choosing a variety with qualities that suit your tastes and storage needs is just one element. Some varieties grow better in certain locations than others, and some are more resistant to pests. When you find the best-tasting, most vigorous and disease-resistant varieties in your garden, the resulting seed will have those qualities.

Each succeeding year, when the seed is planted, a subvariety that is specifically suited to your microclimate and location will emerge. In this way, it is you not nature that selects the desirable traits in a plant; the seeds raised become customized to your site and personal preferences.

Planting only open-pollinated seeds is important in the organic garden because their seeds can be saved. Most hybrid seeds produce a very uniform first-generation crop; genetic diversity among individual plants is extremely low. Saving seed from hybrid plants tends to have very unpredictable results. Frequently the plants grown from saved seed look like one of the hybrid's parents rather than like the hybrid itself.

Seed-saving techniques vary widely depending on the crop. Beans can be dried on the plant then collected and stored, but beets are overwintered in a root cellar and planted out the next spring to bear seed. Tomato seeds may be harvested from

Dried pods and seeds *Save seeds from your favorite and most successful crops to produce plants that suit your own site, climate, and tastes.*

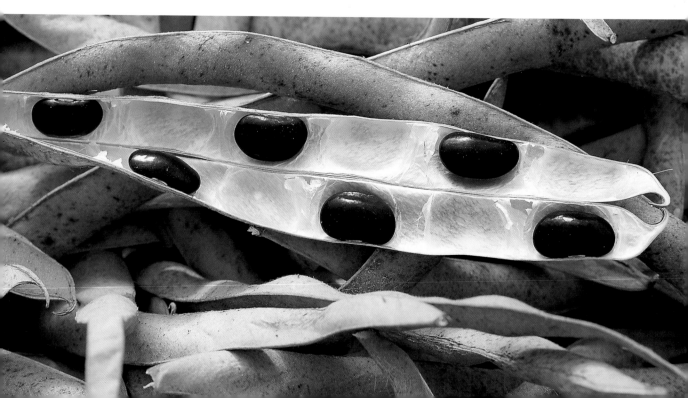

Enjoy now or later
Freshly harvested
vegetables can be used
right away in the kitchen
for a tasty dish or stored,
frozen, or preserved for
use later in the year,
when the growing
season is over.

the fruit and dried (see p. 75), while corn seed should be saved only from plants that have not been cross-pollinated with another variety.

FOOD TO EAT

In nature, animals leave behind their manure after feeding on plants and other creatures. By their very design, fruit plants rely on the animals to eat their fruits in order to spread the seeds in their droppings. This interdependent cycle of feeding differs slightly in gardens, in that fruits and vegetables are harvested for human consumption, and herbivore rather than human manure is usually brought in and added to the compost. The manure from herbivores, especially cattle, horses, and sheep, contains few viable weed seeds, does not have a strong odor, and is the perfect choice for use in the home garden.

When preparing food, save all vegetable kitchen scraps for making compost. Learn to think of apple cores, cauliflower leaves, and potato skins as rich and useful additions to the compost.

Bear in mind the need to preserve some of your harvest (see pp. 276–9). Canning and freezing are common choices, but there are many other methods to consider. Spinach and broccoli can be covered with cold frames, while potatoes, carrots, and beets can be stored in a cool and damp place, like a root cellar. Brussels sprouts can be left in the garden and picked as needed during winter. Parsnips are tastiest when they are left in the ground over winter and harvested in the following spring.

High-value waste *Add lawn and garden waste to the compost where they will be converted into one of the most valuable resources in your garden.*

After the food has been harvested and stored, it is important to think about feeding the soil. Leaving the garden bare over the winter can result in a loss of nutrients and soil erosion during the spring thaw. The best method for preventing this is to plant a green manure that suits your climate. For example, planting winter rye in empty garden beds will provide organic matter for the garden when the soil is dug in the springtime, and its roots will stop erosion during the winter.

MAKING COMPOST

It is essential that every organic gardener maintains a compost pile. All of the waste produced in the garden, the scraps and leftovers from the kitchen, and leaves and grass clippings from mowing can be recycled into a wonderful fertilizer for the garden. Compost feeds the soil and keeps it full of the nutrients necessary to grow crops.

Composting organic debris helps to kill weed seeds, pests, and diseases. As the bacteria aid decomposition, the composting itself generates heat. This speeds up the process and kills pathogens and seeds. The natural process of decomposition sometimes depletes nitrogen levels, but the addition of animal manure will counteract this deficiency. It will also feed the bacteria that use nitrogen as a fuel. A little water needs to be added to the compost pile, but too much brings the decomposition process to a halt.

Building a compost pile in specific layers rather than at random works best (see pp. 46–8). Start with some woody material at the bottom to allow air into the pile, but avoid using it thereafter because woody material takes too long to decompose. Follow this with a layer of green materials such as grass clippings, weeds, and kitchen waste, and then add a layer of manure. Make the following layer from brown materials, such as dried leaves, straw, or dry plant debris after harvest. This layering process is repeated until the compost bin is full.

Achieving a pile of approximately 1yd^3/1m^3 will significantly increase its ability to heat up (see p. 46). You may need to place a cover over the pile to prevent it from becoming too wet. Equally, you may need to water the pile from time to time if it looks likely to become too dry. Turn the pile when it begins to cool down so that the decomposition process can start again. You are likely to find that having two compost bins side by side is very helpful (see p. 44), because it allows a completed pile to heat up while the second compost is in the making.

Use care in what is added to the compost pile (see p. 43). Additional lime may be necessary to maintain proper pH.

GARDENING ON A SMALL SCALE

Organic techniques can be applied to all gardens, whatever their size. You can reap their benefits everywhere, so use them on the smallest of plots, and even when gardening in tubs and pots. It is essential to build soil fertility by making and using compost, and to practice crop rotation.

SMALL PLOTS

When planning the planting in small plots, scale down the numbers of plants you want to grow and choose compact varieties. It is also useful to prioritize which vegetables you plan to grow. For example, fresh organically grown tomatoes are often not available in stores and you may choose to grow them for their fantastic home-grown flavor. Even in small plots, it is important to rotate crops to help prevent diseases and pests. In the small garden, you may choose a three-year rotation plan of vegetables by setting up four small beds, using the fourth bed for perennials. Even in the smallest of gardens, making compost remains central to the organic cycle. A tumbling composter or worm composter may work best if space is limited. If managed properly, a worm composter can be kept indoors (see. pp. 50–1).

CONTAINER GARDENING

It is possible to grow a good portion of your food even if you do not have a yard. Growing plants in containers on a patio or balcony can produce a bountiful harvest. When choosing plants, look for compact varieties, or vines that can be trained vertically or be allowed to tumble over the edge of the container. Many seed catalogs will identify which varieties are best suited for containers. For example, the tomato variety 'Micro Tom' is ideal for container growing. It reaches only 10in/25cm in height

and spread, but bears heavily. Choose heavy-bearing vegetables like summer squash – one plant is often capable of providing enough for a small household.

If you garden in tubs, each spring rotate the crops planted in the tubs and remove the top 4–6in/10–15cm of the soil from each. Replace the soil with compost and work it in lightly. The top layer of soil should be fertile enough to provide essential nutrients to the growing plants. In smaller pots, replace the soil completely each spring. When gardening in containers, it is often necessary to give the plants an extra boost by watering with liquid organic feeds every two to four weeks during the growing season.

Container garden *Climbing beans produce a tasty crop and beautiful flowers as well. They will climb up a string and take little space, yet produce a large harvest.*

CHAPTER 2

SOIL & COMPOST

WHAT IS SOIL?

Soil is the thin layer of the Earth's crust in which plants grow. If the soil is healthy, it in turn can feed the plants that feed us (and the plants will grow well, with fewer pests and diseases). It is an essential cycle that must not be interrupted.

THE IMPORTANCE OF SOIL

In each tablespoon of topsoil, there are more than six million living organisms – three-quarters of soilborne life exists in the top 6in/15cm. When we apply pesticides and herbicides, microorganisms die and fewer minerals are made available by the microbiotic life. At the same time, nonbeneficial microorganisms, which typically are fast colonizers, establish a foothold in the soil. Consequently, the soil is unable to feed plants with the nutrition they need.

The very process of harvesting food removes nutrients from the soil. By returning manure to the garden, planting green manures, and adding compost, we can restore the health of the soil.

KEEP THE SOIL FERTILE
How

1–Raise live stock*
2–Rotate the crops
3–Grow clover, alfalfa and other legumes
4–Save the barnyard manure
5–Pasture rolling lands to prevent washing
6–Add humus – don't burn the stalks
7–Supply needed elements

FARM KNOWLEDGE, VOLUME II, SOILS AND CROPS.
ED. SEYMOUR, E.L.D., DOUBLEDAY, B.S.A.,
PAGE & CO., NEW YORK, 1918

*For today's gardener, this means add composted manure

By testing the soil, we can check that the right elements are present to produce the best and most nutritious harvest. Even if you do not keep livestock, you should be able to obtain composted manure for your plot. Rotating crops is also an essential part of organic gardening.

HOW SOIL BEGAN

To understand soil, it is important to know what it is and how it was created. The Earth is a large sphere of molten rock covered with slowly shifting plates of solidified rock. The forces of nature broke up the outermost layer of this stone into pulverized rock. Over millions of years, the remains of dead plants and animals have decomposed and added humus to the pulverized rock. Nature has slowly built up the surface of the Earth into layers of fine, nutrient-rich soil that feeds plants. Soil is the pulverized rock, mixed with decaying vegetation, manure, and decayed animal matter.

If you watch water flowing in a stream during floods, you will notice the movement of rocks. When the rocks hit one another, chips are broken off and fine rock powder is carried downstream. This material is often deposited in lowland fields. If you look at the forest floor, you will see how last year's leaves are decaying and adding humus to the soil. The new growth of leaves on trees depends not only on soil nutrients, but also on elements in the air. Trees consume carbon dioxide and release oxygen. The carbon that is obtained from the air is converted into wood, bark, roots, and leaves, all of which become part of the soil when they decay.

Farm Knowledge *(1918) devotes the first hundred pages to soil, recognizing its immense importance. Its list of ways to keep soil fertile remains true today.*

RECOGNIZING SOIL LAYERS

Soil types, such as clay or sand, differ according to their location and how they were formed. How the soil is formed also affects soil layers and their thickness. Although soil is made up of many layers, typically you will only see the top two or three layers. The topsoil is generally dark and contains plenty of organic matter. Fungus, insects, bacteria, microbiotic organisms, and worms aerate the soil and release beneficial nutrients in a form that can be utilized by plants. The deeper your topsoil, the better your soil is for gardening.

Subsoil is usually lighter in color than topsoil, because it contains little or no organic matter. To a large degree, its composition determines

Gardener's friends Earthworms help to improve drainage and air circulation around plant roots, as they tunnel through the soil feeding on organic matter.

the rate of drainage and the amount of water available to plants. Gravelly subsoil drains quickly and needs more frequent watering, whereas clay subsoil drains slowly, and less watering is needed; however, clay soils are slower to warm up in the spring, which may delay planting.

Beneath the subsoil is the substrate, which may have several different components. You are unlikely to reach the substrate in your garden except in areas with very shallow soil, or when digging holes for planting large trees.

Cross-section showing soil structure

❶ *Topsoil is rich in organic matter and nutrients. It tends to be darker than subsoil.*

❷ *Subsoil is usually lighter in color than topsoil but is not as rich in organic matter.*

❸ *Substrate is often made of decomposed rock that is rich in minerals. As underlying rock decays subsoil is created. The decomposed rock and rock below it are called parent matter.*

IMPROVING TOPSOIL

When working the soil, take care not to mix different layers of soil, especially when double digging to loosen and aerate the subsoil. Increasing the depth of the topsoil raises the fertility of the beds and will produce better plants. To do this, add organic matter, or convert subsoil to topsoil by growing deep-rooted plants, known as green manure or cover crops. Some vegetables and green manures, such as clover, have very deep roots that reach down into the subsoil. When the plant tops are turned under and mixed into the topsoil, the roots remain in the subsoil and begin to decay. This decomposition helps to break up clay subsoil.

CHOOSING SOIL CONDITIONERS

Some gardeners advocate the addition of soil conditioners to improve soil structure. These are bulk organic materials that are worked into the topsoil (or used as a mulch). In the organic garden, it is important to keep a careful check on what you add to the soil. For example, recycling centers often claim that shredded newspaper is an ideal soil additive that complies with organic gardening principles. However, many newspapers are printed with synthetic dyes, which may leach undesirable chemicals into the soil when added as a conditioner.

Well-rotted sawdust and wood shavings are a good choice if you can be sure they do not come from wood that has been treated with a chemical preservative. Any sort of organic matter that has not been treated with chemicals can be used. Grape pomace, spent hops, mushroom compost, peanut shells, and rice hulls all make good soil conditioners. Matted or manure-coated wool (wool dags) can also be used, although it may sometimes contain the residues of petroleum-based soaps. Very often this sort of industrial waste is free for the asking if you are willing to cart it away.

IDENTIFYING SOIL TYPES

When gardening, it is very useful to know what type of soil you have. There are six types of soil: clay, sand, silt, loam, peat, and limestone. It is also important to test your soil to determine whether it is deficient in nutrients, so that you can assess what improvements are needed.

GETTING TO KNOW YOUR SOIL

Without a soil test, you will not know if your soil is deficient until problems occur. A good approach is to have a newly established bed tested using a professional testing service. You can then add soil amendments to resolve any deficiencies. Later on, you can carry out your own soil tests, with a home-testing kit.

It is important to ask people in your area if they know of any specific soil deficiencies in the locality, because the soil might be deficient in an element that is not normally covered by standard soil tests. If there is something deficient in your area, be sure to ask the laboratory to test for it.

Commercial soil tests are easy and inexpensive. Soil samples can be collected with a purpose-made soil sampler, made up of a simple round tube with a handle, or with a bulb planter, which works almost as well. To take a sample, drive the sampler into the ground and twist it

A flourishing vegetable plot To support a broad range of crops, it is important that your soil remains in peak condition throughout the growing season.

WHAT IS SOIL PH?

It is worth learning how to to tell if your soil is acidic or alkaline, because some plants have a distinct preference for one type or the other. However, most prefer a soil with a neutral pH of 7.0. By looking at which weeds and plants grow well in your garden, you can get a good idea of your soil's pH. For example, sorrel and wild blueberries love acidic soil, while forsythia thrives in alkaline soils. The best method of determining soil pH is to carry out a simple soil pH test, which is available in kit form from most gardening stores.

Brassica bounty Kale and other brassicas need a soil pH of between 6.5 and 7.0, and a feed of bone meal for a steady supply of nutrients.

to scoop up a plug of soil. Avoid picking up any subsoil; if you do find some in the sample, remove it before adding the sample to the collection jar. Use a pocketknife, small spoon, or gloved hands to manage the sample, as your skin pH may influence the test results, and remember to use a glass container, not a plastic or metal one. Always take more than one sample, and try to collect them from random points around the site being tested. Cover the jar that contains the samples and shake it thoroughly to mix the contents. Take out the required amount for the soil test and send it to the laboratory.

Use the remainder of the soil to test for soil type. To do this, reduce the soil level in the jar to about one-third and fill the rest of the jar with water. Shake the jar well and let the contents settle. The sand will rest at the bottom; silt will be the next layer, and clay will settle on the top. The thickness of the three layers can be measured and will indicate the relative proportions of each soil type. If your soil comprises more than 50 per cent sand, clay, or silt, then the dominant one is your soil type. It might also be a loam, sandy loam, clay loam, or a silty loam. If your soil does not separate out into clearly defined layers, add a small amount of powdered eco-friendly detergent to help break up the soil particles.

HOW TO TEST THE SOIL PH

1 *Using a pipette or spoon, add a small sample of your soil to the test chamber. Avoid touching the soil with your hands, as the pH of your skin may affect the results.*

2 *Gently shake the sample so that it mixes well with the testing fluid. Then leave it to stand for a couple of minutes, to allow the contents to settle fully.*

3 *Using the pH indicator chart provided, match the color of your sample to the chart. Green usually indicates alkaline soil; yellow or red indicates acidity.*

IDENTIFYING SOIL TYPES

CLAY

A very heavy soil, clay becomes hard like bricks when dry and holds moisture for long periods of time when it is wet. However, it retains nutrients and is very fertile. In spring, it takes the longest to warm up. Clay soils are made up of the smallest particles. When viewed under a microscope, the thin, flat particles look like pennies heaped together in a pile, which is what makes this soil hard to dig.

SILT

A soil that is somewhere between clay and sand, silt retains moisture and feels slippery when wet. Silt soil retains nutrients better than sand and does not dry out as quickly. This type of soil warms up more quickly than clay during the spring. Silt particles can be likened to a pile of marbles; they are able to retain moisture and nutrients, but they do not stay wet and heavy like the particles found in clay.

SAND

Sandy soil tends to be very light and dries out swiftly. When this soil gets wet, water washes the nutrients away very quickly. During spring, sandy soil is the first to warm up. This type of soil is made up of large particles that are visible to the naked eye. The particles that make up sand can be compared to a very large pile of soccer balls: they allow water to drain out quickly and make the soil easy to dig.

IDENTIFYING SOIL TYPES

LIMESTONE

Also known as calcareous soil, limestone tends to be very rocky and not terribly fertile. Limestone soil has good drainage, and like sand, its nutrients tend to be washed out of the soil quickly by rain and irrigation. The topsoil in limestone soil is usually shallow. As its name suggests, this type of soil contains a lot of lime or chalk and is very alkaline. This makes it difficult if not impossible to grow acid-loving plants in limestone.

LOAM

This soil is made up of a mix of clay, sand, and silt in proportions that produce the most fertile soil. It is friable, quick to drain yet moisture retentive, and contains lots of organic matter. The ideal loam has 40 per cent silt, 20 per cent clay, and the rest is sand and organic matter. None of the components of loam accounts for more than 50 per cent, therefore loam cannot be classed as clay, silt, or sand.

PEAT

A rare soil type, peat is very dark in color and highly moisture retentive. It is quite heavy and can be hard to work. Peat soil is usually low in nutrients and is made up almost exclusively of organic matter. Drainage is necessary in this soil because it is prone to waterlogging. Peat is very acidic, making it unsuitable for growing alkaline-loving plants. It is typically necessary to add lime to peat soil to increase the pH.

IMPROVING YOUR SOIL

Using the soil identification chart on pages 36–7, it should be easy for you to determine your soil type and assess what actions are needed to improve it.

The addition of compost is invariably part of any solution for improving soil. An analogy that suits compost is to picture it as stiff sponges that are not compressed by the weight of the soil. These sponges are able to draw moisture through the soil. Other solutions include green manures (see pp. 57–61) which will break up subsoil as well as clay and silt topsoils.

SAND

To improve the retention of moisture and nutrients in sandy soils, you need to incorporate compost into the soil to fill the areas between the particles of sand. Keep a regular check on the pH of sandy soils because lime is quickly washed out. Water plants growing in sandy soils frequently. Sandy soils need less cultivation than heavier soils; overworking the soil may result in faster nutrient loss. Using a green manure is a quick way to add organic matter to sandy soils. Try to keep something growing in the beds throughout the year. Erosion is swift in sandy soils, and nutrients leach out quickly when nothing is growing in the beds.

SILT

Like clay, silt soils may have drainage problems and become compacted. By adding compost, you can improve the drainage in silt soils and prevent them from turning powdery when dry. The compost allows drainage of water by separating the soil particles. This enhances the soil structure and reduces the likelihood

Preferential treatment Some plants dislike certain soil types. By growing them in raised beds, you can create the preferred conditions for a particular crop.

of compaction. The incorporation of compost also allows air to penetrate the soil and reach down to the roots of plants.

The best time to cultivate silt soils is when they are dry and do not feel slippery when worked between your fingers. Silt must be cultivated well and needs to be mulched to prevent an impenetrable crust forming on the surface. The pH of silt should be checked and adjusted as necessary.

CLAY

With a little work and lots of compost, you will find that clay soils are among the best for growing crops. Working in compost separates the penny-like particles and allows moisture to drain out of the soil, making it lighter and easier to work. This helps clay soil to warm up more quickly in the spring, and reduces the likelihood of it hardening into solid bricks during drought. As the clay becomes easier to work, more air is available to reach the roots of plants.

You will need to test the pH of clay soils and add lime if necessary. An added benefit of working lime or gypsum into clay soils is that the small penny-like particles are bound together and form larger aggregate particles. This improves soil structure. Avoid walking on clay soils because they compact more easily than other types; use a plank if you need to stand on the bed. Cultivate clay soils when they are moist. If you work on them when they are wet, the soil structure will be harmed; working on them when dry is difficult because of the brick-like texture.

LIMESTONE

Working compost into limestone soils improves water retention and creates a deeper topsoil. Limestone soils have large particles like sand, and suffer from nutrients washing out with watering. When cultivating this type of soil, only do so very shallowly, as the topsoil tends not to be

---

PEAT CONSERVATION

Peat moss, which is promoted to improve soil structure, is harvested in Canada, Ireland, Scotland, and England. In some areas this has caused great damage to the delicate ecosystems of the bogs. This threat to the environment is a cause for concern among organic gardeners. The only reason to consider using peat is to increase the acidity of the soil for moisture-loving plants like true cranberries (*Vaccinium macrocarpon*). Look for coco peat and other amendments instead, and try to use peat-free planting pots and seed-starter mixes.

---

very deep. Aim to grow plants appropriate to this soil type or consider building raised beds (see p. 99) so that acid-loving plants can be grown. Erosion takes place very quickly in limestone soils. When nothing is growing in the beds, nutrients leach out more quickly than when the bed is full, so try to keep something growing at all times.

LOAM

If the soil in your garden is loam, you are very fortunate. The widest range of crops will grow in loam with few soil additives.

PEAT

Of all the soil types, peat does not need the addition of compost. To improve drainage in peat soils, it may be necessary to install clay drainage tiles beneath the soil surface or to build raised beds (see p. 99). Test the pH frequently in beds used to grow alkaline-loving plants. If, by chance, peat soil dries out, it takes a lot of slow irrigation to get it wet again. If you drain your peat soils, be prepared to irrigate them during times of drought. Peat is more likely to need the addition of nutrients, so make sure that you have the soil tested and work in the necessary additives.

WHAT IS COMPOST?

Compost is the main soil amendment used in organic gardening and every organic gardener must produce compost. In fact, compost is the most important thing produced in the garden. When you make compost, you are recycling organic matter and using it to feed the soil.

TYPES OF ORGANIC MATTER

When making compost, consider what types of organic matter should be used. For example, some contribute higher levels of nutrients than others, and some make nitrogen unavailable in compost until they have decayed completely.

FROM GARDEN AND KITCHEN

Green garden waste Weeds and plant remains after harvest are just a few examples of green garden waste; however, avoid adding weed seeds (see p. 43). This waste tends to be very rich in nutrients and is an excellent addition to the compost pile. When weeding, green vegetation may be left on the surface of the soil as mulch, but it is better to compost it.

Kitchen waste When preparing vegetables and fruits in the kitchen, keep a small bowl or compost bucket nearby in which to collect all of the peelings and scraps for the compost pile. These scraps may also be used to make worm tea (see pp. 50–51). Orange peel, carrot tops, and melon rinds are some of the best additions to the compost pile. Eggshells may be added to the pile, but crush them first to speed up decomposition.

Leaves It is often a chore to rake and dispose of fallen leaves. If made into leaf mold (see p. 49), they make an attractive mulch and can be worked into the soil to improve its structure and increase the level of organic matter. Leaves have very few nutrients. Many parks and cemeteries will permit gardeners to collect leaves. Some cities that collect leaves make leaf mold available to their residents, but watch out for glass, plastic, and other foreign material that may be present.

Grass clippings Clippings are very nutrient rich. It is best to let them stay on the lawn where they will decompose and feed the grass. In some cases, when mowing the lawn, it is preferable to collect the clippings instead of letting them decompose on site. If the grass is too long when it is mowed or if an area needs to be kept clear for exercise or children's play, the clippings can be composted or used as a mulch in the garden.

If you collect clippings from neighbors, be sure to ask if they treat their lawns with any synthetic chemicals.

Farm fresh *Organic poultry manure is a valuable by-product of keeping chickens. Use it as a compost additive to boost nitrogen and speed decomposition.*

Kitchen waste *Many of the peelings and offcuts from harvested food can be recycled in the composting process rather than thrown away with the garbage.*

LOCALLY AVAILABLE

Hay and straw Hay is rich in nutrients but often contains viable weed seeds. Except for potash, straw has very few nutrients and contains few viable weed seeds, making it an ideal mulch. Straw also has thicker stems that allow air to penetrate a compost pile. Hay added to the compost pile is like any other brown organic matter. It will compact and decompose slowly, releasing its nutrients over a long period of time.

Second-cutting hay generally has few weed seeds and therefore makes an excellent mulch for berry bushes because it slowly releases its nutrients into the soil. Both hay and straw are readily available from local farms or feed stores.

DECOMPOSED MATTER

Compost is decomposed plants and animal manure. Dark and rich, it looks a lot like healthy garden soil. Garden waste and kitchen scraps are piled in a heap, where they decay.
Humus is the material formed by the decomposition of organic matter. When mixed into the soil, humus improves its structure and ability to retain nutrients. A green manure turned into the soil forms humus. Compost breaks down to form humus.

Manure, bovine Cow manure is rich in nutrients and has few viable weed seeds. Well-rotted manure can be used as a mulch or incorporated directly into the soil. It is also good to add to the compost pile. Fresh manure has a pungent smell, and is high in nitrogen, which will burn plants.

Manure, horse Horse manure is rich in nutrients but tends to contain viable weed seeds. Horse manure mixed with shavings takes a long time to decompose. Horse manure mixed with straw is quicker. Use the manure to build a hot compost pile to kill weed seeds.

Manure, poultry Poultry manure is rich in nutrients and does not contain viable weed seeds. It is very high in nitrogen and may burn plants if not composted thoroughly. Poultry manure is typically available mixed with the litter (often sawdust) that the poultry live on. By the time poultry manure is delivered to your garden, the chickens have scratched about in the wood shavings, and the high nitrogen levels in their manure have decomposed the wood. Very fresh manure should be added to the compost, where it will work to speed decomposition.

Manure, rabbit Rabbit manure does not contain viable weed seeds. It is not as rich as other manures and does not contain high levels of nitrogen that can burn plants. Rabbit manure can be used fresh to side-dress plants or incorporated into the beds. Composting this manure reduces its nutritional value.

Manure, sheep Sheep manure is rich in nutrients and does not contain viable weed seeds. It is very heavy and should be mixed with hay or some other organic material before use. It is the finest manure for use in the garden. Well-rotted manure, mixed with hay, can be spread directly on the garden and incorporated into the soil.

Seaweed This nutrient-rich plant provides lots of trace elements and potassium. As it decays, seaweed helps to activate the compost pile. It may also be used as mulch or dug into the soil if the bed is not needed right away. Beware of using very salty seaweed.

Organic melting pot The effects of earthworms, microorganisms, and time produce a rich organic fertilizer from a variety of compost ingredients.

Urine Human urine is rich in nitrogen and potassium. Dilute with water and add to the compost during composting.

PRUNINGS

Soft prunings Add hedge clippings and thorn-free green prunings to the compost pile, or shred them for a mulch.

Woody prunings Shred these prunings before adding them to the pile. Use unshredded prunings as the bottom layer of a compost pile to help aeration. Woody prunings may be left to decay in a heap if you have the space and time to let them rot. Add grass clippings and fresh manure to speed up their decomposition.

MULCHES AND INDUSTRIAL WASTE

Shredded bark A very popular choice for use as a decorative mulch, shredded bark has little

Vintage compost *When it reaches maturity after twelve months or so, rich compost smells sweet and is fine and crumbly in your hands.*

or no nutrients and may rob the soil of nitrogen as it decays. It should be used only as a mulch, rather than incorporated into the soil as an improver. When buying shredded bark, be sure it was not treated with any chemicals to make it decay faster.

Sawdust and wood shavings These have very few nutrients but can make a good mulch. Age them for about twelve months in the open before use or they will rob nitrogen from the soil. Do not to incorporate these into the soil.

Cocoa hulls If they do not contain pesticide residues, cocoa hulls are a good nutrient-rich choice for mulching perennials in the organic garden. They are a by-product of industry and are usually inexpensive. After the shells decay, work them into the soil and add more as mulch on top.

Spent hops This is an industrial organic waste available from breweries. Provided that the spent hops have not been treated with manmade chemicals, they are a good source of trace elements and nutrients. They can be used as a mulch, dug into garden beds or added to the compost pile.

Wool dags These are the waste from the wool-cleaning process. If you can obtain dags that were not treated with any chemicals, they make an excellent mulch that is high in nitrogen. Work them into the soil to increase water retention.

COMPOST REJECTS

These types of organic matter should not be composted:

- Cooked kitchen waste and meat scraps produce a strong odor and attract dogs and vermin to the compost pile.
- Never add protein in the form of meat, chicken, fish, or cheese: it attracts vermin, including rats.

- Paper often has petroleum-based ink and may leach chemicals into the soil.
- Diseased plants or pest-infested plants should be destroyed, especially potato top growth because it may contain diseases.
- Manure from pigs, dogs, and cats may contain diseases that affect humans.

- Weeds with a high seed content should be avoided unless your compost piles reach quite high temperatures.
- Metal objects and plastic will not decompose.
- Roots of invasive weeds should be destroyed or they may grow in the soil when the compost is used.

METHODS OF COMPOSTING

The most fundamental part of organic gardening is to recycle nutrients and organic matter back into the soil by making compost. Fortunately, making compost is easy and inexpensive. Most of what is composted is waste that many people pay to have hauled away with the household garbage.

READYMADE COMPOSTERS

Many people waste money buying extravagant wooden units or ugly plastic bins. This is largely unnecessary as a compost bin need not be ugly or expensive.

Compost tumblers are also heavily advertised, but they do not produce compost any faster than a hot pile. In general, they tend to be very expensive and should only be considered where vermin are a problem or space is at a premium. Do not add to the tumbler during the composting process.

COMPOST BINS FROM FENCING

If you have any carpentry skills, a compost bin can be made from wood quite easily. Many home improvement centers and local hardware stores stock 8ft/2.5m lengths of pre-assembled fencing. Cedar and redwood are the most resistant timbers. Choose a style that complements your home's architecture and that you find attractive. One that has small gaps between the pickets is preferable because it will permit air to penetrate the pile more easily.

Choose fencing that is 36in–4ft/90cm–1.2m in height and make sure that it has not been made from pressure-treated or preserved wood. Buy four 8ft/2.5m lengths and eight L-brackets with screws. This will be enough to make two bins. Cut each of the lengths of fence in half, and using the L-brackets, re-attach the two halves at a 90° angle with the decorative pickets on the outside. When this is done you will have four

ASSEMBLING YOUR OWN PANELS

1 *Take an 8ft/2.5m length of fencing and saw it in half through the struts to make two 4ft/1.2m pieces. Cut a second length of fencing in the same way.*

2 *Position the first pair of 4ft/1.2m lengths at right angles to each other. Screw them together with two L-brackets. Repeat with the second pair.*

3 *Stand the two right-angled pieces of fencing together to form a square compost bin. Repeat the whole process from Step 1 to make a second bin.*

L-shaped pieces of fence that can be set up to provide the two compost bins. Do not worry about attaching the two L-shaped pieces of each bin together, as this is rarely necessary. Just stand two L-shaped pieces of fencing on the ground so that they form a square.

Site the bins in a sheltered location, such as under trees, or use covers to protect them from excessive rainfall or the drying effects of the sun. In areas with summer drought, sprinkle water on the compost if it shows signs of drying out. Make sure the bins are also within easy reach of the kitchen and the vegetable garden, which produce the most compost ingredients.

MAKING COMPOST

There are two ways to build compost piles. One is to build a pile carefully in layers so that it heats up; this is called a hot compost pile. The other way is to make a cool compost pile by continually tossing whatever organic matter you have onto the pile; then you just wait patiently for the compost ingredients to break down. The results are the same but the time it takes to produce useful compost differs. A carefully layered pile that heats up may be ready within two months, while a cool compost pile may take a year or more.

BUILDING A COOL COMPOST PILE

A cool pile may or may not heat up. You add the ingredients as they become available, a little at a time. It is particularly important that the compost bins are convenient to the kitchen, because at the end of each day you need to add your vegetable scraps to the pile. Two bins are needed for a cool compost: one to build up slowly during the year, and one to hold the previous year's finished compost.

Start a pile by laying small woody branches and sticks at the bottom of the bin. This will assist in allowing air to infiltrate the pile. Add

> ## COMPOSTING TIPS
>
> - Add as much as possible at one time.
> - Add a mix of lush green material and tough brown material.
> - Keep the pile moist but not wet or waterlogged. Cover the pile if necessary.
> - Build air into the heap, by placing branches at the bottom and mixing straw into the middle to let air penetrate the pile.
> - Avoid outside inputs; only add amendments to cure nutrient deficiencies in the soil.

garden debris, grass clippings, and kitchen waste to the pile. If you are including lots of green materials in your compost, add in some hay or straw. The straw is rigid and will encourage air to infiltrate the pile. After collecting the garden debris, such as plant remains after harvest and fall leaves, start building the second pile. By the following spring, the bottom of the first pile should be ready for use. The top of the pile may not be decomposed yet.

Spring is the time to turn the pile to improve decomposition. In areas with summer drought, it is often helpful to turn the pile in early winter before the rains. Remove both halves of the compost bin and set them up next to the existing pile to form another bin. Using a garden fork or round-nosed shovel, turn the pile over into the bin. The bottom of the pile should be well composted and can be used immediately. Consider adding an activator, such as manure, at this stage. The combined effect of turning the pile and an application of activator will speed up the process and produce a completed compost.

Throughout the summer, continue to add organic matter to the second bin. Worms tend to quickly find their way into cool compost piles and move in to eat the nutritious organic matter. They will help with decomposition and add their manure to the pile.

SPEEDING UP THE COOL COMPOST PILE

The biggest complaint about cool composts is that they take too long to produce useful compost. To speed decomposition, add as much organic matter as possible at one time. Include green and brown organic matter in equal amounts, then apply manure. Chopping up organic matter increases its surface area, which helps it to decompose more quickly. Use a spade to break up large or thick pieces and smash tough stalks. Put tree and bush prunings through a shredder or run over them with a lawnmower to break them down. Finally, to speed decomposition, turn the pile in the fall and mix in some manure to activate it.

BUILDING A HOT COMPOST PILE

Making a hot compost pile is a little more complicated because it is usually built all at once in layers to ensure a good even mix of green and brown organic matter and manure. In order to heat up, the pile needs to be large enough in size and shape. A pile measuring about 1yd³/1m³ is

Starting over By the time your first compost pile has matured, a second pile should already be in the making to ensure a steady supply of rich organic matter.

optimum. It is important to keep the pile near this size, because if it becomes too large, air will have trouble penetrating the pile and reaching the middle. Equally, if it is smaller, the pile will not heat up properly.

To build the pile, begin with a layer of small woody branches and sticks at the bottom of the bin. On top of this, put a 4–6in/10–15cm layer of green, succulent organic matter, such as grass clippings, soft kitchen waste, and weeds. On top of this layer, add 1in/2.5cm of fresh manure; bovine, sheep, or horse manure works best. Unless there is a lot of soil on the roots of weeds already on the pile, add a 1in/2.5cm layer of garden soil to introduce soil-borne organisms. The final layer is made up of 4–6in/10–15cm of brown organic matter. Straw makes an ideal choice because it allows air to infiltrate through its stems. Other semi-rigid brown organic matter

COOL VERSUS HOT COMPOSTS

METHOD	ADVANTAGES	DISADVANTAGES
Cool pile	The pile can be built slowly as materials become available. It is easier to build, because it is not necessary to add the material in layers. Resulting compost is more fertile because undecomposed material traps nutrients which are released later into the soil.	The pile takes longer to produce compost (possibly up to one year) because the decomposition process is much slower. Weed seeds and diseases may not be killed.
Hot pile	Compost is produced very quickly (in as little as two months) thanks to the high temperature reached. Weed seeds and diseases are usually killed. Roots and woody material are generally broken down thoroughly.	A lot of organic material is required all at once to build up the pile in layers. High temperatures release nutrients that may be washed out of compost quickly. High temperatures can also evaporate ammonia, resulting in reduced nitrogen levels and an unpleasant odor.

also works well, but avoid any woody material. Continue adding layers to the pile in the same order: green organic matter, manure, soil, and brown organic matter.

When the pile nears the top of the bin, make brown organic matter the final layer. The purpose of layering is to ensure a good mix of compost ingredients. Mixing the material is often difficult but produces the best results.

Once the compost pile has begun the decomposition process, do not add any more material to the pile. Check the temperature of the compost regularly by using a purpose-designed thermometer. A temperature of between 130°F/54°C and 140°F/60°C will kill weed seeds. Keep an eye on the moisture content of the pile too. If the pile is getting very wet or waterlogged, use a waterproof cover or large wooden panel to protect it. If the pile is too dry, water it liberally.

FINISHING A HOT COMPOST PILE

As the decomposition process sets in, the pile slowly heats up and eventually reaches a plateau. Once the temperature begins to drop, it is time to turn the pile. This will incorporate air into the pile and encourage further decomposition.

Remove the two sides of the compost bin and set it up alongside the existing pile. Place a layer of woody material at the bottom of the newly set up bin. Using a garden fork or round-nosed shovel, turn the pile over into the bin. Do not add any fresh organic matter. The pile will heat up again, typically to a hotter temperature than the first time. Again, check the moisture content and cover the pile to keep it dry or water the pile, as necessary.

When the temperature drops to within the soil/air temperature range, the composting process has slowed to a point where the compost is ready for use. The organic matter will continue to decompose either in the bin or in the garden where it is used.

Garden recycling *Compost bins are used to recycle weeds, kitchen waste, and garden debris into rich organic matter that can be used as a garden fertilizer.*

MAKING SEED COMPOST

In order to produce compost for seed starting, a further step is necessary. Take a portion of the compost to make a new, small pile in the spring, and keep it covered for up to a year. Compost used for seed starting should be two years old and thoroughly decomposed.

In areas with very cold climates, bag up the compost in the fall and store it in a root cellar or basement so that it is available in late winter. Burlap or cloth will keep the compost moist during storage. For best results, sieve the soil through ¼in/0.5cm screening before using.

SOIL FEEDS

Maintaining the soil is easily accomplished by growing green manures, incorporating compost or by adding mulch, which will later rot and add nutrients to the soil. Leaf mold and worm castings are valuable additions to the soil, and liquid feeds are used to supplement container plants.

MAKING LEAF MOLD

Leaf mold is a very useful product in the garden. It can be used as mulch and later worked into the soil. Leaves from any deciduous trees are suitable, but avoid any diseased leaves. When starting a new bed, a thick 3–4in/8–10cm layer may be spread over the surface to deter weeds. Seeds and seedlings may be planted directly in the leaf mold. It can even be used as potting mix if left to decompose for two to three years.

Begin by setting up a bin for the leaves. A section of wire fencing works best. Use canes to stake it in a circle with a diameter of between 36in/90cm and 10ft/3m, depending on how many leaves you have.

In the fall, collect the leaves from your land; it does not matter if they are damp. If you need more leaves, ask permission from neighbors and public gardens to collect theirs. Some gardeners use a bagging lawnmower for collection. This adds grass which speeds decomposition and reduces the labor of raking. Fill the bin with leaves and keep the pile moist.

Leaf mold may be ready as early as spring, but can take until the following spring. The process of decomposition is unlike composting. Fungus breaks down leaves into leaf mold, whereas bacteria break down organic matter into compost. This fungal process takes longer and depends on the leaf types being composted as well as the temperature and climate.

ORGANIC TEAS

Where conventional gardeners add a liquefied chemical fertilizer, organic gardeners make "manure tea." Using liquid organic feed is not a common practice in organic gardening, except in feeding container plants. Most often, the soil is fed with compost which, in turn, feeds the plants. In some cases, certain plants need an extra boost and are fed directly by the gardener. For more information, refer to page 50–3.

Decomposed leaves Leaf mold makes a wonderful mulch and can be used to add organic matter to the soil. It is made by fungus breaking down the leaves.

MAKING LIQUID FEEDS

Making a liquid organic feed is quite easy. Choose the appropriate ingredients depending on what nutrients are needed by your plants.

Compost tea For a general and well-balanced liquid feed, make compost tea. Put a cloth bag of finished compost into a bucket or garbage can filled with water. Cover and let it sit for three to four days. Remove the bag of compost and apply it as mulch in the garden. The liquid should be diluted with water until it has the color of weak tea. Using it full strength may burn plants.

Manure tea For a high-nitrogen feed, make manure tea. Dry manure works too but has significantly less nitrogen than fresh manure. Sheep manure produces the best results, but bovine and horse manure make a satisfactory liquid feed. Site a garbage can away from the house where the odor will not be offensive, and fill it with water. Place a few shovels of fresh manure in a burlap sack or cloth bag, and suspend it in the water with a rope. Cover the can and leave it steep.

After several hours, a very mild feed may be obtained and can be used directly undiluted. Better yet, leave the bag for about two weeks. The water will heat up like a hot compost pile. If the water is hot, the tea is not ready. When the water returns to the ambient temperature, it is ready to be used. Manure tea should not be used as a foliar feed. It may be used at full strength or diluted to a weak tea color, depending on the amount of nitrogen necessary.

Nettle or comfrey tea Nettle makes a feed containing iron, magnesium, sulfur, and nitrogen; comfrey makes a high-potassium tea. Place 1–2lb/450–900g of leaves in a cloth sack and submerge in a large bucket of water. Let the bag steep for one or two weeks before use. Nettle tea should be diluted 1:15 with water.

USING A WORMERY

Worm composting is very easy and takes little space. It is ideal for gardens where space is at a premium. Worms eat kitchen waste and other organic material and produce castings for use in

MAKING A LIQUID FEED

1 *Put the organic material in a cloth bag or burlap sack and tie it closed securely. Fill a large, clean plastic or metal container with water.*

2 *Secure the bag to an overhead batten and steep it in water for three days to two weeks depending on the organic material being used to make the tea.*

3 *When the water becomes dark brown in color, it is ready to use. Always dilute the tea before applying it, as full-strength tea may burn plants.*

Commercial wormery
The worms live in the lower layers of the worm composter and come to the upper layers to feed. Once established, a small wormery will house around 30,000 worms and will be able to accept 1–2lb/450–900g of kitchen scraps per day.

the garden. Worm composting does not produce any offensive odors and may be done on porches, patios or even under the kitchen sink. If you wish to make worm compost, I strongly recommend one of the black plastic wormeries available for purchase. Typically, they come with excellent instructions. They are round bins raised on legs and fitted with a drain to remove worm tea. The best models have three or more perforated bins that stack. Wooden and other non-watertight containers rarely produce worm tea.

To start a worm composter, fill the bottom bin with compost or coco peat and introduce red worms from your compost pile or purchase appropriate worms from a supplier. In the middle bin, add kitchen waste. When the middle bin is full, add kitchen waste and organic matter to the top bin. The worms will work their way up as they digest the scraps. When the bottom bin is fully converted, and most of the worms have moved onto the middle bin, remove the bottom bin and use the worm castings. Return this empty bin to the top of the stack. Make sure that the composter is sufficiently moist, but leave the cover on to keep out light and excessive moisture. Any excess water drains through and can be used as liquid feed. The worms need to be kept warm but not hot; they prefer a temperature of 60–70°F/16–21°C. To keep the process working in winter, bring the wormery into a garage or basement with a temperature above 50°F/10°C. Very cold weather will kill the worms.

COMMERCIAL LIQUID FEEDS

Any purchased liquid feeds, such as fish emulsion, should be diluted exactly as directed. These feeds tend to be very concentrated and there is a risk of burning plants. Fish emulsion is a good general fertilizer, containing nitrogen, phosphorus, and potassium (shown as NPK on labels). It is often applied with seaweed and makes a useful foliar feed if sufficiently diluted. Be sure to choose an organic fish emulsion that has no additives.

USING LIQUID FEEDS

The use of liquid feeds is a temporary solution to poor plant growth; it is not a common practice in organic gardening. Ideally, you should feed the soil with compost, and let the soil feed the plants. If plants are growing poorly, a crop can often be saved by using a liquid feed. The deficiency in the soil should be corrected for future crops.

Liquid organic feeds are most useful when growing container plants and raising vegetables in tubs or planters. Applications of liquid feed can be made by pouring it onto the soil near the roots of plants or by spraying it onto the vegetation. It should only be applied to moist soil. Plants growing in containers, tubs, or planters can be watered regularly with very dilute liquid feeds, but the feeds can be used in a less diluted form when a problem is discovered in the garden.

To apply liquid feeds, create a small depression in the soil around the base of the plant and fill it with a small amount of feed. Alternatively, bury a small plant pot in the soil near the roots of the plant, and pour the feed into it; you will see it quickly penetrate the soil.

Strawberry planter Container-grown plants benefit from liquid feeds which compensate for the limited amount of soil available to their roots.

Worm tea The excess "tea" produced by worms as they work through the compost can be drawn off and used as a liquid fertilizer.

APPLYING FOLIAR FEEDS

When you notice visible deficiency in the leaves of a plant, use a foliar feed to provide an immediate boost. Pour a very dilute mixture of liquid feed in a watering can fitted with a spray rose or in a spray bottle. You might find it useful to add 1 tablespoonful of vegetable oil to help the feed adhere to the foliage. Apply it directly to the leaves in the early morning when dry weather is forecast; rain or overhead watering will wash away the benefits of a foliar feed. Make sure that the leaves are not in direct sunlight when applying a foliar feed.

SOIL & COMPOST ADDITIVES

When making compost it is important to address any soil deficiencies. Testing your soil is the only way to ensure that the soil has appropriate amounts of nutrients. A soil test may indicate a number of deficiencies, such as low nitrogen levels or a lack of phosphorus, calcium or boron.

WHAT IS A DEFICIENCY?

A plant that is lacking a much-needed nutrient will grow poorly, be subject to diseases, distortion of growth, and leaf discoloration. Typically the lack of nutrients is caused by a deficiency in the soil which is remedied by supplying the necessary additive to the compost. Some plants may have specific needs. To address these, add the supplement directly to the soil near the plant. Again, a soil test is the only way to be certain there are no soil deficiencies.

The soil additives listed below are organic. They are found mostly in a form that will be slow to decompose, so they will not act as a "quick fix" like chemically based fertilizers. They remain in the soil and slowly release nutrients. Microbial action as well as time and moisture break down these additives. Many of them are mined from the earth, and collecting them causes some environmental damage. Before using an additive make sure that it is acceptable to your organic certifying agency. Rules vary across the United States and, indeed, between countries, such that additives advocated in one region may be banned in another. Please take this into consideration when choosing additives.

Garden waste that is composted will recycle some of the nutrients derived from these additives into the finished compost. With time and soil tests, you may find that some soil deficiencies in your garden have been eliminated.

TO ADJUST pH

The optimal pH for the average soil is between 6.5 and 7.0. Some plants are acid loving and require a lower pH. Others prefer alkaline soils with a higher pH.

Lime Made from pulverized calcium carbonate, this is added to the garden to increase the pH of the soil. It also provides calcium. Limestone is the most common form of lime. Another form, oystershell, contains nutrients and micronutrients and is also used to adjust pH and add calcium. The particles are of different sizes, so they break down at different rates, providing immediate as well as long-term results. Dolomite lime provides both magnesium and calcium.

Peat Peat is used to lower the pH of the soil. It also improves the soil structure. The use of peat is not permitted under organic standards in some countries; elsewhere its use is discouraged (see p. 39). Try using pine needles or coco peat as an alternative for lowering pH.

Coco peat Made from the husk fiber of coconuts, this additive has the same properties as peat, but it is not quite as effective for lowering the pH.

Pine needles These are often used as a mulch around acid-loving plants or to adjust the pH of

SUPPLYING ADDITIVES

- Supplying additives is the easiest solution for satisfying nutrient needs and correcting nutrient deficiencies in the soil.
- For a garden that is deficient in some nutrients, add the supplements to the compost pile as it is being built (see pp. 45–8).
- For plants that require higher levels of some nutrients, mix the supplement into finished compost as you add around the plants.

Lime This soil additive is often used to increase the pH of acidic soils. There are several forms of lime which may be used and all are a good source of calcium.

alkaline soil. Use pine needles instead of brown organic matter to make a low-pH compost.

MOST COMMON ADDITIVES

Bone meal This is made from finely ground animal bones. It is a good source of phosphorus and calcium and encourages root development if worked into the bottom of holes before planting trees and bushes. Bone meal also contains many trace elements.

Blood meal Trace minerals and lots of nitrogen are released into the soil by incorporating blood meal (dried, pulverized animal blood). Even though it is high in nitrogen, blood meal does not burn plants when mixed into the soil.

Fish meal This is a balanced fertilizer containing nitrogen, phosphorus, and potassium. An application on a garden bed will slowly release nutrients during the entire summer.

Animal manure Well-rotted organic manures are good additives to mix directly into the soil where increased nitrogen levels are necessary. For details of different manure types, see pp. 41–2.

Wood ashes The nutrient content of ashes depends on the types of wood being burned. Typically it is high in potassium. If small, woody prunings are burned, the ashes may contain a fair amount of minerals. Add ashes in moderation to the compost pile or spread them directly on beds.

Crushed eggshells Eggshells are a wonderful source of calcium and are especially useful around brassicas. Add them to the compost pile, or work them into the soil with compost around vegetables that require higher calcium levels.

Gypsum Gypsum contains calcium and sulfur. It also increases pH, but to a lesser degree than lime. It is good for improving structure in clay soils, and very effective in alkaline soils that are

Salty harvest Either purchased dry or harvested fresh from the coast, seaweed is an excellent fertilizer additive, mulch, and soil improver.

high in salt. It can be added to the compost pile or can be spread on the beds and worked or watered in.

Seaweed or kelp Seaweed is high in potassium and an excellent source of trace elements – it contains more than 70 minerals, vitamins, and enzymes. It is also an organic fertilizer additive. Add seaweed to the compost pile, use it as mulch, or work it into the soil. If you collect it from the beach, choose only fresh wet pieces from the surf and rinse off the salt – beware of high salt levels. Dried seaweed can be purchased.

Greensand For the slow release of potassium and trace minerals, add greensand to compost. It is not a quick remedy for potassium deficiency.

Rock phosphate Also called colloidal phosphate, this is an excellent source of

phosphorus and calcium. Given the opportunity, choose the soft type rather than the hard type. Soft rock phosphate provides both immediately available phosphorus and the long-term release of phosphorus and calcium, but the hard type does not provide phosphorus immediately.

Rock dust Also called azomite, this is a good source of potassium, calcium, magnesium, and iron. It contains many trace elements as well as aluminum silicate. Aluminum has recently been linked to the development of Alzheimer's disease, but further study has to be conducted to establish whether a link exists. Azomite is not processed and is thought to be a "safe" soil additive.

Epsom salts Also called magnesium sulfate, this is a good source of magnesium but is not permitted by some organic certifying agencies.

GREEN MANURES

Green manures, also known as cover crops, are grown to improve soil fertility, and to protect the soil from erosion when crops are not being grown. These deep-rooted plants suppress weeds, prevent soil crusting during long, hot summers, and bring nutrients to the surface from below.

USE OF GREEN MANURES

The practice of planting green manures began more than 2,000 years ago, and is still an important way to enrich the soil. Green manures should be worked into your plant for crop rotation (see pp. 78–81). Plant a green manure whenever a crop has been harvested and you do not intend to use the bed for other crops for at least thirty days. From the table on pages 58–9, you can see that many options are available. In warm weather, consider growing buckwheat, or, if nitrogen is needed, buckwheat mixed with soybeans. In fall, try planting winter rye.

UNDERSOWING CROPS

Undersowing is a form of companion planting (see pp. 118–19): a green manure is sown in a bed after the main crop is well established, and remains after the main crop has been harvested. Undersowing can be very advantageous, for example when a green manure of legumes is desired for winter. Legumes are difficult to get established in cold weather, and undersowing gives them a good head start. But undersowing must be timed well, or the green manure may be competition with the main crop. Generally it is a good idea to allow six weeks between planting the main crop and undersowing.

Prior to undersowing, clear the bed of weeds and loosen the surface of the soil. Broadcast the seeds by hand under the foliage of the crop. A few examples of good companions are dwarf white clover or oats sown under tomatoes, sweet clover around winter squash, and beans under corn.

Winter rye Plant winter rye in the fall, immediately after harvesting crops. It may be turned under in the spring or allowed to grow to maturity for the grain to be harvested.

RECOMMENDED GREEN MANURES

NAME	CONDITIONS	COMMENTS
Buckwheat *Fagopyrum esculentum*	Warm weather	Excellent for crowding out weeds. Produces lots of organic matter quickly. Attracts bees. Provides habitat for beneficial insects. Matures in 30–40 days.
Winter rye *Secale cereale*	Cold weather	Hardy winter crop. Good for sowing in fall. Prevents soil erosion. Chokes out weeds.
Winter wheat *Triticum aestivum*	Cool weather	Chokes out weeds. Stabilizes soils in winter if planted in fall.
Spring wheat *Triticum aestivum*	Warm weather	Chokes out weeds.
Oats *Avena sativa*	Cool and warm	Plant at any time of year for green manure. Prevents erosion. Will not regrow in spring.
White/Sweet clover *Melilotus alba,* *M. officinalis*	Cool weather	Long taproots open up soils. Fixes nitrogen.
Red clover *Trifolium pratense*	Cool weather	Attracts bees and fixes nitrogen. Requires high calcium and good drainage.
Persian clover *Trifolium resupinatum*	Cool weather	Ideal permanent seeding in erosion prone areas. Fixes nitrogen. Dense growing. Crowds out weeds.
Crimson clover *Trifolium incarnatum*	Cool weather	Shade tolerant. Fixes nitrogen. Good cover crop in beds used to grow grains.
Rape *Brassica napus*	Cool weather	Breaks up clay soils extremely well with long taproot. Chokes out weeds.
Mustard *Brassica hirta*	Cold weather	Great for loosening heavy clay soils. Fast growing.

RECOMMENDED GREEN MANURES

NAME	CONDITIONS	COMMENTS
Common vetch *Vicia sativa*	Cool weather	Fixes nitrogen. Chokes out weeds and tolerates mowing. Feeds beneficial insects.
Hairy vetch *Vicia villosa*	Cool weather	Fixes nitrogen. Best for cold climates. Feeds beneficial insects. Chokes out weeds.
Fava or broad bean *Vicia faba*	Cool weather	Fixes nitrogen. Strong roots break up hard soil and bring up nutrients.
Cowpeas *Vigna sinensis*	Cold weather	Fixes nitrogen. Chokes out weeds. Tolerates shade. Discourages nematodes if incorporated after bloom.
Pinto beans *Phaseolus vulgaris*	Cool weather	Fixes nitrogen. Requires good drainage. Heat and drought tolerant.
Soybeans *Glycine max*	Warm weather	Fixes nitrogen. Often mixed with buckwheat.
Alfalfa *Medicago sativa*	Cool and warm	Fixes nitrogen. Does not like acidic soils. Provides habitat for beneficial insects.
Fenugreek *Trigonella foenum-graecum*	Cool weather	Seeds germinate at very cold temperatures. Quick growing. Deep roots break up soil.
Sudan grass *Sorgum bicolor* var. *sudanense*	Warm weather	Excellent organic matter producer. Vigorous and chokes out weeds extremely well. Discourages nematodes.
Sparky marigold *Tagetes patula*	Warm weather	Grown for nematode control. Adds organic matter.
Oil radish/Dakon *Raphanus sitivus*	Cool weather	Mow before incorporating into the soil. Discourages nematodes. Long taproot penetrates subsoil.

BENEFITS OF HUMUS

Adding humus to the soil has the following results:

- Improves drainage
- Aerates the soil
- Allows water to penetrate the surface
- Retains moisture
- Loosens heavy soils
- Helps heavy soils warm up in the spring
- Prevents loss of nutrients from light soils

ADDING ORGANIC MATTER TO TOPSOIL

Planting green manure and turning it into the soil is a quick way to add organic matter. The above-ground vegetation decays and forms humus.

When the tops are turned under, the roots are left in the ground to decay, and help to deepen the topsoil. There are two ways to incorporate the vegetation into the soil. The first is to turn under green moisture-filled growth. This stimulates microbiotic activity, but adds little humus to the soil. The second is to mow the green manure and leave it to dry for a day or two before turning it under. Although it takes much longer for the dry vegetation to decay, it adds more humus to the soil and makes organic material available for a longer period of time to feed future crops grown in that area.

Which method is better? This depends on your situation. It may be difficult to try to plant a bed where dried vegetation has recently been turned under. So if you intend to plant the bed very soon, turn it under green. If you want to increase the long-term fertility of the bed, turn it under dried.

BREAKING UP THE SUBSOIL

Many green manures have deep roots that break up compacted subsoil. While topsoil is generally light and filled with lots of humus, subsoil is usually heavy and lacks organic matter. When the roots of deep-rooted cover crops spread out and penetrate the subsoil, they loosen it and break it up so that it is aerated. Future crops then find it easier to extend their roots into the subsoil to obtain minerals, nutrients, and water. When the roots decay, they leave behind organic matter in the subsoil. Improved air circulation allows oxygen to reach deeper into the soil and assist with the breakdown of organic matter.

NITROGEN FIXING

Some green manures extract nitrogen from the air and fix it in nodules on their roots. These nodules slowly release the nitrogen into the soil for use by future crops. These green manures are legumes, just like beans and peas. In order for them to fix nitrogen, they require a special type of bacterium in the soil. This bacterium is called an "inoculant." The bacterium and the legumes have a symbiotic relationship. There are many strains of bacteria, and the right one must be chosen to match the legume being grown. Once legumes have been grown in a bed, it is rarely necessary to inoculate again. For legumes to fix nitrogen, a pH of 6.5 to 7.0 is preferred, and there should be no deficiency in cobalt, which is a catalyst for the chemical reaction.

PREVENTING EROSION AND NUTRIENT LOSS

When soils are left unplanted, rain falls on the bare earth and washes away its nutrients. Sandy and alkaline soils are particularly susceptible to nutrient loss and erosion. Heavy soils are compacted. Planting a green manure will prevent erosion. Nutrients that might otherwise be washed out will be used by the green manure, and then returned to the soil when the cover crop is turned under. Minerals spend more time in plant roots and vegetation than they do in the soil when the bed is kept planted throughout the year. Try to plant a cover crop as soon as possible after harvesting from a bed. The deep roots of some green manures collect nutrients from deep down in the soil and bring them to the surface where they will be available to future crops raised in the bed.

STIMULATING SOIL MICROORGANISMS

As mentioned above, turning under moisture-filled green vegetation stimulates microbiotic activity in the soil. This activity helps to break up organic matter in the soil and makes the nutrients available to future crops grown in that bed. It also breaks up woody and undecomposed organic matter into rich humus that will wick water out of heavy, moisture-retentive soils and retain water in light, powdery soils. Even peat soils are improved by cover crops that are turned under when lush and green, because this stimulates microbiotic activity and improves drainage.

SOWING AND TURNING UNDER

To sow a green manure, prepare the bed as you would for vegetables (see pp. 128–31). Broadcast the seeds by hand and rake to cover the seeds lightly with soil. If sowing a large area, use a handheld seed broadcaster to make the job easier. Dragging tree branches across the area makes quick work of lightly covering the seed. If it is dry, water the area after planting. Little other care is necessary until it is time to turn the crop into the soil.

Use a garden fork or spade to turn the crop under when green. Mowing just before turning under makes the job easier, but is not necessary. To increase the humus level in the soil, mow the cover crop and let it dry before working it in. For very large areas, you may find a tiller useful. As a general rule, green manure is ready to be turned under when it flowers, but before it sets seed. Research the cover crop you choose and incorporate it at the appropriate time.

Digging in When a cover crop has flowered but not yet set seed, it is time to incorporate it into the soil. It can be dug in green, or mowed and allowed to dry before being incorporated.

CHAPTER 3

PLANNING THE

ORGANIC GARDEN

THE IMPORTANCE OF PLANNING

After soil fertility, planning is the most important step to a successful organic garden. Crop rotation and choosing varieties that suit your location and climate are fundamental to organic gardening. They are more help in growing healthy plants than the use of beneficial insects or organic fertilizers.

ASKING QUESTIONS

Rotating crops discourages diseases and many pests. Rotation also allows soil fertility to be maintained or improved. Heavy-feeding crops can follow crops that feed the soil. But before drawing up a plan of crop rotation, you must decide what to grow.

Which fruits and vegetables do you and your family like? And which are most nutritious? Which varieties should you choose? What will grow in your climate? These are all questions that must be answered first.

Heirloom fruits and vegetables are old varieties that are open pollinated. Unlike many modern varieties, they tend to grow very well without chemical fertilizers. Most of the old varieties were developed before the invention of pesticides, and many of the heirlooms are resistant to pests in the conditions where they were developed.

FOOD FOR THE HOME

It is important to plan your garden so that it provides for you own nutritional needs and those of your family. A well-balanced diet is essential for good health. It is also worth taking into consideration the new science of functional foods. These provide phytochemicals that can lessen the risk of cancer as well as of heart disease and other serious illnesses, and are necessary for good health. Do not worry if this subject is new to you

or if you find it confusing; it is explained in more detail later in this chapter (see pp. 88–9).

Planning the garden so that there is something to harvest throughout the year ensures that you have a fresh supply of organic vegetables during winter. Many plants are quite cold hardy and can be harvested from greenhouses and cold frames all winter long. You will need to assess how much you and your family are likely to consume of any particular fruit or vegetables, so that you can devote the appropriate amount of space to them in the garden.

It is also useful to consider companion

Well-planned plot *To make the most of your vegetable plot, take time to assess the quantity and variety of plants that you want to grow.*

PARTS OF A FLOWER

Plants that have male and female reproductive parts on the same plant are called monoecious; those where male and female parts are borne on separate plants are known as dioecious.

❶ Ovary The ovary, at the base of the flower, is where seeds form. In fruiting plants, the fruit is the mature ovary; inside the ovary are ovules.

❷ Petal Thin leaves that form the colorful blossom of the flower. Sepals are leaflike coverings over the flowerbud before it opens.

❸ Stamen The male reproductive parts of the flower, made up of anthers and filaments. The anther is the location of the pollen, and the filament extends from the base of the flower and holds the anther.

❹ Pistil Made up of the stigma (receives pollen), style and ovary, this is the female reproductive part of the flower. The style is the tube that holds the stigma and transmits pollen into the ovary. The stigma receives the pollen and is generally quite sticky.

planting at the planning stage. If you grow certain vegetables and fruits in close proximity to one another, one plant can provide nutrients needed by a neighbor, or discourage pests that would otherwise be attracted to that neighbor.

LANDSCAPING

Finally, when considering the overall plan for your garden, take time to think about landscaping. There is a wonderful selection of plants available, from which you can choose edible plants that are decorative, as well as ornamental plants that are edible, to landscape your site. Flowers are an essential part of this plan, for they attract beneficial insects and provide habitat for predators in the garden. Toads and frogs, birds, and beneficial insects, all of which feed on pests, are encouraged to live in your garden.

BASIC BOTANY

Some plants have complete flowers, containing both male and female reproductive organs (highlighted in the box). Other plants have incomplete flowers, that is to say, they possess only one set of sexual organs. All flowers are held on a stalk or stem, which usually has leaves. Alternatively, leaves form on leafless stalks or emerge directly from the roots.

Seed is formed when pollen from the anthers is deposited on the stigma and the stigma conveys this pollen to the ovary where fertilization takes place. The stigma must be at the right stage of development to accept the pollen. In self-fertile flowers, this stage is reached before the blossom opens. If this is not the case, the plant depends on an external pollinating agent, which is usually an insect. Other plants rely on the wind to carry pollen to the stigma.

CHOOSING PLANTS

Deciding what to grow can be very difficult, but it is easy to come up with answers if we consider what our ancestors grew and why. Our grandparents and great grandparents were much more concerned with the quality of vegetables in the garden. Quantity was of less concern.

ASSESSING SUITABILITY

Our ancestors chose to grow things that worked well together; after one crop was harvested, another could be planted in its place. They also learned to plant so that the preceding crop fertilized the following one. These are useful factors that we should bear in mind when planning the organic garden.

Another key factor when deciding which plants to grow is that some vegetables can be purchased from a store, while others are not available on the shelves or are simply unpalatable. For example, the taste of store-bought tomatoes cannot compare to that of home-grown varieties. Lettuce or strawberries picked fresh from the garden taste better than those offered in stores. When planning your garden, start on a small scale, growing only the vegetables that have a short lifespan or that are not available in shops. In subsequent years, you can expand your range of garden produce to match your diet and taste.

CLIMATE AND LOCATION

When choosing plants, take practical factors into consideration. You may love artichokes, but it may not be possible to grow them if you live in a cold climate with short summers. If this is the case, search out a variety that matures more quickly or consider using a cold frame or greenhouse. Vegetable varieties often differ in their tolerance of climates and locations. For example, some varieties of dry bean are prone to mold and produce poorly in the humid heat

 ## CLIMATES AND ZONES

Climate is an important consideration when planning. You should determine the date of the average last spring frost in your area, and that of the average first fall frost. The number of days between these two dates is your growing season. When buying seed, consider the number of days it takes the plant to mature. Most seed companies will list the number of days required from sowing to maturity.

Similarly, when choosing perennials, trees, and bushes, it is important to consider your climate – both the severity of the winter and how hot it gets in summer. In particular, you need to know the average minimum temperature for your area. The United States Department of Agriculture Plant Hardiness Zone Map divides North America into zones which correspond to average minimum temperatures. Many gardening books and catalogs indicate plant hardiness by giving a range of zones in which a plant may successfully be grown.

of warm areas, but they grow remarkably well in temperate climates. Other varieties will not mature in the short summers of cold climates, and prefer hot climates.

For consistently good results from your crop, choose the variety that is most appropriate to the growing conditions in your particular climate, location, and soil type.

SAVING SEED

After growing an open-pollinated variety successfully, you may notice that some individual plants grew better than others. These are the ones that are likely to prefer the climate and soil conditions of your site, and so you should save their seeds for use when planting in the next year. By selecting seeds from those plants that grow best in your garden, you are choosing a subvariety that is well suited to it. However, if you repeat the practice of seed saving year after year, that particular strain of the variety will differ slightly from the seed that you originally purchased and sowed. As well as site suitability, seeds may also be chosen for their color, form, flavor, or time of harvest – the beauty of saving seed is that you set the criteria.

THE EFFECTS OF AGRIBUSINESS

In the last couple of decades, large commercial concerns have started to take over the food-growing industry, buying up most of the seed companies. They mix up chemical fertilizers in the laboratory and advertize them to farmers and home gardeners alike.

In order to make profits, these big businesses have hybridized new varieties of vegetable, then patented and promoted them. These hybrids are rarely chosen for their taste or nutrition. More often, they are selected for their uniform appearance, shipping ability, and ease of growth under chemical control. These hybrids tend to produce a crop that is ready for harvest at the

Saving seed *Seedheads can be hung upside-down in the warm sun to dry. Protect the heads with paper bags to keep out light and to catch any seeds that fall.*

same time – a necessary feature for commercial farmers – whereas the home gardener wants the exact opposite of this, namely a harvest over an extended time.

HYBRIDS IN THE GARDEN

Some hybrids grown for their taste still create problems for organic gardeners. The plants tend to be very uniform and are ready for harvest all at the same time, rather than over an extended period. The hybrid crop rarely produces any individuals that grow better than others because it lacks diversity; hence, the benefits of saving seed from open-pollinated varieties is lost.

If you save seed from a first-generation hybrid between two true-breeding varieties (these plants are referred to as F1 hybrids), the resulting seed

Open-pollinated varieties provide diversity of color and flavor.

tends to revert to some of the parents' characteristics. The second-generation, or F2, hybrid is likely to be very irregular. If successive generations are selected repeatedly, the hybrid can be "stabilized" to produce plants that are very close to the parent. At this point the plant is referred to as a new open-pollinated variety.

IMPORTANCE OF GENETIC DIVERSITY

Open-pollinated seeds are usually a better choice for the organic garden than F1 hybrids. They have a greater genetic diversity among individuals, which is a strength when adverse conditions occur. For example, some individual plants may be resistant to disease or able to survive pest attack. If a crop is damaged, you can still expect some harvest, albeit smaller than expected, rather than no harvest at all.

The importance of genetic diversity is well illustrated by the following tale. In 1970, most commercial farmers in the United States were growing the same hybrid variety of corn. When corn blight attacked this non-resistant variety, more than 15 per cent of the entire US crop was destroyed. Vast amounts of corn were lost because the commercial variety lacked genetic diversity. In contrast, small farmers who were growing open-pollinated varieties of corn lost little if any of their crop. Following the blight, the large-scale seed suppliers offered open-pollinated varieties to commercial farmers for the next year's planting. Sadly, little has been learned from this incident because, today, these suppliers are once again selling hybrids to commercial growers.

The founder of Seed Savers' Exchange, an organization that preserves heirloom varieties, has likened the offering of these uniform hybrids to a burglar stealing the key to a single apartment and finding that the key opens every other apartment in the building. Many commercially grown crops are of a similarly small genetic diversity. Most of the major commercially grown cash crops are hybrids, which have virtually identical genes.

GENETICALLY MODIFIED FOODS

Instead of increasing genetic diversity, large-scale seed producers opted to produce chemicals that combat the pests and diseases, for which they charge the commercial growers dearly. More recently, the major chemical companies that make pesticides have come up with a new idea – genetically modified seed, commonly referred to as a genetically modified organism (GMO). Instead of hybridizing seed, these companies now inject the DNA of viruses, bacteria, fish, animals, and other vegetables into the DNA of vegetables in the hope of creating a "better" variety.

Seed producers claim that genetically modified seed is necessary to "feed the world." In reality, there is no evidence that the harvests have increased in size; in fact, studies show that the harvests produced from genetically modified seeds are sometimes smaller. You may wonder why this work is being done. The answer is profits. The primary factor that is introduced in the process of genetic engineering is pesticide and herbicide resistance. For example, a soybean has been produced that can withstand virtually unlimited doses of the most popular brand of

Raising wheat *With growing concerns over GMOs in wheat and other commercial crops, many organic gardeners are choosing to raise their own.*

pesticide. When one of these seed companies sells its seed to a commercial grower, it issues a contract to license the seed. Not only does this contract require the grower to use the company's pesticide, it also forbids them from saving seed for the next year's planting.

Besides the obvious concerns about the possible adverse effects of such huge doses of pesticide on people eating produce from these seeds, another concern exists. When the complete eradication of pests is attempted by using chemicals, the genetic diversity of the pests inevitably results in the survival of the resistant individuals only. These individuals breed and reproduce, eventually creating a strain that is resistant to the pesticide. Considering the rapid rate of reproduction in the insect world, the widespread use of pesticides, such as that seen in the midwest of the United States, may result in resistant strains in as little as five years.

CREATING RESISTANCE
This concern about the rise of a resistant strain is analogous to documented medical data from Mexico. Doctors in that country in the past prescribed penicillin for every little ailment. When patients were diagnosed with a viral infection such as a cold, it was customary to prescribe penicillin as a preventative measure in order to discourage opportunistic infections. A study carried out in 1997 indicates that the overuse of penicillin has resulted in the creation of resistant bacteria; the number of cases of antibiotic-resistant pneumonia rose from 14 per cent in 1994 to 25 per cent in 1997 – compare this with a few decades ago, when there were no known resistant strains of pneumonia.

Perfect fruit Working with a resistant variety by using organic rather than chemical controls, you can achieve a harvest of perfect peaches and nectarines.

A recent study shows that tobacco budworm (*Heliothis virescens*) will be completely resistant to *Bacillus thuringiensis* (Bt) within three to four years (see p. 172)[1], because of the prevalence of Bt corn. When a chemical company executive was confronted with this information, he replied, "We can handle this problem with new products. The critics don't know what we have in the pipeline. Trust us."[2]

In the United States, the Environmental Protection Agency (EPA) has recommended that a percentage of farmland be planted with conventional corn to slow down the process of resistant pest formation. Areas of non-genetically modified corn will provide a habitat for pests.[3] It is ironic that an organic method of pest control (Bt) has been used to create a super-pest that is much harder to control.

UNSEEN GENES
Genetic engineering has gone far beyond the genetic manipulation of hybrids, and the safety of genetically engineered food has not yet been determined. Hybridizing involves human assistance in a natural process; genetic engineering may have unforeseen consequences. No study has proved that GMO foods are safe.

Any plants may face infection with genetically modified genes, through the natural process of insect or wind pollination. There have been several documented incidents of genetic drift, resulting in at least one court action. There is no easy solution to this problem.

[1] Gould, F., Anderson, A., Jones, A. et al. *Initial frequency of alleles for resistance to* Bacillus thuringiensis *toxins in the field populations of* Heliothis virescens, Proceedings of the National Academy of Sciences, 94, pp. 3519–23, 1997.

[2] Pollen, Michael. *Playing God in the Garden*, New York Times Sunday Magazine, October 25, 1998.

[3] *Ibid.*

HERITAGE & HEIRLOOM VARIETIES

Heritage and heirloom varieties of vegetables and fruits are old open-pollinated varieties that have long been in cultivation. They refer to historic and ethnic varieties or to varieties that have been passed down through generations of a family or culture.

BENEFITS OF OLD VARIETIES

Growing old and open-pollinated varieties have many advantages for the organic gardener. First and foremost, the seed from these vegetable plants can be saved and replanted. This has

Traditional crop *Parsnips have long been common kitchen garden vegetables. They keep well in root cellars or stored in the ground over winter.*

several benefits. There is no reason to go out and purchase new seeds every year when they can easily be collected in the garden, and they have the advantage of being organically grown. It is often difficult to find organically grown seeds, and it is essential to use organic seeds.

Seed companies often discontinue older varieties of vegetables and replace them with modern hybrids, which are more profitable for them to sell. You may find that your favorite tomato or bean has suddenly been discontinued or withdrawn from stock. In fact, between 1984 and 1991, 45 per cent of the open-pollinated seeds available for sale were removed from seed catalogs and replaced with F1 hybrids. Many of the older varieties have been selected for traits that make them more suitable to specific climates and locations than the current commercial varieties. The taste of the old varieties is often unique, whereas most of the vegetables sold in stores have a "standardized" taste.

OPEN-POLLINATED VARIETIES

While all heirloom and heritage seeds are open pollinated, not all open-pollinated varieties are old. A good example is the 'Sweet 100' tomato, a hybrid that was stabilized over many years. The seed of the F1 generation was saved and grown out again. The individual plants closest to the F1 generation were chosen to be the parents of further generations. After more than six generations, the hybrid was stabilized so that the seeds come true to type.

Some hybrids have qualities that are not found in the open-pollinated varieties. You may choose to stabilize them yourself in your garden. You may consider some of the newer open-pollinated varieties, which can offer wonderful qualities for the vegetable garden.

REGIONAL VARIETIES

Among heirloom plants, regional varieties are most suited to being grown in certain areas. 'Vermont Cranberry' is an example of a regional variety of dry bean. It is noted for growing extremely well within a short growing season. There are regional varieties for almost every area of the world and it is worth your while to seek out the varieties that are common to your area, and consider growing them. Typically they will be resistant to the pests and diseases found in your area and be able to produce an abundant crop in your climate.

When choosing varieties, look beyond plants that are propagated by seed. There are many perennials, trees, and bushes, as well as potatoes, artichokes, asparagus, and garlic, that are asexually propagated. These plants are reproduced by division or other vegetative methods rather than by fertilization. While all the arguments in favor of open-pollinated seeds do not apply to these plants, the other benefits still weigh heavily in favor of the heirloom, heritage, and regional varieties. Older vegetable varieties often grow better without the use of chemical fertilizers and pesticides, and are likely to be more pest resistant. Most important of all, they produce a wonderfully flavorsome harvest.

Golden pears Like many heirloom fruit varieties, these pears are deliciously sweet. Because of their resistance to disease, they also thrive with relatively little care.

WHAT IS AN HEIRLOOM VARIETY?

It is difficult to accurately define an heirloom, but there are three primary guidelines:

- Heirlooms must be open pollinated. Seed saved from one year will produce plants that are largely like their parents, or "true to type." The edible parts of the plant will taste basically the same as their parents. There is room for biodiversity in open-pollinated varieties; this is not so in F1 hybrids where almost all individuals are identical. Asexually propagated plants are exempt from this guideline.
- Heirlooms must have withstood the test of time. The amount of time required is rather arbitrary, but some standard expectations have developed. Plants started from seed are generally considered heirlooms if they have been cultivated for more

than fifty years. Bushes and perennials require fifty to seventy-five years, and trees are considered heirloom varieties if they are still valuable after seventy to one hundred years.

- The variety should have a history. This may include its association with a particular ethnic group and its cuisine. The variety may have been an

important crop for a society or a treasured fruit or vegetable passed down through one family. It may have a historical link with a particular event in a certain culture.

Many varieties have been grown for a long time but their histories have been lost. Nevertheless, they are still considered to be heirlooms.

Some of the more recent varieties of asexually propagated plants are also worth considering, but choose carefully. You may find yourself raising the latest and best variety that can be harvested green, shipped over long distances, and that needs doses of pesticides to yield a decent crop – in other words, a variety bred to please commercial growers rather than organic gardeners.

GOVERNMENTAL THREAT TO BIODIVERSITY

One of the most serious threats to heirloom seed is governmental pressures for the elimination of varieties that are almost identical in appearance and taste. The Common European Catalogue removed 1,500 varieties from its lists in 1980, claiming they were identical. What governments

overlook is the fact that many similar-looking varieties possess different qualities of pest and disease resistance because of their ancestry. For example, a variety that has long been grown in England is better suited to that country's climate than a variety that looks and tastes similar but has been developed and grown in southern Italy for the last fifty years. The climates, pests, and diseases are not identical, so the resistance levels are bound to differ between varieties.

Some countries have gone so far as to make it illegal to supply varieties that are not recognized by the government. In these countries gardeners seeking specific varieties have to join a seed-saving group, in order to exchange (rather than purchase) restricted seeds.

BREEDING VARIETIES FOR YOUR GARDEN

Saving seed from the best plants in the garden will result in a selection that is especially well suited to your particular location and climate. Saving seed is easy for most vegetables. The hard part is choosing the individual plants from which to harvest seed.

SELECTING THE BEST PLANTS

You need to be a constant observer in your garden. If a few individual plants bear fruit earlier than the others, you can select for that trait by saving seed only from those individuals. You get to decide what qualities constitute "best." For one gardener the quality might be flavor but for another it might be pest resistance or drought tolerance, depending on your location and climate, as well as on the types of pest and disease present in your area. Whatever your criteria, make sure that you save seed only from healthy, disease-free plants that are hardy or heat tolerant in your garden. Choose several plants from which to save seed – this helps to protect the genetic diversity of the variety. Always label your seed plants so that they do not get accidentally harvested for the table. It often helps to keep a journal recording your seed selection and the reasons why you chose them.

SAVING SEED

The first step is to determine if the plant is an annual, a biennial, or a perennial. Perennials are most often propagated asexually; however, some are propagated from seed like annuals.

Annuals are the easiest plants from which to harvest seeds. They flower and produce seed in one season. Many of them are self-pollinating, although some require cross-pollination. Those that cross-pollinate must be isolated from different varieties and other vegetables in the

SAVING TOMATO SEEDS

1 Take several fully ripe tomatoes and slice them to expose the seeds and pulp. Squeeze the pieces and use your thumb to remove all of the pulp and seeds.

2 Smear the pulp and seed mixture on a dry paper towel. Spread them out evenly for quicker drying and leave them in a well-ventilated, dark, warm area.

3 When the seeds appear dry, place them in a paper envelope to finish drying. Once dry, they can be transferred to an airtight jar. Label and date the seeds.

same family, otherwise the resulting seed may be an unexpected hybrid. A good way to accomplish this is to separate insect-pollinated plants in a screen enclosure and to pollinate by hand. Choose a flower from one plant, peel back its petals and brush the pollen against the stigma of the flowers of the plant you will use to harvest seed.

Wind-pollinated plants need to be separated from each other by a significant distance in the garden for successful results; alternatively, they must come into flower at different times. A greenhouse is occasionally required for growing plants for seed (see pp. 96–8).

Propagating garlic *Although garlic sets seed, it is best propagated by division. Separate the individual cloves of a garlic bulb and plant them in the fall.*

Multiple beds Divide large plots into smaller beds and rotate crops from year to year. You may choose to include flowers in your rotation plan.

Biennials are plants that require two growing seasons to flower and set seed. Some may be left in the ground over winter, while others must be harvested and replanted in the spring. All the above information about self-pollination and cross-pollination applies equally to biennials.

HARVESTING SEED

Timing is essential when harvesting seed: unripe seed will not germinate, and seed that is left on the plant too long is likely to become damp or damaged by pests. Typically, you should harvest seed at the end of the growing season, long after the point when the plant would normally have been harvested for the table. In come cases, the seeds need to be extracted from the fruits (see Saving tomato seeds, p. 75).

Water is the enemy of all seeds. Dry seeds thoroughly in a dark, warm area, such as a cupboard, but check that it is well ventilated so as to encourage free air circulation. Spreading seeds thinly on a fine-mesh screen works well. After the seeds are dry, store them in a canning jar, or similar container, and label and date them.

TESTING SEED VIABILITY

Most seeds remain viable for a long time, but others, like carrots and parsnips, germinate well only in the following spring. Test the germination rate of your seeds first before relying on them for your spring planting. To do this, plant ten seeds indoors in a flat and see how many germinate. Another method is to put the seeds on a wet paper towel inside a plastic bag and leave them in a warm spot. If you have less than 50 per cent germination, discard the seeds or grow a crop just for the purpose of producing fresh seeds.

CROP ROTATION

Crop rotation is one of the most important factors in planning the organic garden – even in the smallest of gardens. The order of rotation should aim to have heavy feeders follow those that nourish the soil. Rotation also breaks the cycle of soilborne pests and diseases.

BASIC PRINCIPLES

Once you have a good idea of what you plan to grow in your garden, it is time to plan the order of crop rotation. Although it is more difficult to rotate crops in a small plot, you must persevere in order to discourage pests and diseases. Crop rotation is essential to achieve success when gardening organically.

Plants that feed the soil should be followed by those that take nutrients from the soil. Let us start with a simple example of a two-year plan where only corn and beans are to be grown. Beans are legumes that fix nitrogen into the soil,

Simple rotation Sweet corn and beans make a good choice for simple crop rotation. The beans fix nitrogen in the soil, on which the corn thrives in the next year.

THREE-YEAR ROTATION PLAN

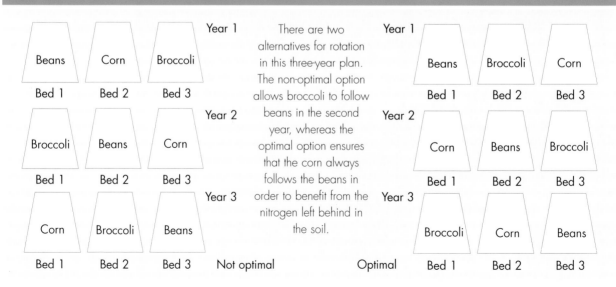

	Year 1		
Beans	Corn	Broccoli	
Bed 1	Bed 2	Bed 3	

	Year 2		
Broccoli	Beans	Corn	
Bed 1	Bed 2	Bed 3	

	Year 3		
Corn	Broccoli	Beans	
Bed 1	Bed 2	Bed 3	
			Not optimal

There are two alternatives for rotation in this three-year plan. The non-optimal option allows broccoli to follow beans in the second year, whereas the optimal option ensures that the corn always follows the beans in order to benefit from the nitrogen left behind in the soil.

Year 1

Beans	Broccoli	Corn
Bed 1	Bed 2	Bed 3

Year 2

Corn	Beans	Broccoli
Bed 1	Bed 2	Bed 3

Year 3

Broccoli	Corn	Beans
Bed 1	Bed 2	Bed 3

Optimal

and corn needs nitrogen to grow well. You can create two beds, and alternate the crop grown in each bed every year. In this way, the beans leave nitrogen behind to be used by the corn.

Now suppose that you choose to introduce a third crop, such as broccoli. This would provide you with two possible rotation plans (see three-year rotation plan, left). The real question here is which is the best order to rotate them? One option would be for the first bed to be sown with beans, followed in the next year by broccoli, and then by corn in the third year.

A second option would be for the corn to immediately follow the beans every year. The latter option is preferable because the corn has a greater need than the broccoli for the nitrogen left behind by the beans. Also, experience has shown that brassicas are not good preceding crops for heavy feeders such as corn.

GROUPING THE CROPS

There is no crop-rotation plan guaranteed to produce perfect results because every garden has a different selection of crops. It is up to you to

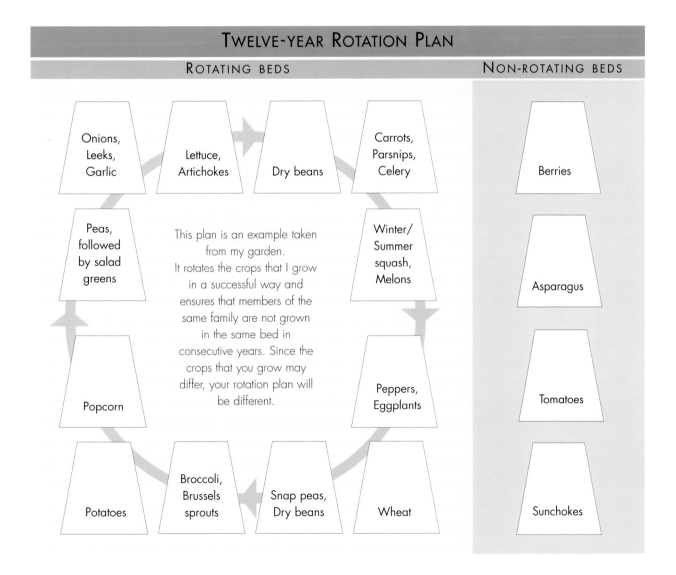

TWELVE-YEAR ROTATION PLAN

ROTATING BEDS   NON-ROTATING BEDS

Onions, Leeks, Garlic

Lettuce, Artichokes

Dry beans

Carrots, Parsnips, Celery

Berries

Peas, followed by salad greens

This plan is an example taken from my garden.
It rotates the crops that I grow in a successful way and ensures that members of the same family are not grown in the same bed in consecutive years. Since the crops that you grow may differ, your rotation plan will be different.

Winter/ Summer squash, Melons

Asparagus

Popcorn

Peppers, Eggplants

Tomatoes

Potatoes

Broccoli, Brussels sprouts

Snap peas, Dry beans

Wheat

Sunchokes

Broad beans *Plant broad beans as a green manure or as a crop to harvest for use in the kitchen. They are an ideal preceding crop to heavy feeders.*

work out one that best suits your garden and the crops you want to grow. The easiest way to accomplish this is to use slips of paper labeled with the names of the vegetables and fruits. Cut the pieces of paper in proportion to each other so that the size of each slip reflects how much you want to grow of that particular crop.

Arrange the slips of paper on a table in front of you, with similar vegetables grouped together by family (shown below):

- *Chenopodiaceae*/Goosefoot family: beets, spinach, Swiss chard
- *Asteraceae*/Daisy family: endive, chicory, artichokes, sunflowers, sunchokes, lettuces
- *Convolvulaceae*/Morning glory family: sweet potatoes
- *Brassicaceae*/Mustard family: kale, radishes, cabbages, Brussels sprouts, kohlrabi, broccoli, rutabagas, turnips, cauliflower
- *Cucurbitaceae*/Gourd family: watermelons, melons, cucumber, summer squash, winter squash
- *Poaceae*/Grass family: wheat, corn, rye
- *Papilionaceae*/Pea and bean family: beans, peas
- *Alliaceae*/Onion family: onions, leeks, garlic
- *Polygonaceae*/Buckwheat family: buckwheat
- *Solanaceae*/Nightshade family: peppers, eggplants, potatoes
- *Apiaceae*/Carrot family: celery, carrots, parsnips

Many gardeners group their vegetables based on how they are grown, rather than by their botanical family. On this basis, a grouping of root crops would comprise potatoes *(Solanaceae)*, radishes *(Brassicaceae)*, carrots *(Apiaceae)*, and beets *(Chenopodiaceae)*. The drawback here is that although it may aid in cultivation and harvesting, it does not assist with the prevention of pests and diseases. For example, you might choose to have root crops (including rutabagas) followed by greens (including kale), and then cabbages; this would result in brassicas being grown in the same bed for three consecutive years and would allow diseases that plague brassicas to flourish. For this reason, the better method is to group vegetables based on their botanical family and to rotate the families.

PLANNING YOUR ROTATION

With the paper slips separated out into vegetable families, you can develop your own crop rotation plan. If any of the groups are particularly large, divide them into two smaller sections to make them more manageable. Your goal should be to have all the groups at approximately the same size. If a family only contains one crop, move it to a smaller group to create a more even balance.

With the equal-sized groupings of paper in front of you, start to arrange them in a logical order. Begin with the legumes (beans and peas), which feed the soil. Follow them with heavy feeders like corn. Put brassicas before legumes. Potatoes are a suitable crop to follow corn because they tolerate poor soil. And since potatoes produce so much foliage that they inhibit the growth of weeds, follow them with, say, a crop of onions, which are difficult to weed.

Once you have arranged your cards on this basis, you might find that you have an arrangement similar to the twelve-crop plan illustrated on page 79. This is a good start but the question remains: how do the rest of the crops fit into the rotation plan? Highlighted in the box to the right are some key rules for crop rotation.

RULES FOR CROP ROTATION

- Never follow this year's crop with another member of the same family.
- Arrange your plan so that heavy feeders always follow legumes, which enrich the soil.
- Potatoes yield best after corn.
- Grain crops do best after legumes.
- Root crops often take a lot out of the soil, so put them before legumes.
- Having brassicas follow onions is beneficial.
- Tomatoes are narcissistic and do not like to rotate.
- Squashes and cucumbers are beneficial to most following crops.

Bumper harvest Summer squash do not need high nitrogen levels, and leave plenty of nutrients in the soil for crops raised in the bed in the following year.

THE HEALTH-GIVING GARDEN

A well-balanced diet is essential for good health. The basic principles of good nutrition are very simple but need to be clearly understood to ensure a diet made up of vitamins, minerals, fiber, protein, carbohydrates, and fat. Here are a few basic guidelines to improving your diet.

EAT ORGANIC FOOD

Studies have shown that many chemical pesticides and herbicides leave a residue on plants. This residue may be toxic to humans and can remain in the soil to be taken up by plants. Thereafter, it enters into our diet. Conventionally grown food may be genetically modified, and the potential dangers of this are still yet to be discovered. No study has proven that GMOs are safe. Hormones given to animals are passed on in their milk and flesh to humans.

One final concern is that many conventionally grown crops are fertilized with a manmade nitrogen/phosphate/potash (NPK) fertilizer. Crops grown this way, especially root crops, contain less of the trace elements present in organically grown vegetables. Given these facts, it is clear that carcinogens and other chemicals are unwelcome ingredients in our diets. Instead, we should eat nutritious organic food for good health.

EAT FRESH FOOD

The longer food is stored, the fewer nutrients it retains. Canning and freezing are forms of dead storage, and the nutritional content of the food decreases rapidly. It is best to eat food while it is still fresh, or to preserve it using live storage methods, such as root cellaring, lactic fermentation, or preserving in oil or vinegar (see pp. 276–9). Nothing beats eating food that is

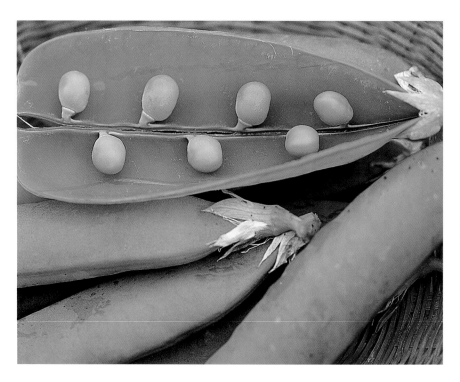

Fresh from the pod
Peas are the easiest vegetable to freeze and they retain almost all their nutrition. They have a high content of vitamin C and phytochemicals. Peas also contain vitamins B1, K, folic acid, potassium, and fiber.

Mediterranean pyramid When planning your meals, allot portions of different types of food according to this diagram. Eat less of the foods at the top of the pyramid and more of the foods at the base. Restrict consumption of red meat and sugars, and eat more grains, fruits, vegetables, and legumes. Be sure to drink plenty of water; wine is permissible in moderation.

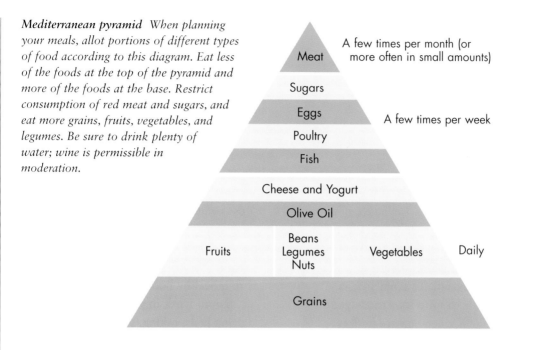

Meat — A few times per month (or more often in small amounts)

Sugars

Eggs

Poultry — A few times per week

Fish

Cheese and Yogurt

Olive Oil

Fruits | Beans Legumes Nuts | Vegetables — Daily

Grains

newly harvested from the garden, so try to extend your harvest well into the winter by using cold frames, greenhouses, and by choosing very cold hardy vegetables. When buying meat, it is worth asking whether it was frozen during transport, as freezing may result in significant nutrient loss.

EAT UNPROCESSED FOOD

In terms of nutrient loss during storage, the issue of food processing should be raised. For example, wheat that has been ground for flour is nutritious, but most flour sold in stores has had the germ or outer shell removed, which is where most of the nutrients are concentrated. The remainder of the wheatgrain, the endosperm, is ground for flour. However, it lacks nutrients to such a degree that iron, B vitamins, and folic acid are added before the flour is sold. Wholewheat flours make a much better choice than chemically enriched flours. Similarly, most raw vegetables provide more nutrients than cooked vegetables, because the heat breaks down nutrients and enzymes. Uncooked foods also provide more fiber. As for ready prepared convenience foods,

eat them as infrequently as possible, if at all. These foods are usually heavily processed and have lost much of their nutritional value.

EAT A VARIETY IN MODERATION

The only way to achieve a proper balance of nutrients is to eat a wide variety of foods. The saying "Too much of a good thing" holds true: too much of any good nutrient can build up to toxic levels. Most people restrict their intake to just a few types of vegetable, even though a wide and diverse range of foods is readily available.

Moderation means that no foods need be blacklisted from your diet, unless for medical reasons; instead, they can be eaten in proper proportions with other foods. The nutritional pyramid above illustrates how to allot portions of different types of food to maintain a well-balanced diet. Foods at the apex of the pyramid are limited to small amounts that may be eaten occasionally, while those at the base can be eaten daily in larger amounts. Place greater emphasis on nutritious foods, and less on others. Portion control is also necessary for good health.

IMPROVING YOUR EATING HABITS

Change your diet slowly. If you change your diet rapidly to eliminate unhealthy eating habits, the end result will probably be failure. You are more likely to suffer from cravings for much-loved foods and gradually revert to an unhealthy diet. Slow changes work better and are more likely to last. Begin by reducing the portion size of foods that should have less emphasis in your diet. At the same time, increase the portions of foods that should have more emphasis. Introduce new vegetables to balance your diet, and vary the foods used in your meals to ensure a good balance and to keep your meals interesting.

Aim to reduce and eventually avoid snacks. Snacks tend to be the least nutritious foods you eat. They are convenient when you are hungry and, more often than not, you find yourself eating them out of habit rather than hunger.

Well-planned nutritious meals need not be elaborate or time consuming to make. Studies have shown that several small meals are healthier than three large meals a day. Moreover, eating several small meals a day will reduce your dependence on snacks. One widely recommended meal plan for good health is six small meals which provide a daily allotment of milk, protein, carbohydrate, fruits, and vegetables.

GARDENING FOR EXERCISE

Feeding your body well is only one half of good health; the other half is getting proper exercise. A combination of nutritious food and exercise is the key to a healthy body. And what better way to exercise than to work in your organic garden? Double digging beds, raking, weeding, and harvesting can be just as good exercise as walking, swimming, and other sports.

Ruby stems Plant Swiss chard (left) in a cold frame in early fall to extend the harvest well into winter.

Cherry ripe Eaten fresh or baked in pies and tarts, cherries (right) are packed with goodness. They are an excellent source of beneficial phytochemicals, vitamin C, and fiber.

VITAMINS & MINERALS

Vitamins are derived from plants and animals. They are organic substances that assist the body in processing other nutrients, like proteins, fats, and carbohydrates. Minerals, unlike vitamins, are inorganic substances and do not break down. They assist enzyme function in the body.

VITAMINS

In addition to helping the body break down nutrients, vitamins are also used in the formation of blood cells, nervous system chemicals, and in the production of DNA. They are needed by the human body in extremely small quantities. Remember that too much of any nutrient can reach toxic levels – this can pose a very real danger if vitamin supplements are overused.

MINERALS

Iron, copper, and other minerals are similar in function to vitamins. They help the body to break down nutrients, by assisting enzymes in their activities. Minerals are usually not broken down by cooking or preserving food, but some leach out of foods that are cooked in water. They can be divided into two categories: macrominerals, that are needed in large quantities, and trace elements.

VEGETARIANISM

If you choose to eat only a vegetarian or vegan diet, it is important that you take supplements of vitamin B12. This vitamin is only available from animal foods but it is essential to your diet for the formation of red blood cells. Anemia, pale skin, loss of balance, and general weakness are just some of the symptoms that can be caused by a deficiency of vitamin B12.

TOP 10 VEGETABLES IN VITAMINS AND MINERALS

1 Broccoli
2 Spinach
3 Brussels sprouts
4 Lima beans
5 Peas
6 Asparagus
7 Artichokes
8 Cauliflowers
9 Sweet potatoes
10 Carrots

One of the Top 10 Vegetables *Carrots are high in minerals and beneficial phytochemicals, including vitamins, and easy to store for use throughout the year.*

VITAMINS AND MINERALS FOR HEALTH

VITAMIN	BENEFIT	MINERAL	BENEFIT
Vitamin A	Healthy skin and hair, good night vision, bone and tooth development, needed for reproduction.	**Macrominerals** Calcium	Builds bones and teeth, aids in blood clotting, aids absorption of B12, activates some enzymes.
Vitamin B1/ Thiamin	Aids breakdown of fats, proteins, and carbohydrates.	Chloride	Activates some enzymes, necessary for stomach acid; regulates body pH.
Vitamin B2/ Riboflavin	Aids breakdown of fats, proteins, and carbohydrates.	Magnesium	Needed to build bones and make proteins; aids in nerve operation.
Vitamin B3/ Niacin	Catalyst for energy production in cells.	Phosphorus	Builds bones and teeth; breaks down fats, proteins, and carbohydrates.
Vitamin B6	Helps the body use fats and proteins; catalyst in red blood cell formation.	Potassium	Needed to regulate balance of water and dissolved solids inside cells.
Vitamin B12	Necessary for formation of red blood cells; helps nervous system functions.	Sodium	Needed to regulate balance of water and dissolved substances outside cells.
Vitamin C	Helps prevent breakdown of other vitamins; blocks some cancer-causing chemicals; helps in collagen formation.	Sulfur	Needed to build amino acids and many proteins.
Vitamin D	Aids in bone and tooth formation; aids in phosphorus and calcium absorption.	**Trace elements** Chromium	Needed to metabolize sugar.
		Copper	Needed for red blood cell formation and for building many enzymes.
Vitamin E	Aids in cell formation, including muscle and red blood cells; prevents vitamin A breakdown.	Fluoride	Aids in formation of teeth and bones.
Vitamin K	Helps with blood clotting.	Iodine	Needed for reproduction, and for proper function of thyroid.
Folic acid	Combined with B12, aids in the formation of red blood cells.	Iron	Helps red blood cells to carry oxygen.
Pantothenic acid	Aids breakdown of fats, proteins, and carbohydrates; aids in regulating nerves.	Manganese	Breaks down carbohydrates, proteins, and fats. Necessary for brain function.
		Selenium	Antioxidant interacts with vitamin E, prevents breakdown of vitamin A.
Biotin	Aids breakdown of carbohydrates.	Zinc	Building block of many enzymes.

FUNCTIONAL FOODS

Strictly speaking the term "phytochemical" applies to all chemicals synthesized by plants, including starches, sugars, oils, and vitamins. However, when people refer to phytochemicals they are usually talking about a particular group of chemicals which are physiologically beneficial to humans by providing protection against cancer and other diseases.

WHAT DO PHYTOCHEMICALS DO?

There are literally hundreds of different phytochemicals present in vegetables and fruits. Scientists are only now beginning to identify many of them, and to understand how they work. It is hoped that by increasing our intake

TOP FRUITS, VEGETABLES, AND NUTS FOR GOOD HEALTH

1	Strawberries	12	Onions
2	Tomatoes	13	Garlic
3	Peppers	14	Blueberries
4	Apples	15	Raspberries
5	Cabbages	16	Blackberries
6	Beans	17	Plums
7	Cherries	18	Lettuce
8	Winter squash	19	Walnuts
9	Apricots		
10	Peaches	plus the Top 10 Vegetables
11	Grapes	listed on page 86

listed on page 86

High-ranking *High in beneficial phytochemicals, peppers come in a range of striking colors and shapes. Their crisp skins and succulent flesh can be eaten raw or cooked. Hot peppers are especially high in phytochemicals.*

of physiologically beneficial phytochemicals, our diet may be used to protect the body against disease. Many of the compounds identified so far are antioxidants which bind with highly reactive substances, called "free radicals," that damage DNA. It is believed that these free radicals are among the factors responsible for cancer and heart disease. Other phytochemicals have been shown to boost the immune system, or block the action of viruses.

Although scientists have only recently identified physiologically beneficial phytochemicals, humans have long been eating large amounts of them. This is important because these compounds are needed in rather

Tasty cabbages Grow brassicas in the garden for a year-round supply of nutritious food which is rich in vitamins, minerals, and phytochemicals.

large quantities for good health. One of the easiest ways to increase the beneficial phytochemical content in our diet is to eat more raw vegetables and fruits. When food is cooked, many of these delicate phytochemicals are destroyed.

Another good way to increase our consumption is to choose vegetables that are high in phytochemicals. The top ten vegetables (foods that have the highest content of vitamins or minerals, see p. 86) are also high in health-promoting phytochemicals. To complement these vegetables, it is important to include some fruits and nuts for a well-balanced supply of phytochemicals (see box, left). In addition to these, consider adding the following produce for a highly nutritious, well-balanced diet: potatoes, cantaloupes, tangerines, mangos, persimmons, pineapples, and watermelons.

PLANNING A YEAR'S SUPPLY

Planning the organic garden so that there is something to harvest throughout the year will enable you to have fresh vegetables in winter. Some vegetables are tolerant of cold weather (cold hardy) and may be harvested in the winter, while others may be harvested from a root cellar.

EXTENDING THE HARVEST

The primary premise in having vegetables to harvest all winter long is quite simple: extend the growing season as long as possible by using a combination of cold hardy plants with cold

EXTENDING THE HARVEST

There is a significant difference between extending the growing season and extending the harvest season. In order to extend the growing season, you will need a greenhouse, heating equipment, overhead plant lights, and a lot of labor to coax plants; however, more often than not the results are unsatisfactory.

In contrast, extending the harvest season is quite easy and economical. Plants are grown during the summer and fall and then protected from the cold throughout the winter for a later harvest.

Cold hardy kohlrabi *A member of the brassica family, kohlrabi is well suited to live storage in a root cellar and will not lose any of its valuable nutrients.*

frames and unheated greenhouses; and then extend the harvest after the plants are grown. Heating a greenhouse or using other expensive and complicated strategies is not necessary.

Start the plants and get them growing in warm weather. When the cold sets in, they should be ready for harvest. Rather than removing them from the ground, however, protect them from the cold – right there in the garden – for a later harvest. Crop protection, in this case, means that the vegetables should be sheltered under cold frames, greenhouses, soil, hay bales, snow or some other method of insulation (see pp. 94–8).

Another benefit of winter harvesting is that it cuts down on the need for preserving food. The labor of canning, freezing, and so on, is not necessary when the vegetables are stored right where they grew in the garden.

LABOR-SAVING PLANNING

Planning for a year-round harvest actually makes your work in the garden easier because it eliminates the effort needed for a major spring planting as well as the frantic rush to harvest and preserve crops in fall. By successional planting, the effort is spread out through the entire growing season, with some vegetables planted in spring, others in summer, and still others in the fall. The harvest is not all in the late summer and fall, but instead is spread out across the entire year. Dismiss the idea of "putting the garden in" during spring. With a year-round harvest, there is always something to plant and something to harvest. For example, when you carry out your weekly harvest of lettuce, replace the mature plants with seedlings that you have started indoors. Instead of it being time to thin the beets, it is actually time to harvest some beet greens for salad or soup. When the peas are done in early summer, seize the opportunity to replant the area with some radishes or bok choi.

If you miss planting something because you are busy or the weather is poor, there is no need to worry: just skip that planting and continue with the next. This means that if you are too busy when the peas are finished to replant the area with a summer crop, all you have to do is plant the area later, when you have time, with a fall crop. If your corn failed to germinate because of the weather, you need not bother trying to plant it again if it is too late – simply refer to your crop rotation plan and plant something else (such as buckwheat) in its place.

The garden is always there and something will always be ready for harvest. There is no need for one small problem to overturn and destroy your plans; you just need to change them a little.

Non-stop salads
Grow lettuce in a bed that you can cover with a cold frame in winter. Weekly sowings of lettuce and other greens will permit fresh salads throughout the year in most climates.

SUCCESSION PLANTING

Succession planting is the practice of planting a small amount of the same vegetable in several sowings spaced a few weeks apart to ensure a continuous harvest. When starting seeds, be sure not to plant them out too early without protection, and also note the number of days to maturity, so that you can calculate the last sowing date.

Sowing recommendations

Lettuce Sow every three weeks indoors
Other salad greens Sow every one to two weeks
Spinach Every week in early spring/late summer
Radishes Every week
Beets Every two to three weeks
Carrots Every two to three weeks
Peas Early spring and mid-summer

When harvesting greens from cold frames in winter, be sure that they are not frozen. Remove any snow from the cold frame and let the plants warm up before harvesting them during the warmest part of the day. The chart opposite lists recommendations of crops that can provide an extended harvest season with protection.

ROOT CELLARING

Some vegetables and fruits store extremely well in a root cellar or other form of live storage (see pp. 276–9). Few of them lose nutrients during storage and some will even increase in nutrition and taste. Harvesting vegetables as needed from a root cellar is easier than canning or freezing. The most important requirement of a root cellar is for it to be kept cool and moist. The best vegetables to store in a root cellar are root crops, cabbages, kohlrabi, and winter squashes. Belgian endive can be stored in a root cellar for later forcing. This will produce delicious fresh greens in the middle of winter.

Growing under glass If frost threatens, place cloches over tender plants. In spring, they can be used to start seedlings early, directly in the garden.

PLANNING THE PLANTING

Having considered nutrition, harvesting, and your family's preferences, it is time to make a rough estimate of what to grow and in what quantities. Assess how much of each crop your household is likely to eat in a year, and from this determine how many plants of each crop are needed. Only experience will provide the answer. A small yard will certainly provide enough space to grow all of the grains, fruits, and vegetables needed to feed a small family. To complete a well-balanced diet for your household only dairy, meat, and possibly some grain will need to be bought in.

EXTENDED HARVEST CROPS

SEASON	CROP
Year-round	Minor salad vegetables
	Endive and arugula
	Chicory and radicchio
	Spinach
	Parsley
	Kale
	Onions
	Leeks
Through mid-winter	Lettuce
	Swiss chard
	Beet greens
	Broccoli
	Brussels sprouts
	Chinese cabbage
	Kohlrabi
Through entire winter	Carrots
	Parsnips
	Celery

COLD FRAMES

Cold frames are very simple structures with glass tops that are used to extend the growing and harvest seasons of crops in the garden. They are most often used to start seedlings earlier than usual in the spring and to extend the harvest of cold hardy vegetables into the winter.

CLOCHES

These are the simple, portable predecessors of cold frames. They are bell-shaped covers, made from glass, which can be placed over individual plants. They come in various sizes, ranging from models that are small enough to sit on a 3in/8cm pot to 15in/35cm domes which cover larger plants in the garden.

The use of cloches allows seedlings to be started in garden beds earlier in the spring. When frost threatens to damage tender plants, place a cloche over them. Similarly, mature plants can enjoy cloche protection in the fall to prevent their demise on cold nights. Always remember to remove cloches on warm days because they heat up quickly in the sun. When it is only moderately warm, simply tip up the edge of a cloche on a stone or brick to allow air to enter and prevent overheating.

COLD FRAMES

There are both semi-portable and permanent versions of cold frames. The portable ones are more useful for season extension, especially if they are the same width as your garden beds. If you are purchasing a cold frame instead of building it yourself, be sure to buy a model fitted with an automatic vent opener. This device opens the lid to release the warm air and let in cool fresh air if the cold frame starts to overheat on a warm day.

You can make a simple cold frame in your garden by arranging hay bales along your garden paths and covering the beds with old storm windows. If the frames are painted brown, these windows will blend in with the site and be unobtrusive. On warm days, move the windows slightly to create a 1–2in/2.5–5cm crack between them to allow air to circulate. During cold nights, push the windows together to eliminate the cracks and keep the heat in.

Glass pyramid *Traditional glass-framed cloches are prized for their ornamental value as well as their practical use in potagers and kitchen gardens.*

Homemade frame
A simple cold frame can be made in your garden from old storm windows and spare timber. Paint it dark to blend in with the surroundings or white to reflect the light.

If you require a more permanent version of a cold frame, construct one from wooden frame walls that are staked into the ground. Again, old storm windows can be used to cover the frames. Attach them with hinges at one side and consider providing an automatic venting arm to the other side. A good location for this type of cold frame is against the sunniest side of your house foundation. This will provide some additional heat gain and provide an ideal place to start seedlings in the early spring. Be sure to enrich the soil in these permanent cold frames just as you would for any other bed in the garden.

HOTBEDS

One variation of a permanent cold frame is a heated frame, or hotbed. These contain a source of heat that is either electrical or organic; traditionally, fresh manure was used to generate the heat in the early spring to start seedlings. Hotbeds need to be taller than cold frames if manure is used to generate the heat; this will also have the additional benefit of bringing the top to a convenient height for working the bed.

To build a manure-based hotbed, place a 24–30in/60–75cm layer of fresh manure mixed with straw at the bottom of the bed. Wet the manure and cover it with 12in/30cm of garden soil. Close the glass cover of the hotbed and wait for one week. The temperature will rise quickly and then begin to drop. Once the temperature has fallen to 75°F/24°C, the bed is ready to be planted. It will stay warm for several weeks.

A much simpler solution is to use electric heating cable. Dig out the frame to about 12in/30cm deep and place a 4in/10cm layer of coarse gravel at the bottom to ensure good drainage. Employ a professional electrician to place the cable in equally spaced parallel lines and cover it with a layer of wire mesh to protect it from gardening tools. Add a layer of fine sand followed by another 6in/15cm of garden soil. Check the temperature of the bed regularly.

GREENHOUSES

Greenhouses are simply elaborate cold frames that are large enough to walk into. They can be used to start seedlings and grow crops that are not hardy in your climate. In some cases, they are used to extend the harvest season of certain crops into the winter.

GREENHOUSE STYLES

There are two basic styles of greenhouse: heated and unheated. The purpose of heated greenhouses is to extend the growing season. Seedlings can be started very early in spring, and long-season crops can be grown in short-season areas. Many plants can be grown year round. If you garden in a cold climate, a heated greenhouse will enable you to grow lemons, oranges, and other crops that require hot climates. The use and operation of heated greenhouses can be a little complicated at first. Unheated greenhouses are much simpler to use, in that they are just like cold frames.

CHOOSING A GREENHOUSE

It is important to choose a greenhouse that suits your purpose. The most common mistake is to choose a small greenhouse. You will find all too quickly that you have outgrown it. Whatever size you think you will need, you are well advised to buy one that is at least 50 per cent larger. You will never regret this initial higher cost.

Greenhouses come in many forms. Freestanding is probably the best choice unless you have a south-facing wall, which is ideal for a lean-to style greenhouse. Whether building a greenhouse yourself or buying a kit, automatic ventilation is essential. A greenhouse may overheat rapidly while you are away and literally cook your plants to death.

SITING A GREENHOUSE

If you intend to attach your greenhouse to your home or another building, try to locate it on the south side. Eastern or western orientation is acceptable but not as good, because nearly half the day's sun will be lost. There is little point in positioning a greenhouse on the shady north side of your home. Whether your greenhouse is freestanding or attached, orient the ridgeline from east to west. This allows the greenhouse to receive the maximum amount of sunlight during winter.

LIGHTING

Choose the sunniest spot on your property, away from the shadows of trees and buildings. Remember that more sun is better than too little sun. During the sunniest months of the year, if shading is necessary, you can install shade cloth or blinds, or wash the glass with shading paint to reduce excessive sunlight. During the least sunny months, and especially during late winter and early spring seed starting, supplemental light may be necessary. Full spectrum 4ft/1.2m fluorescent lamps work well. It is important that the lights are kept 1–3in/2.5–8cm away from the foliage to discourage the seedlings from becoming leggy.

TEMPERATURE AND VENTILATION

Ventilation is essential not only to prevent overheating but also to reduce excessive humidity that causes rot and fungal diseases. Automatic roof vents are the best solution for this problem. These are worked by a non-electric temperature-controlled piston that opens a hatch in the roof to allow hot air out. Even when temperatures are not too high, open the windows (weather permitting) to reduce excessive humidity.

In a large greenhouse, sometimes a small amount of heat will be needed. In order to start seedlings in the spring, place heat mats beneath the trays to assist germination. Large greenhouses are often more prone to draughts but a small heater is sufficient to counteract this problem.

WATERING

In cool greenhouses used for harvest extension, watering is rarely necessary, but if you are starting seedlings or maintaining perennial plants and trees, regular watering is essential. Over- and underwatering both cause significant problems. At cool temperatures, plants need little if any water, but more is needed as soon as temperatures soar.

An easy solution is to set up a drip irrigation system in the greenhouse. You can run it more frequently and for longer periods of time in hot weather than cold weather. If you are raising potted plants, you may find that capillary matting fulfils your watering needs.

SUPPLEMENTING PLANTS WITH NUTRIENTS

When growing plants in a greenhouse, two methods are commonly employed. One is to grow plants in pots and the other is to grow them in the soil that forms the floor of the greenhouse. The drawbacks of using the soil floor are that the soil quickly becomes depleted of nutrients. A lack of crop rotation may result in soilborne pests and diseases too. The best solution to this problem is to excavate some soil and replace it with compost each year when cultivating. If plants are grown in

*A **small greenhouse** Growing a wide variety of plants in your greenhouse will create a balanced environment which will help control pests and diseases.*

Raised beds *If your garden suffers from waterlogged ground, build raised beds that ensure good drainage. The improved growing conditions are worth the labor involved.*

pots, you may find that the reduced amount of soil available requires you to supplement the plants with liquid organic feeds. Making your own liquid feed is a simple process (see pp. 49–53) and the feed can easily be applied when watering your plants.

CONTROLLING PESTS AND DISEASES

Within the confined space and warm environment of a greenhouse, any pests or diseases, such as mold and mildews, will thrive. Therefore it is especially important that you remove dead and diseased matter from the greenhouse promptly. Cleaning the greenhouse thoroughly on a regular basis is also a good preventative measure. Good gardening practices with an eye toward hygiene are the best defense against problems.

One downside of automatic venting is that pests are permitted to enter and, sadly, screens do little to combat the problem. Planting flowers and plants that attract beneficial insects alongside your crops is the best method of pest control. Aphids, whiteflies, and red spider mites are the most common greenhouse pests.

POLYTUNNELS

Often called floating row covers, polytunnels are made by stretching thin plastic over metal or fiberglass hoops. The hoops are driven into the ground and the plastic is anchored with stakes. They are often covered with shade cloth or a screen to protect plants from insects. Netting is often placed over hoops to protect berry plants from birds. Some polytunnels are as large as greenhouses but most are a mere 3ft/90cm high.

RAISED BEDS

When planning the garden it is important to think about good drainage. Raised beds are one method of planting in a wet site. They offer the additional benefit of being able to create a bed with specialized growing conditions for certain plants, like a low pH for blueberries.

BUILDING A FRAME

The first step in building raised beds is to make a frame. Railroad ties suit raised beds well; they age to an attractive dark color and blend in well with the color of the soil. Be sure not to choose pressure-treated wood which contains arsenic and other toxic chemicals.

Set the frame on the ground on the site you have chosen for your raised bed. The sod must be removed and the soil leveled without digging deeply enough to disturb the compacted earth that will be under the frame. Gravel is often used to level the underlying soil surface. If you are using a wood frame, you may need to drive stakes into the ground on the inside of the bed to attach to the wood.

Loosen the soil and sod in the bottom of the bed with a garden fork, then fill it with soil or compost. If the raised bed is being made to grow a particular crop, use soil or compost that has been enriched with soil amendments specifically suited to that crop (see pp. 54–6).

FRAMELESS BEDS

To build a frameless raised bed, remove the sod from the bed in brick-like pieces. Stack these pieces grass-side down, along the outline of the bed. These "bricks" make it easier to form irregular shapes. Very often these beds last for years before erosion takes its toll. You can seed edges that start to slope, but be careful not to tread on these sloping edges.

MAKING A FRAMELESS BED

1 Mark out the site of the bed using pegs and string. Cut out brick-shaped pieces of sod and stack them grass-side down until they are needed.

2 Place the "bricks" along the sides of the bed to form a surrounding wall. Loosen the soil, without disturbing the subsoil, then fill with compost and soil.

3 If you are growing a specialized crop, incorporate the necessary soil amendments to ensure ideal growing conditions. Water the bed well.

EDIBLE LANDSCAPING

The goal of organic gardening is to create a natural balance of planting through diversity. There is a vast array of plants that are not only ornamental but also edible, and edible plants which are also ornamental, which can be used to landscape around your home.

DECORATIVE FRUITS AND FLOWERS

It was quite usual for our grandparents to have apple trees, cherries, blueberries, raspberries, and other fruiting plants interspersed with flowers and vegetables around their home in a beautiful and decorative way. Many trees have beautiful blossoms and foliage, but they also provide wonderful nutritious food for the table. With a little imagination and effort, even the vegetable garden can be laid out to enhance the beauty of your land and home. A large manicured lawn is not the only ideal of beauty.

Edible landscaping is simply utilizing edible plants (namely, fruit trees and bushes, herbs and vegetables) which have decorative value, and decorative plants which are edible (even many flowers).

Rosehips *Many roses produce hips after they flower. These can be used to make syrup or jelly or, if left on the bushes, will attract wildlife in winter.*

FILLING THE YARD WITH FOOD

When planning the landscaping around your home, take time to consider where you spend time outdoors. A perfectly natural choice might be to have alpine strawberries along the walk from the front door to your mailbox. Then, on your way to checking the mail each day, you can pull up a few weeds at the same time as harvesting a handful of strawberries for breakfast. Either side of the path that runs from the car to the back door is another choice location for planting edibles. On your arrival home, you could harvest some basil and tomatoes to mix in with mozzarella and olive oil to make

a wonderful salad for supper. If you spend a lot of time on the porch or deck during the summer, why not surround it with a narrow vegetable bed, interspersed with flowers and a few shrubs that produce fruit? If a patio needs some shade, plant a nut or fruit tree that will also yield fruits in summer and a display of blossom in spring.

Another consideration in landscaping your property is fencing. Instead of building a fence to keep the dog in the back yard, why not plant a thick informal hedge of, say, *Rosa rugosa*. It forms an impenetrable barrier, and produces hips that are a good source of vitamin C. Alternatively, grow a thick patch of raspberries to create green "fencing". The hedge will also porvide a welcome shelter for birds, who will find food in a diversity of plantings. Against the background of your hedge, plant a mix of flowers that will provide color from early spring through fall, or plant a vine or flowering climber like kiwi or trumpet vine to climb the wall.

HIGHLIGHTING AND SCREENING

If you want to keep your compost bins from full view but need them to remain close to the kitchen where they will be used, plant a few shrubs or climbing plants around them to act as a screen. Perhaps there is an attractive architectural feature on your property that can be accented with landscaping? Try flanking the front door with two columnar evergreens that will sway attractively in the wind and frame the entry. If there is a wet area on your plot, consider digging a bed to grow true cranberries.

When choosing ornamentals to plant in the garden, search for those that produce edible fruit. Most people think of a dogwood tree as purely ornamental, but cornelian cherry *(Cornus mas)*

produces edible red fruits. A honeysuckle is a beautiful fragrant bush, but you can just as easily choose a variety that produces edible fruit *(Lonicera caerulea* var. *edulis)*. The chart below lists bushes and trees that are generally considered ornamentals, but have edible varieties.

YEAR-ROUND TEXTURE

Finally, you also need to think about how the landscape will look during the different seasons of the year. In winter, the yard can still look attractive if the landscape has been planned well. Trees and bushes with striking bark or colorful stems and branches add a welcome splash of interest in winter. European mountain ash trees *(Sorbus aucuparia)* produce orange berries that attract birds, and corkscrew willows *(Salix matsudana* 'Tortuosa')* have a more beautiful form in winter than when they are in leaf. Many roses bear huge hips or thorns that remain on the plants into winter; the rosehips are a sure magnet for birds. Evergreen plants can also be put to good use for structure in winter. Choose those that best offset the "starkness" of leafless trees.

EDIBLE ORNAMENTALS

Please note that only the varieties specified below are edible.

Sugar maple *(Acer saccharum)*: make maple syrup/maple sugar

Milky Way kousa dogwood *(Cornus kousa 'Milky Way')*: papaya-tasting fruits

Cornelian cherry *(Cornus mas)*: eat red fruits

Honey locust *(Gleditsia triacanthos)*: dried "beans" are cooked or ground as flour

Kentucky coffee tree *(Gymnocladus dioica)*: use as coffee substitute

Orange daylily *(Hemerocallis fulva)*: eat unopened flowerbuds

Edible honeysuckle *(Lonicera caerulea* var. *edulis)*: eat the blue tear-shaped berries

Staghorn sumac *(Rhus typhina)*: use berries to make a drink

Rose *(Rosa* spp.)*: make syrup or jelly

Nasturtiums (Tropaeleum majus) *The flowers are a tasty addition to salads and the buds make a peppery substitute for capers.*

PLANS & PLANTING IDEAS

The first step in landscaping your yard is to draw a plan. Exact dimensions are not important. Pace off the space and draw a rough plan locating buildings, paths, boundaries, existing trees and shrubs, and any contours in the land. Note which areas receive the most sun.

AVOIDING HAZARDS

If you live in an old property, one important consideration is lead. Lead paint was commonly use for house-painting, and any soil lying close to the walls may be filled with paint chips. If you are concerned that this may be the case, have your soil tested for lead. Look for other areas where you should avoid growing edibles: for example where the water runs off the driveway, washing away the oil drips from the car. With these things in mind, mark out any areas unsuitable for growing food, and use these parts of the garden for decorative plantings or lawns.

LOCATING VIEWS

Next, on the plan, mark out the direction of views. Highlight any favorite views, and identify from where they are best appreciated. Note down any unsightly views, and plan to plant some trees or shrubs of suitable size to block them off.

Flowers in the vegetable plot Use brightly colored flowers to liven up vegetable plots and add interest. They will also attract beneficial insects to the garden.

SMALL CITY PLOT

Today the choice of decorative edible plants is greater than ever before. For the boundaries, plant raspberries along the back fence, or mingle them with hazelnuts and thornless blackberries. If you like honeysuckle, there is even a Russian fruiting variety that has blue berries with a wonderful distinctive flavor. Flank a garden path with strawberries or lingonberries, the fruits of which make a tasty sauce that is the perfect accompaniment to roast venison or lamb.

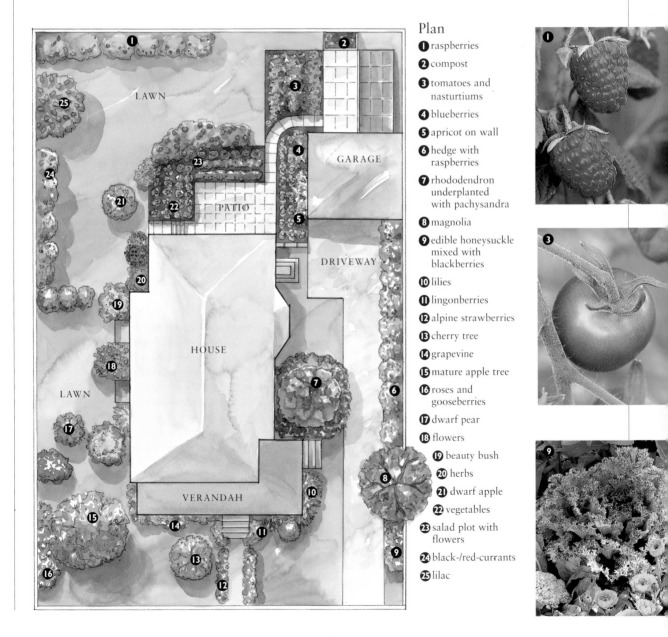

Plan

❶ raspberries

❷ compost

❸ tomatoes and nasturtiums

❹ blueberries

❺ apricot on wall

❻ hedge with raspberries

❼ rhododendron underplanted with pachysandra

❽ magnolia

❾ edible honeysuckle mixed with blackberries

❿ lilies

⓫ lingonberries

⓬ alpine strawberries

⓭ cherry tree

⓮ grapevine

⓯ mature apple tree

⓰ roses and gooseberries

⓱ dwarf pear

⓲ flowers

⓳ beauty bush

⓴ herbs

㉑ dwarf apple

㉒ vegetables

㉓ salad plot with flowers

㉔ black-/red-currants

㉕ lilac

LARGE CITY PLOT

Raspberries are planted outside the fence along the alley, and are a joy to pick when arriving home by car. The terraced back yard leaves lots of room for children to play under the cover of the existing trees. The three raised beds are in the sunniest spot in the yard. The large cherry produces more fruit than a family can eat, and the fruit left on the tree attracts birds all winter. The herbs are grown in partial shade on one side of the house along with rose of Sharon and plants that attract bees and other beneficial insects. The front yard is left more formal with no vegetable production. The pine trees along the south side provide a supply of pine nuts. The row of hemlocks at the rear of the property blocks the prevailing winter wind.

Plan

❶ kiwi fruits
❷ herbs
❸ cherry tree
❹ grapes
❺ hemlocks
❻ raspberries
❼ hostas
❽ crab apples
❾ flowering dogwood
❿ apple tree
⓫ blueberries
⓬ white pines
⓭ lilac bush
⓮ rhododendron
⓯ evergreen
⓰ rose bush
⓱ azaleas
⓲ columnar arborvitae
⓳ andromedas
⓴ rose of Sharon
㉑ mint
㉒ astilbe
㉓ sugar maple
㉔ herbs
㉕ climbing roses
㉖ achillea
㉗ flowering annuals
㉘ yew
㉙ vegetables
㉚ garlic

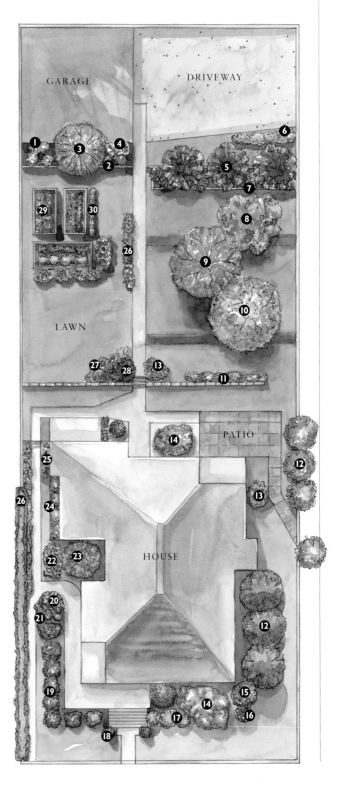

I once lived in a city house where my dining room was so close to that of my neighbor that we could see each other sitting down to dinner. Although we were friends, we both felt my arrangement lacked privacy. The solution was to plant a dwarf apple tree and a honeysuckle to block the view.

In the same house, a dreaded black walnut tree cast shade over virtually the entire back yard. Moreover, its roots produced a chemical that retards the growth of many vegetables, especially tomatoes. This made gardening quite difficult, and also obscured a view from my upstairs rooms of a nearby river. However, after the tree had been removed I discovered that the upstairs bathroom was exposed to the neighbor, so shades had to be installed, depriving the room of sunlight!

Fruit orchard *Apples tolerate a range of soils and climates. Choose a variety that is hardy in your climate and a rootstock that is compatible with your soil type.*

PLANNING THE PLANTING
The next step is to choose the location of trees, followed by bushes and perennials. When choosing trees, bushes, and perennials, it is very important to consider your climate. Some varieties may not grow where you live.

Most good nurseries are able to provide information on the cold and heat tolerance of the plants and trees for sale. Plants are usually listed in catalogs by zone or by average minimum winter temperature. In your own garden, the exact low will depend on several factors:
- Wind: A windy spot allows trees and bushes to desiccate and results in less cold tolerance.

● Exposure: The sunniest spots in the yard in winter are the warmest. A sunny spot may be an entire zone warmer than a spot that is shaded in winter.

● Elevation: Cold air slides down hills and collects in low spots. A location that is 300ft/90m away but with a drop of 15ft/4.5m in elevation may be 20°F/–7°C colder in winter than a high spot.

● Buildings: Garages, houses, and other structures may block the wind as well as absorb the warmth of the sun during the day and radiate it back out at night. This process may allow someone with average minimum temperatures around –25°F/–32°C to grow peaches.

Edible flower border Calendulas and anise hyssop are not only edible flowers that can be used in salads but they also attract beneficial insects to the garden.

SITING TREES

When choosing sites for trees, try to locate them where they will not shade the garden when they mature. Although trees are quite small when you plant them, many of them quickly grow tall and spread wide. In terms of views in your garden, try to site trees so that they block bad views and frame good ones. The most important thing to remember with trees is to start slowly, and not try to plant an orchard in one year. As your plan develops, it will become clear that some existing landscaping needs to be removed. Wait until some of the new plantings are well established before removing existing plantings. Making dramatic changes, such as the removal of several trees and bushes all at once, will not be attractive. It is better to make these kinds of change gradually, replacing the plants removed with your new choices.

LARGE SUBURBAN PLOT

This one acre of land produces nearly all of the food needed by a large family for a well-balanced diet. The gardens are in bloom for most of the year. Flowers and bushes attract birds and bees that pollinate vegetables. Hedges and unmowed areas provide habitat for birds and beneficial insects. Bushes have been planted in groups of threes. Note the five peonies in an L-shape – only three are seen at once. No long straight paths are used; a turn in the path creates visual interest and makes the space seem larger.

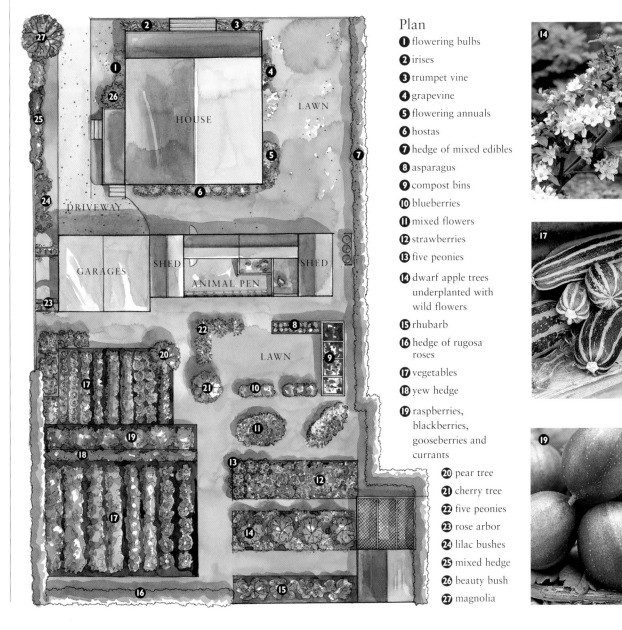

Plan

1. flowering bulbs
2. irises
3. trumpet vine
4. grapevine
5. flowering annuals
6. hostas
7. hedge of mixed edibles
8. asparagus
9. compost bins
10. blueberries
11. mixed flowers
12. strawberries
13. five peonies
14. dwarf apple trees underplanted with wild flowers
15. rhubarb
16. hedge of rugosa roses
17. vegetables
18. yew hedge
19. raspberries, blackberries, gooseberries and currants
20. pear tree
21. cherry tree
22. five peonies
23. rose arbor
24. lilac bushes
25. mixed hedge
26. beauty bush
27. magnolia

THREE-ACRE SUBURBAN PLOT

This plot is designed to grow enough food to feed a large family. The visual appeal of the property has been achieved with a mix of edibles and ornamentals. All of the annual flowers and vegetables are grown together. Perennials, which need less care, are planted all around the property, but annuals which need watering and weeding are kept in one location, near a water faucet in the area that receives the most sun.

Plan

1. black walnut
2. phlox
3. tree hydrangea
4. rose
5. sugar maple
6. blue spruce
7. hostas
8. crab apple
9. magnolia
10. evergreen hedge
11. rose of Sharon
12. mixed flowers
13. lily of the valley
14. pine tree
15. apple trees
16. ivy
17. peach tree
18. pear tree
19. mature catalpa tree
20. peonies
21. perennial herbs
22. rhubarb
23. currants
24. gooseberries
25. sorrel
26. hedge with mature trees
27. compost bins
28. vegetables and grains
29. vegetables and flowers
30. forsythia
31. elderberry
32. serviceberry
33. edible honeysuckle

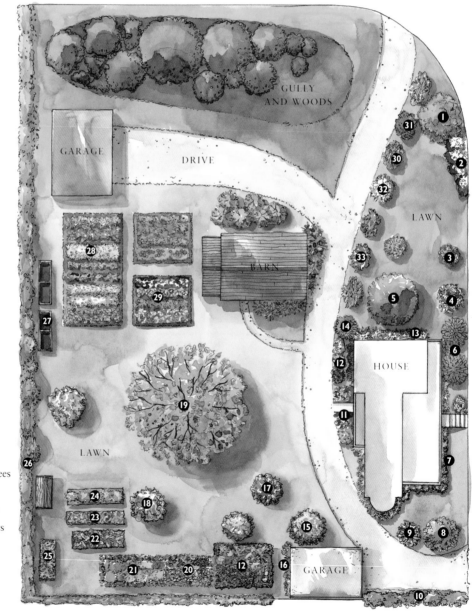

Heirloom potato This unusual variety, known as 'All Blue', stores very well and the potatoes can be kept in a root cellar throughout winter.

Another consideration with trees is the climate. In cold areas, consider planting evergreen trees to the windward side of the home. If the cold winter wind comes from the north, a band of trees will deflect the wind, keeping the home warmer and helping to reduce fuel costs for heating. In summer, the home may be cooled by planting large deciduous trees to the south (see garden plan opposite, item 5). In the winter, the trees will have no leaves and let the sun into the home, but in summer the shade will keep the home cooler.

SITING FRUIT BUSHES

Once the trees are identified on the plan, mark down the site for cane and bush fruits. These are less permanent than trees, but more permanent than vegetable beds. When planning where to put cane and bush fruits, consider whether you will plant flowers and vegetables with them, or keep them separate. A patch of raspberries growing against a fence at the edge of the drive is unlikely to be interplanted with vegetables, but blueberry bushes around the patio will probably be mixed with flowers and more decorative vegetables.

Start with a few bushes, as you can always add more later. Also consult your plan for a year's supply of food, to help you decide on quantities. Many nurseries give significant

Hidden from view *Use scrambling evergreen climbers and shrubs to screen off unsightly objects, such as a compost bin, that might otherwise come into full view during winter.*

discounts for ten or more plants, but few households could manage to consume the amount of fruit produced by ten bushes of gooseberries, raspberries, blueberries, currants, and so on. For fruiting hedges, plant the bushes very closely. In borders, however, space them wider than recommended to leave room for planting flowers and vegetables.

CREATING WINTER INTEREST

Now is the time to take into account any non-vegetative features of the landscape that become more visible during winter. Will the bare compost bin be an unwelcome sight from the kitchen window in winter? Will the fence be an eyesore when the leaves fall off the forsythia in the fall? The visual appeal of garden features in winter is more important than in summer, when vegetation

softens and hides them. A bench might look abandoned in winter, so try to give it some visual appeal. This may simply mean siting a hedge or dwarf fruit trees around it or moving it nearer to another feature to form a focal point.

ORNAMENTAL VEGETABLES

Many vegetables are quite attractive and suit ornamental beds. For example, tomatoes were originally thought to be poisonous and were grown only as ornamentals. They remain a good choice for ornamental beds today. Many flowers attract beneficial insects, and by mixing them with vegetables in ornamental beds, pests can be much less of a problem. Perennial herbs, such as sage and rosemary, are good choices for incorporating into ornamental beds.

SMALL FARM

A small kitchen garden close to the home produces enough fruit and vegetables for family use. The land is separated into "outdoor rooms." For example, the area of berry bushes is surrounded on all sides by tall trees, and has two entrances. The large vegetable garden is surrounded by hedgerows, a wetland, and a pond. These outdoor rooms bring a more intimate feel to the land because it is broken up into smaller spaces.

Plan

❶ kitchen garden
❷ black walnuts
❸ Japanese maple
❹ sugar maple
❺ kiwi fruits
❻ roses
❼ apple tree
❽ dogwood hedge with trees
❾ peach trees against wall
❿ gazebo covered with vines
⓫ vegetables
⓬ soft fruits
⓭ white pines
⓮ hardwood trees
⓯ vegetables and grains
⓰ trellised grapevines
⓱ sugar maple
⓲ nut trees
⓳ apple trees
⓴ evergreen windbreaks

COURTYARD GARDEN

This very small garden appears much larger than it is, yet from the house, the end cannot be seen. Likewise from the bench at the rear, the front can not be seen. The curved arrangement of plantings and the height of the trees leaves something hidden, something to be discovered. Here the focus is on ornamentals, but a small vegetable garden has been included. Most of the ornamentals chosen are edible. The herbs and several flowerbeds are all within reach of the kitchen. The dwarf cherry, apple, and pear trees provide seasonal food for the table. Together with the Japanese maple and fruit bushes, they give the garden structure, and lead the eye to the roses at the rear.

Plan

❶ rose hedge

❷ vegetables

❸ dwarf cherry tree

❹ dwarf apple tree

❺ primulas and lupins

❻ hydrangeas

❼ climbing and bush roses

❽ quince bush

❾ bay tree

❿ clematis

⓫ potted evergreens

⓬ strawberry planter

⓭ chives

⓮ tomatoes

⓯ flowers

⓰ rosemary

⓱ parsley

⓲ grapes and kiwi vines

⓳ flowers and herbs

⓴ herbs

㉑ currants and gooseberries

㉒ japanese maple

㉓ thornless blackberries

㉔ pear espalier

㉕ figs

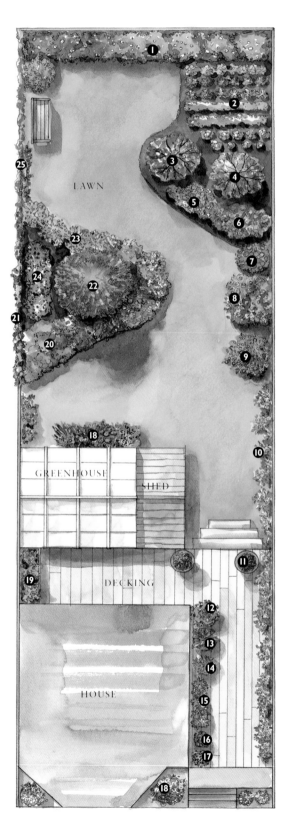

PLANTS FOR SCREENING AND STRUCTURE

When considering how to screen a wonderful porch from the harsh summer sun, or cover an unattractive compost bin, it is important to consider the options available. When an architectural feature such as an entrance deserves accent, the right choice of tree or bush can make all the difference. Plants that provide structure and screening should not be an afterthought, but integral to the landscaping design. The individual choices you make depend on your situation, but it is worth visiting other gardens in your area to see what plants and devices have been used.

To screen a porch from sun, so that it can be enjoyed throughout summer, consider planting trumpet vine, or grapevines that will not only shade but provide fruit. Nothing beats the wonderful scent of wisteria. For a shady location or to create some privacy use Dutchman's pipe.

Choose tall trees to flank an entrance and low bushes to line the walk to an entry. Using a pair of bushes or trees this way breaks one important rule of locating plants in the landscape.

THE RULE OF THREES

Trees and bushes look best grouped in threes. You would need a large even number of bushes to look as attractive as an odd number. It is hard to determine why this is the case, but almost everyone who looks at a landscape agrees with this rule. When planning to plant bushes that have a separation between them, you will find that an odd number always look better. Where bushes are planted closely and touch one another, as in a close planting of gooseberries, this is not a concern. An even number looks fine because it becomes one line of vegetation, not several individuals.

Colorful screen
The annual sweet pea (Lathyrus odoratus) *can be trained on canes or trellis to create a woven screen of color and a sweet summer scent.*

HERB PLANS & PLANTING

Herbs can be mixed into the vegetable garden or ornamental beds. However, many gardeners choose to create interesting beds exclusively of herbs. These can be designed into formal or informal plans and are guaranteed to attract many beneficial insects into the garden.

COOK'S DELIGHT

Locate the herb garden near your kitchen and pick from it frequently as you cook. Herbs that are perennials should not be worked into annual vegetable gardens. The decision as to formal or informal arrangements should match the character of the home and the garden as a whole. If formal hedges of privet surround the garden, consider a classic knot garden or chessboard pattern for herbs. If raspberries, gooseberries, and evergreens are mixed with tall trees to form the boundaries of the garden, consider a less formal

design. A cartwheel pattern can fit in with both formal and informal gardens and homes.

Many herbs prefer to grow in sun, but there are some that prefer shade. For this reason, you will probably need to have herbs in two different areas of the garden. In general, annual herbs tend to require direct sunlight and do best in the vegetable garden or worked into a sunny perennial plan. Any herb that is used in great quantity, such as basil or parsley, should be grown in the vegetable garden so that there is enough room to produce the amount needed.

Some herbs are useful the whole year round. Use this to your advantage by growing these herbs in containers or pots that can be brought indoors during the winter. Some of them can be quite ornamental: for example, a pyramidal rosemary can be trained and pruned into a perfect shape, making a welcome decoration in the home during winter.

LAYING OUT A HERB BED

1 Plan a formal herb bed by laying out strings to delineate the edges of the beds and paths. The edging should be secure. Remove topsoil from any paths.

2 Install the edging and fill any cracks between the pavers with sand or mortar. Prepare the beds for planting by working in lots of well-rotted compost.

3 Plant the herbs in the bed, keeping in mind the size that they will reach at maturity. Any paths can be filled with a thick layer of gravel to deter weeds.

CREATING A HERB BED

Formal herb gardens are often bordered by manicured low hedges of boxwood *(Buxus sempervirens)* or walls made of warm red brick or stone. Most large formal herb gardens feature a central statue or fountain, while smaller plans may feature a particularly eye-catching plant, such as a bay tree in a planter. Most of the work involved in creating these gardens is planning the borders and paths. Stone, brick, or gravel paths together with hedges or walls form the infrastructure of the garden. It is worthwhile spending time and effort initially to build these features well so they will need little maintenance in later years.

The first step is to design the bed. Decide on the type of border and preferred material, then lay out the route of the paths. Choose a central feature, such as an ornament or striking plant that will draw the eye to your design. The next step is to lay out the masonry features in the garden. Brick and stone paths and walls should be built on undisturbed soil. Excavate the turf and set the pavers on a bed of sand. Walls measuring more than 12in/30cm in height will need special footings for support. Consult a reference book or a professional for advice on masonry construction.

After the structure has been completed, plant any hedge borders or other edging plants that are needed. The final step is to dig the beds between the paths and the edge of the garden. Give perennial herbs a good start by single or double digging the beds; then you are ready for planting out. There are many herbs to choose from, but try to place tall ones at the center or back of the spaces, and low-growing herbs for the edges. Also consider carefully the colors of your choices.

Purple-leaf basil This is one of the many tasty basils available. Grouped together, these plants provide a strong contrast to lighter-colored foliage in the bed.

FORMAL HERB GARDENS

Formal herb gardens are generally symmetrical in shape, based on
a repeating geometric pattern. They are usually edged with paving
stones or loose materials such as gravel to separate the paths from
the beds. The plantings are often symmetrical too, chosen carefully
to repeat the colors and sizes of plants (see plan below). Also
illustrated is a classic knotwork bed; its intricate pattern is
accentuated by a simple planting of just three types of plant.

Knotwork plan
❶ thyme
❷ rosemary
❸ boxwood
❹ stone pavers

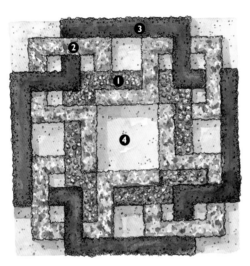

Symmetrical plan
❺ boxwood
❻ bunching onions
❼ pyramidal rosemary
❽ marjoram
❾ hyssop
❿ bee balm
⓫ parsley
⓬ flowering urn
⓭ garlic
⓮ angelica
⓯ lemon verbena
⓰ thyme
⓱ cilantro
⓲ chives
⓳ sage
⓴ lovage
㉑ feverfew
㉒ epazote
㉓ Egyptian top onions
㉔ stevia
㉕ dill
㉖ sweet Cicely
㉗ mint
㉘ ornamental fountain

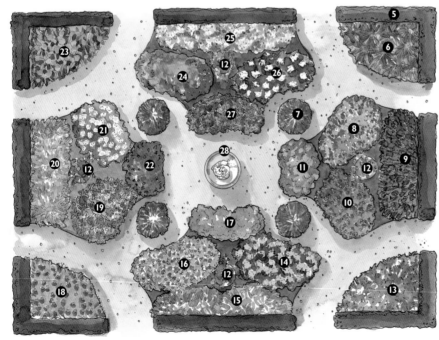

INFORMAL HERB GARDENS

Creating an attractive informal herb garden is much easier than a formal garden. All that is really necessary is to:

● Place tall items at the rear of beds that are up against a building or wall, or in the center of beds that are viewed from all sides.

● Ensure that the colors of the herbs and their flowers complement each other. The beds can be of any shape, and are easily created by preparing the soil as you would for a vegetable bed – then let your imagination run wild. Look at the example below for inspiration.

Natural drift plan

❶ dill
❷ bay
❸ fennel
❹ lovage
❺ juniper
❻ borage
❼ chives
❽ sorrel
❾ rosemary
❿ spearmint
⓫ tarragon
⓬ sage
⓭ basil
⓮ parsley
⓯ coriander
⓰ thyme
⓱ creeping thyme

Cartwheel plan

⓲ basil
⓳ spearmint
⓴ parsley
㉑ thyme
㉒ chives
㉓ sage
㉔ oregano
㉕ dwarf lavender
㉖ boxwood

COMPANION PLANTING

Companion planting is the practice of locating particular plants near one another because they enhance plant growth, discourage pests and diseases, or have some other beneficial effect. It also includes ensuring that "bad companions" are kept apart.

WHEN TO USE

Companion planting is much less effective at discouraging soilborne pests and diseases in the vegetable garden than crop rotation, and wherever possible, you should practice crop rotation (see pp. 78–81). The real benefit of companion planting is in perennial beds where crops cannot rotate.

In fact, very little research has gone into the benefits of companion planting and most of the information is anecdotal. However, the tradition of planting certain crops together extends back thousands of years. With this kind of history, companion planting is certainly worth considering. Though some of the folklore surrounding the practice might make you dismiss this concept as nothing more than an "old wife's tale," more often than not these companion plantings are based on fact.

Marigolds as a companion to vegetables
The powerful scent produced by a row of marigolds growing next to a patch of cabbages will help to keep many pests away from the crop.

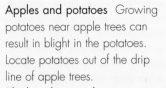

COMBINATIONS TO AVOID

Apples and potatoes Growing potatoes near apple trees can result in blight in the potatoes. Locate potatoes out of the drip line of apple trees.

Black walnuts and many vegetables, especially tomatoes Black walnut trees *(Juglans nigra)* produce a chemical in their leaves called juglone. When it rains, this chemical is washed off the leaves and onto the soil below. Juglone inhibits the growth of many plants, including tomatoes, apples, potatoes, and blackberries. The roots of black walnut trees also produce toxins.

Brassicas and tomatoes When tomatoes are planted close to brassicas, their growth is poor and they do not produce well.

Grass around apples and pears The root tips are the quickest-growing parts of young apple trees and are present near the surface of the soil. Chemicals excreted from the roots of grass can retard the growth of these root tips, therefore the area close around young apple trees should be kept free of grass.

Maples and wheat The roots of maple trees produce a toxin that deters the growth of wheat, but their leaves have a preserving effect on apples and potatoes.

Spruce trees The effects of spruce trees maintain a presence in the soil long after the tree is gone. While they retard the growth of other trees, they encourage the growth of strawberries.

SUGGESTED PAIRINGS

The best idea is to experiment with companion planting in your garden, and to keep using those that have beneficial effects.

French marigolds French marigolds *(Tagetes spp.)* have many benefits in the garden. Dutch scientists discovered that the roots of marigolds excrete a substance that kills soil nematodes. In Holland, chemical sprays were being used with some success to combat a problem of nematode infestation in rose beds. The Dutch Plant Protection Service tried using French marigolds and found that the nematodes were controlled in the beds that were interplanted with marigolds and roses. The beds that were not interplanted still suffered from an infestation of nematodes.

This is one of the many uses of marigolds in the garden. They are also grown in greenhouses used for tomatoes to discourage whitefly. The scent of marigolds is offensive to many insects and other pests. One year I surrounded an entire garden bed with marigolds, and while there was no conclusive evidence that there were fewer pests, the decorative effect was so striking that the following year I planted French marigolds around all the vegetable beds. It might have been coincidence, but I found that squirrels raided less from the garden that year.

Parsley and carrots Mixing parsley and carrots deters carrot flies because of the masking aroma of the parsley.

Tomatoes and asparagus Tomatoes repel asparagus beetles. Tomatoes planted in the asparagus bed after the spring harvest will protect the asparagus plants during their summer growth season, and the fernlike foliage of the asparagus will provide an attractive backdrop for the tomatoes.

Borage and strawberries Planting borage around strawberry beds makes potassium, calcium, and other minerals available in the soil.

Pyrethrum *(Tanacetum cinerariifolium)* This is a common organic insect repellant; a powder is made from its flowers and has been used for thousands of years. Growing this wild plant in your garden can discourage many pests.

Cilantro The scent of cilantro repels aphids.

Stinging nettle *(Urtica dioica)* As its name suggests, stinging nettle is somewhat painful to touch, but it is an excellent deterrent of pests.

BENEFICIAL WILDLIFE

Inviting wildlife into your yard or garden will bring many benefits. Some insects and animals are predators which will eat the numerous pests that invade the garden. All that is necessary is to attract these predators with flowers and herbs, and provide them with a habitat in which to live.

PLANTING FOR BENEFICIAL INSECTS

Traditional American and English gardens shared similar planting styles, which mix flowers, vegetables, herbs, and fruit trees and bushes. It was common to find garlic growing with roses, and tomatoes being grown for their decorative value interspersed with marigolds, zinnias, and herbs.

It rarely occurs to most gardeners today that the beneficial insects, which were attracted by this mix of flowers, herbs, and vegetables in traditional gardens, are the reason why pests were rarely a problem. Today most gardeners avoid planting carrots alongside the tomatoes, or siting the fritillaries in the same bed as cabbages. The current preference for large mowed lawns provides very little habitat for beneficial insects. In the past, the number of pests in the garden was kept under control by planting a varied garden which attracted natural predators.

FRIENDS OR FOES?

The most effective means of controlling pests is to welcome beneficial insects and birds into the garden by providing them with a habitat. Birds, bees, and ladybugs are just some of the many predators that will keep pests out of the garden.

Attracting beneficials Plant an area to flowers that are known to attract beneficial insects. An area of lawn can be unmowed and sprinkled with flower seeds.

Welcome predator Spiders enjoy a carnivorous diet of flies, caterpillars, and other garden pests, making them a welcome visitor to the organic garden.

Planting flowers that attract these predators is a simple step in the right direction to controlling pests. Another option is to plant flowers and bulbs that ward off pests, such as onions and sage which repel carrot fly, and some other pests. For more information on specific beneficial insects, please refer to the section on pests and diseases in Chapter 4 (see p. 173).

ATTRACTING BIRDS

One of the best ways to encourage birds is to create a habitat for them to build nests and to provide them with food when it is scarce.

Lavender *The delicate scented flowers of lavender attract bees and butterflies to the garden. Leave their seedheads for the birds to enjoy in the late summer and fall.*

Plant trees and shrubs that produce berries that can be eaten by birds throughout the winter, encouraging them to live near your garden. European mountain ash trees are a good example. They produce wonderful orange-red berries that birds enjoy feeding on. Rosehips, especially from *Rosa* spp. and *R. rugosa*, also provide nutritious food. Snowberries and the black berries that form on ivy are also a good source of food for many birds.

During the growing season, many plants provide seeds for birds. The flowerheads of golden rod, lavender, and globe thistles all provide food. Find a spare corner of your plot for growing sunflowers and millet, so that the seeds can be saved as winter feed for the birds.

Dense hedges make an excellent nesting site for birds. The leaves and debris that collect under dense hedges is a wonderful habitat for opossums. They may even overwinter under the

hedges if it is not too wet. When planting hedges, leave about 36in/90cm of width to provide ample room for the bushes to grow and provide habitat. The composition of hedges depends on the type of hedge you prefer. For formal hedges, choose slow-growing bushes such as yew *(Taxus baccata)* or holly *(Ilex aquifolium)*. This will reduce the necessary labor in clipping and maintaining them. Let the seeds or berries remain on the bushes through the winter to provide food to the birds.

Informal hedges can be composed of a variety of bushes. Forsythia *(Forsythia* spp.) is a favorite nesting place for birds, and hawthorn *(Crataegus monogyna)*, raspberries, gooseberries, currants, and blackberries are all good choices too. Use just one species to make up three-quarters of the hedge, then mix in the others to complete the planting. For example, starting at one end of a hedge, plant 75 per cent *Rosa rugosa* mixed with raspberries for the first 30ft/9m; then plant

75 per cent gooseberries mixed with holly, blackberries, and an apple tree in the next 30ft/9m. Repeat this process until the entire length of the hedge has been done. After every 10ft/3m, include an evergreen to provide winter protection for nesting birds.

Providing birdhouses for nesting and birdbaths for drinking and bathing will further encourage birds to live in your garden. Squirrel-proof birdfeeders filled with black oil sunflower seeds in addition to a thistle feeder will provide necessary winter nutrition and encourage migrating birds to return in the spring.

ATTRACTING BEES

Bees are wonderful to have in the garden. They pollinate squash and other vegetables, and feed upon small insects. Different flowers attract different types of bees. This is supposedly because different varieties of bees have different tongue lengths. Growing a wide range of different flowers will attract many varieties of bee.

It is important to do this because more than one-third of the food we eat is bee pollinated, and we need all kinds of bees in the garden. Most of the above listed methods of attracting birds and beneficial insects to the garden will also attract bees.

Waste not An upturned lid of an old garbage can, filled with water and placed on the ground, provides a drinking pool for birds and small creatures.

BENEFICIAL PREDATORS

There are several different classes of predator, and attracting them requires different methods.

Animals	Insects
Bats	Ladybugs
Birds	Ground beetles
Frogs	Hoverflies
Toads	Centipedes
Opossums	Lacewings
Porcupines	Earwigs

ATTRACTING BATS

Bats feed on a wide range of flying insects, including flies and mosquitoes that attack humans. Bats are mammals and look very much like winged mice. They hibernate during the winter; if you find a family roosting in your home – they usually settle in the eaves of a roof – do not disturb or try to remove them from your property, as they are a protected species.

They can easily be attracted to nest in your garden by providing a simple bat house, which can be made or purchased. Contact your local bat conservation society for more information.

Silvery seedhead
Dandelions have bright yellow flowers that attract insects. Harvest the young foliage for wonderful early spring salads, but leave a few seedheads for birds to enjoy.

ATTRACTING FROGS AND TOADS

Frogs and toads eat slugs and small insects; they even eat some snails. A small pond is a great way to encourage them; however, it is not essential. Water is only necessary for them to breed. They will live and hibernate happily in sheltered dark damp places where they are safe from predators.

ATTRACTING HEDGEHOGS

Native to Europe, hedgehogs feed on caterpillars, slugs, and millipedes. As noted above, hedges are wonderful habitat for hedgehogs. They do not like wet places, and are found in cities and the country. You may not know you have hedgehogs in your garden because they hide during the day and hunt at night. If you do not have hedges, leave a shady section of unmowed lawn where they can hide during the day. A small heap of brush will also provide them with a good home. Encourage hedgehogs to hibernate in your yard in winter by leaving wet cat food or dog food for them near the hedges or brush.

FLOWERS TO ATTRACT BENEFICIAL WILDLIFE

When considering which flowers to plant in order to attract beneficial insects and animals into your garden, start by planting the wildflowers that are native to your local area. Try creating different styles of habitat. For example, a woodland edge is by far the most attractive area to beneficial insects. Beneath some tall trees, plant an understory of bushes and flowers. Choose shade-tolerant varieties that will provide pollen in early spring, when food is scarce. Other popular habitats are lawns and grass. Leave a section of the lawn unmowed and allow weeds and meadow flowers to flourish. Here are some plants that are recommended.

Bulbs for naturalizing in lawns
Anemone *(Anemone nemorosa)*
Glory of the snow *(Chionodoxa spp.)*
Snow crocus *(Crocus chrysanthus)*
Species crocus *(Crocus spp.)*
Winter aconite *(Eranthis spp.)*
Snowdrop *(Galanthus nivalis)*
Star flower *(Ipheion spp.)*
Snowflake *(Leucojum spp.)*
Grape hyacinth *(Muscari)*
Daffodil *(Narcissus spp.)*
Scilla *(Scilla siberica)*

Wildflowers
Try to use only wildflowers that are native to your area.
Yarrow *(Achillea millefolium)*
Queen Anne's lace *(Anthriscus sylvestris)*

Snapdragon *(Antirrhinum majus)*
Columbine *(Aquilegia spp.)*
Bachelor's buttons *(Centaurea cyanus)*
Daisy *(Leucanthemum spp.)*
Coreopsis *(Coreopsis tinctoria)*
Foxglove *(Digitalis purpurea)*
Purple coneflower *(Echinacea purpurea)*
Baby's breath *(Gypsophila elegans)*
St. John's wort *(Hypericum perforatum)*
Flax *(Linum usitatissimum)*
Birdsfoot trefoil *(Lotus corniculatus)*
Baby blue eyes *(Nemophila menziesii)*
Poppy *(Papaver somniferum)*
Phlox *(Phlox drummondii)*
Black-eyed Susan *(Rudbeckia hirta)*

Annuals and biennials
Hollyhock *(Alcea ficifolia)*
Calendula *(Calendula officinalis)*
Aster *(Callistephus chinensis/Aster novae-angliae)*
Celosia *(Celosia spp.)*
Cosmos *(Cosmos spp.)*
Foxglove *(Digitalis purpurea)*
Sunflower *(Helianthus annuus)*
Heliotrope *(Heliotrope arborescens)*
Morning glory *(Ipomoea tricolor* var. 'Heavenly Blue'*)*
Alyssum *(Lobularia maritima)*
Marigold *(Tagetes spp.)*
Feverfew *(Tanacetum parthenium)*
Mexican sunflower *(Tithonia spp.)*
Flowering tobacco *(Nicotiana spp.)*
Zinnia *(Zinnia spp.)*

Orchards
Buckwheat *(Fagopyrum esculentum)*
Clover *(Trifolium spp.)*

CHAPTER 4

WORKING THE

ORGANIC GARDEN

CREATING NEW BEDS

Preparing new beds is an important step in gardening. The effort and time you invest digging and enriching the soil will result in bountiful harvests. Make sure that the size, position, and shape of the plots suit your overall design, and that the beds are easily accessible.

THINKING AHEAD

When breaking ground for new beds the first thing to consider is their size and shape. I usually make mine about 4ft/1.2m wide so that they can be worked from the edges without stepping on them. The soil quickly becomes compacted if it is trodden on and will need double digging again to restore the soil structure. Short gardeners may find a width of about 36in/90cm more manageable. If you plan to put a cold frame over the bed, make the width the same as that of your cold frame. If you build simple cold frames using hay bales and storm windows, allow enough space between the beds for the bales as well as room to walk (see pp. 94–5).

In small yards, irregularly shaped beds work best as they can incorporate awkward corners and combine several small areas of land. Curved beds can bend around the corner of a house or patio, or follow the course of a path or contour of the land. Provided that they are not too wide, curved shapes are just as suitable for the organic vegetable garden as regular ones. If the site requires a wide bed, build a small stepping-stone path to the center to avoid walking on the soil.

MARKING EDGES

Once you have decided on the size and shape of a bed, mark out the edges with string. To achieve straight edges, drive stakes into the ground along the perimeter and tie string tightly between them.

Curved bed *A series of shaped flowerbeds or vegetable plots suits a symmetrical garden design, or they can be used to accentuate the contours of a site.*

Mark out curved beds by laying string or a garden hose directly on the ground. Stand back to view the overall shape, then adjust the outline until the desired shape is achieved. Following the outline, slice through the sod with a garden spade or half-moon edger.

A common mistake is to mix sod into the bed. If the area where you are creating a new bed is covered with sod, remove the sod and add it to the compost bin, leaving behind as much soil as possible in the bed. Once you have removed all the sod from the new plot, the surface is likely to be lower than the level of the path around the bed. Do not worry about this now; the process of double digging and incorporating compost will make up for this difference in levels. When establishing new beds, it is especially important to test the soil for deficiencies and to establish its pH level (see p. 34). This is the most appropriate time to carry out these tests.

DOUBLE DIGGING

Although it may appear to be a laborious technique, double digging repays the time and effort spent as it ensures a thorough cultivation of the soil. As well as being used in the preparation of new beds, double digging is a good solution for beds with poor drainage or where a hard layer of subsoil has formed. Once it has been double dug, a bed is unlikely to need this treatment again. The process involves turning the soil in two separate layers, and mixing in compost and additives. There are three purposes to double digging:

- To loosen compacted soil, which allows plant roots to grow with ease.
- To improve drainage, which reduces waterlogged soil and enables the bed to warm up earlier in the spring.
- To allow air to penetrate the soil, which is necessary for plant roots to grow.

 ## RULES FOR DIGGING

There are several rules for digging the soil that apply to both single and double digging.

- Do not dig the soil when it is wet as you are likely to damage the structure and cause compaction. If the soil sticks to your shovel, fork, or boots, it is too wet to cultivate. Wait until it dries out or dig the beds in the fall instead of the spring.
- Do not dig the soil when it is too dry. It will be very difficult to dig and the wind will carry away your topsoil. You may need to water the area before digging. Allow several days of watering before trying to dig in very dry clay soil.
- Use a D-handled spade that is suited to your height (see pp. 270–2). Let the weight of your entire body provide the force to drive the blade into the ground, not muscular force from your foot. When lifting a spade of dirt, do not toss it but let it slide off your spade where desired. Both of these techniques take less effort and allow you to dig longer.
- When digging, you may need to step on the bed. To avoid compacting the soil, always stand on a large board that is long enough to reach across the width of the bed. This will spread your weight across the surface.
- Always remove weed roots from the bed.

DOUBLE DIGGING A BED

1 Mark out the edges of the bed with stakes and string. Once you have obtained the desired shape and size, cut the sod around the edge of the bed using a spade. Lift and remove the sod, leaving behind as much soil as possible.

   You may find it useful to divide the bed into 10–12in/25–30cm strips across the width of the bed, using wooden stakes to mark the width of each trench.

2 Excavate a trench of soil from the bed. The trench should be about a spade's length deep and wide. Your excavated trench should measure about 12in/30cm wide by 12in/30cm deep. Put the soil to one side, either in buckets or a wheelbarrow. It will be used at the other end of the bed to fill the trench left there after digging.

3 Using a garden fork, loosen the subsoil in the bottom of the trench. Work along the length of the trench, plunging the tines deep into the heavy subsoil to break it up. The subsoil should be loosened to a depth of 12in/30cm. The total depth of the loosened soil will be about 24in/60cm below the surface. Add a 2in/5cm layer of compost or organic matter to the bottom of the trench. This will work its way down into the subsoil and create topsoil.

4 Using a spade, begin digging the second trench about 6in/15cm wide and 12in/30cm deep, adjacent to the first. Toss the soil on top of the compost in the first trench. Add a 1in/2.5cm layer of compost on top of the soil in the first trench. Finish digging the second trench, about 6in/15cm wider (again to a depth of 12in/30cm) and toss it on top of the compost in the first trench.

5 The first trench now contains soil (6in/15cm), compost (1in/2.5cm), soil (6in/15cm), compost or organic matter (2in/5cm), and loosened subsoil (12in/30cm). The second trench is empty. Repeat steps 3–4 until you reach the other edge of the bed. Loosen the subsoil in the last trench and cover it with a 2in/5cm layer of compost. Add half the soil from the wheelbarrow, cover with a 1in/2.5cm layer of compost, then add the balance of the soil.

6 Rake the bed smooth with a garden rake and add a 2–3in/5–8cm layer of compost to the top of the bed. Now is the time to add and gently work in any soil amendments that are necessary. A soil test will indicate which, if any, soil amendments should be added. Only if the bed is showing severe signs of compaction, or if drainage is poor, will it be necessary to double dig the bed again. This most often happens in heavy clay soils.

RENOVATING EXISTING BEDS

Double digging rarely has to be repeated once a bed has been established. Provided that the soil does not become compacted or waterlogged, light cultivation of the top layer of the bed, without disturbing the soil structure, is all that is needed to maintain and improve a bed.

ANNUAL TOPSOIL IMPROVEMENT

When a crop is harvested, nutrients are removed from the soil. These nutrients need to be replaced before the bed is replanted. The technique shown on the opposite page allows the gardener to aerate and loosen the soil without repeating the labor-intensive work of double digging. The first essential step is to remove weeds and debris from the previous crop. Make sure that the weeds are removed in their entirety, roots and all; add them to the compost pile. However, if the previous crop was a legume, leave its roots in the bed because they contain nodules of nitrogen. Using a garden rake, smooth the bed and remove any rocks or other debris from the bed.

Close planting Well-nourished soil will support abundant quantities of closely planted vegetables to provide food throughout the year.

CHECKING FOR DEFICIENCIES

Now is the time to test the soil, if you think that there may be any deficiencies of nutrients (see pp. 32–4). Then spread an even layer of well-rotted compost over the entire bed. On top of this, spread any required soil amendments, such as lime (to increase the pH) or rock dust (a good source of potassium, calcium, magnesium, and iron). If you apply fresh manure or other soil amendment that may burn, allow the bed to rest for several weeks before planting.

The next step is to work the compost into the bed using a garden fork. This process also helps to loosen the soil and eliminate any compaction that may have occurred during the previous season. Start from the edge and work toward the center of the bed, so that soil is pushed toward the center rather than onto the paths. The majority of the compost should remain close to the surface of the soil where it is needed most.

The third step is to smooth the bed and break up any clods of hardened earth that remain near the surface. Mix the compost into the top

BED WIDTH

For practicality, the maximum width for your beds should be no more than 4ft (1.2m). This ensures that all parts of the plot can be reached from the edges, allowing you to incorporate compost and organic fertilizers without having to step off the garden path and tread onto the soil. You will also be able to carry out planting, routine duties such as weeding and watering, as well as harvesting, without causing compaction.

2–3in/5–8cm of soil using a garden rake or "four-tine refuse hook" (this looks like a rake but has four, widely spaced long teeth), or use a garden fork with a slight twisting action. The final height of the bed will be about 3–4in/8–10cm above path level. The bed is now ready for planting. If it is the end of your growing season and you do not wish to plant crops in the bed at this time, consider planting a cold hardy cover crop to prevent erosion and to further nourish the soil (see pp. 57–61).

MAINTAINING A BED

1 After clearing the bed of weeds and residue from the previous crop, spread well-rotted compost in an even layer about 2in/5cm deep over the surface of the bed.

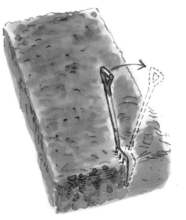

2 Plunge the fork tines to their full depth. Gently rock the fork to loosen the soil so that the compost sifts down. Work across the bed in rows 3in/8cm apart.

3 Break up any remaining clods of earth and mix the compost into the top layer of soil, using a light hoeing action. Using the back of the rake, even out the surface.

SOWING & PLANTING OUT

Now that the beds have been prepared it is time to plant them. Whether transplanting seedlings or sowing directly in the garden, you must consider the spacing of the plants in the bed. The best choice is equal spacing of plants to completely cover the bed.

NATURAL SEED DISPERSAL

In nature, seeds are sown in many ways. Birds scatter them with their droppings; the wind carries seeds over long distances; and animals carry seeds with burs. When planting, remind yourself that nature does not plant seeds in tidy little rows with walking paths between, so try to follow suit. In nature, soil is rarely left bare. Planting in rows leaves large areas of bare earth, which only encourages weeds to grow and rain to wash away nutrients. Instead, plant the seeds or seedlings at equal distances from each other in the bed and close enough that the leaves of mature plants will touch and leave no bare earth visible. This will crowd out weeds and allow the roots of the plants to stabilize all the soil in the bed to prevent erosion and nutrient loss. The canopy of leaves over the bed will prevent sunlight from reaching the soil and causing evaporation and germination of weed seeds; the bed will require less watering and weeding.

ASSESSING PLANTING DISTANCES

The optimal plan for spacing plants in a bed is hexagonal spacing (see below), where each plant is equidistant from every other plant. Much closer spacing can be achieved this way, which results in a greater harvest from less space as well as less labor digging, weeding, and watering. The exact distance between the centers of each plant is determined by what is being grown. Spinach may be spaced just 7in/18cm apart while pepper

Hexagonal spacing
When the plants mature, their foliage will create a canopy that prevents light from reaching the soil, which can cause moisture loss.

plants might require a spacing of 18in/45cm.
Any planting scheme that covers the bed with
vegetation and avoids exposure of bare soil is
a valid plan to consider.

SOWING SEED OUTDOORS

Direct seeding is the process of starting seeds
directly in the garden beds. Many vegetables
will not survive transplanting and must be sown
directly in their permanent locations. Other
vegetables are so easy to get established that
they need not be started inside. As a general rule,
when seeds are sown in the garden, they should
be planted to a depth equal to their length. For
example, a bean seed that is ¾in/2cm long
should be planted ¾–1in/2–2.5cm below the
surface of the soil. Some seeds need light to
germinate, so it is best to consult planting
directions specific to the vegetable being grown.

HEXAGONAL PLANTING PLAN

When seeding directly in the garden, follow the
hexagonal planting illustrated on the opposite
page. Sow one seed at each corner of the
hexagons and one in the center of each. You may
find it easier to mark a line across or along the
length of the bed using string attached to stakes.
Using the recommended spacing for the vegetable
seed being sown, make holes in the bed with a
dibble or narrow-bladed trowel, and place a seed
in each. Sometimes it is easier to make a furrow
along the entire row, rather than a series of
planting holes. Do not cover the seeds with soil
yet, or it will be difficult to assess how to plant
the next row to achieve a hexagonal pattern.
Move the string the appropriate distance over
and plant the next row, offset from the first so
that all the seeds are equidistant. Continue this
process until the whole bed, or allotted area of
the bed, has been planted. Now, using a rake or
handtool, cover the seeds with a thin layer of
soil. It is a good idea to water the bed if the

Seed drill *Where recommended planting distances
are minimal, you may find it easier to make a furrow
rather than a series of planting holes.*

soil is dry, but take care not to deluge the soil
so that the water uncovers the seeds or washes
them away. Always label the area sown to
identify the vegetable and variety planted.

Sowing in a cold frame should be treated just
like sowing outside in a bed. By sowing cold
hardy vegetables in a cold frame, you can start
them much earlier in the spring (see pp. 94–5).

BROADCASTING SEEDS

Cover crops are usually broadcast by hand. This
can be difficult to do evenly without practice.
Even seeding, however, is not essential with cover
crops. Simply grab a handful of seed, and while

Constant harvest *When one crop of vegetables is harvested, replace it with another crop, using seedlings that were started indoors.*

gently waving your arm back and forth, let the seed slip between your thumb and index finger and land on the bed. Rake the bed lightly to cover the seeds.

USING A BROADCAST SEEDER

If you are seeding a large area, a broadcast seeder is essential. Also known as a broadcaster, this seeder is made of a canvas, metal, or plastic hopper that drops seed onto a spinning plate to sow the seed evenly. The speed with which you turn the handle determines the width of the path sown; your pace determines how densely the area is covered. The opening can be adjusted to suit the size of the seed.

USING A PLATE SEEDER

Another common tool for direct seeding is the plate seeder. It is only appropriate in the largest of gardens. This seeder has a hopper that picks one seed at a time and drops it down a chute into a furrow created in the soil. The seeder has a flange or chain to cover the seed with soil. There are two drawbacks with this tool: you must walk on the bed to use it, and the spacing and depth can be very difficult to control.

HARDENING OFF SEEDLINGS

Seedlings that have been started indoors need to move out to garden beds when the weather and conditions are appropriate. Many plants can suffer root damage and must be transplanted with care. After growing indoors, seedlings are not accustomed to the harsh conditions outdoors and have to be acclimatized in a process called

Broadcast seeder *Use this style of seeder for large areas. The seeder disperses seed evenly via a spinning plate that is operated by hand.*

Plate seeder *Seeds are sown individually in furrows created by the seeder as it is pushed along the ground; a flange or chain then covers the seed with soil.*

STARTING SEEDS

Home-made seed mix

Try making your own seed mix for soil blocks (see pp. 140–2), using compost and coco peat (or peat moss). Remember to keep the ingredients fine. A good way of doing this is to put the finished mix through a ¼in/0.5cm screen; this type of screen is generally available at hardware stores.

The composition of a good mix for soil blocking consists of:

- 3 parts well-rotted compost
- 1 part garden soil
- 4 parts coco peat

Use compost that is about two years old and quite fine (see p. 48). The garden soil should be fine textured and fertile; harvest it in the fall, before the ground freezes (in cool climates). The coco peat has good moisture-absorbing abilities and will help to hold the block together. If your garden soil is heavy, you may find it helpful to mix in a little sand.

Mix the ingredients thoroughly in a bucket and then add enough water to moisten the mix well. You will learn to judge the right amount of water with experience.

Sterilizing equipment

It is important to sterilize seed-starting trays, pots, and equipment prior to use. Wash them well and dip them in a dilute bleach solution. Allow the equipment to dry and then rinse them well with water.

Sowing extra seeds

When sowing seeds directly in the garden, it is important to remember that germination does not have a 100 per cent success rate. This may cause gaps to appear in the bed, allowing bare soil to be visible, and creating an opening in the canopy of foliage. For this reason, sow seeds more closely together or sow more seeds than necessary. The extras can be thinned out later and, depending on the vegetable, they can be used young in the kitchen or composted.

Germination

Some seeds need special treatment to assist germination. Some need to be scarified – nicked with a sharp knife – to allow moisture to penetrate; others need to be soaked in water overnight. Some plants need light to germinate and others require total darkness. Some

seeds even need to be wrapped in moist paper towels and refrigerated until they sprout. Specific advice on the germination of seeds is given under individual entries in Chapter 5 (see pp. 178–269). Most seeds will germinate better indoors if their trays are covered with a clear plastic dome, which should be removed immediately after germination; otherwise damping off (see p. 143) may occur.

Booster feeds

As seedlings grow in trays indoors, there may come a time when they use up the nutrients in the soil block and need an additional boost to keep growing well. A good choice for a booster is an organic liquid feed of fish emulsion. Be sure to dilute it exactly according to the manufacturer's instructions and bottom-water the seedlings with the feed.

"hardening off." Starting a couple of weeks before transplanting, set the young plants outdoors for an hour or two each day. They will gradually adjust to the stronger light and wind. As the time for transplanting draws near, let the seedlings stay outdoors for longer periods; the differences in temperature will prepare the plants for life in the garden. Once the seedlings have hardened off, they are ready for transplanting.

TRANSPLANTING SEEDLINGS

In the same way as you would mark out the bed for sowing seeds directly outdoors (see pp. 134–5), use string and pegs to mark out the planting rows in a hexagonal pattern. With a hand trowel or dibble, make a hole in the soil that is wide and deep enough to receive the seedling. Some seedlings, such as tomatoes, prefer to be planted very deep, but many vegetables will not survive if they are planted too deeply in the ground. Most seedlings need to be set at the same soil level as when they were growing in a soil block.

SOWING IN HOTBEDS

When starting seedlings in hotbeds, make sure the soil in the hotbed is about 75°F/24°C before sowing. Sow the seeds very closely in the hotbed, equidistant in a hexagonal pattern. The seedlings must be transplanted into the garden when they are small, before the roots grow together. To transport the seedlings, hold them by one leaf and dislodge the roots by lifting with a wooden plant marker. If seedlings are spaced far enough apart, they can be dug out with a trowel.

Remove the soil block from the tray with a spatula or bricklayer's trowel and place it in the hole. Push the earth around the soil block and firm it gently. Water the seedlings thoroughly after planting, taking care not to wet their foliage. After the initial watering, let the soil dry out somewhat to encourage the roots to develop. This "mini-drought" will prompt the roots to branch out and head downwards through the soil in search of water.

Getting a head start
If protected by a cold frame, tender vegetables can be started much earlier in the spring.

SOWING INDOORS

There are many reasons to sow seeds indoors. Some plants need to be started indoors in winter, otherwise they will not be able to mature and produce fruit before fall. Others are started indoors to provide an early harvest, and some plants need special cultural conditions to be able to germinate.

USING SOIL BLOCKS

The best method of sowing indoors is to use soil blocks, which have many advantages over seed trays and pots:

- Plant roots are not disturbed when transplanting (see p. 139) because they are contained within the soil block.
- The plant is unlikely to become potbound because each block is surrounded by air.
- Soil blocks are inexpensive and easy to handle.

- The use of soil blocks is good for the environment because it decreases the use of disposable plastic trays and peat pots.

The concept of using soil blocks has been around almost as long as agriculture itself. When pots and containers for planting were scarce, soil was packed into pots and then turned out onto a flat surface, in the same way as a child builds a sandcastle at the beach using a bucket and sand. By this method, many more seedlings can be started with only a few pots.

There have been improvements on this method that have resulted in a special tool called a soil blocker. This tool is available in cubes of several different sizes, from ¾in/2cm to 4in/10cm; the most useful size for the home gardener is the 2in/5cm version. Smaller cubes may save some space but they tend to be more

Making soil blocks
Ensure that the mix is thoroughly moist, but not waterlogged, to make soil blocks that will not fall apart when you work with them.

difficult to handle. Equally, larger cubes can be very difficult to handle and often fall apart. For plants that will need a lot of soil, start them in 2in/5cm blocks and transplant them into 4in/10cm blocks when the seedlings require more root space.

MAKING SOIL BLOCKS

Using a soil blocker is easy if the seed mix you are trying to form into blocks has the right proportions of soil, compost, and coco peat. You should be able to purchase a commercial organic mix that is specifically designed for the purpose. If possible, choose a mix that does not contain peat moss, the harvesting of which causes damage to wildlife habitat and the environment. Alternatively you can make your own seed mix (see p. 138), which is just as effective.

Practice makes perfect: if you are new to making soil blocks, make an entire tray of blocks and then toss the soil back into the bucket. The first step is to put 4–5in/10–13cm of the properly moistened seed mix in the bottom of a shallow flat-bottomed tub. It is also essential that the mix is not too dry or moist. When squeezed it should not feel like a drenched sponge, but should release a little water. Hold the soil blocker by the metal flange, not the handle, and drive it forcefully into the mix. With the blocker pressed against the bottom of the tub, twist it back and forth – clockwise and counterclockwise – several times. This loosens the soil from the bottom of the tub and allows the blocker to be removed easily. Lift the blocker and ensure the holes are full of mix before gently pressing the blocks out onto a tray.

SOWING IN SEED BLOCKS

Start seedlings in soil blocks arranged on a rigid tray. Choose one that will last a long time and that can withstand rough handling. The tray should also be completely watertight. I prefer a heavy rigid tray that is about 1in/2.5cm deep, with sloped sides. Place the filled soil blocker on the tray, and gently push down on the handle as you lift the tool, keeping the mix in contact with

SOWING SEED IN SOIL BLOCKS

1 *Place the filled soil blocker flat on a rigid watertight tray. Lift the blocker carefully while pushing slowly down on the handle to release the blocks.*

2 *Gently drop one or two seeds into the dimple on the top of each soil block. Push a little of the seed mix over the top of the seeds so that they are lightly covered.*

3 *Place the seed tray in your sunniest window or under an artificial light. Consider covering it with a plastic dome. Make sure that each tray is clearly labelled.*

141

the bottom of the tray. Place the blocker directly on the tray and lift it slowly as you push the blocks out so that they do not break apart.

Always start an entire tray at once so that the seedlings will be approximately the same size, then the lights can be placed as close to the seedlings as possible without actually touching them.

In the dimple in the top of each soil block, place one or two seeds. Use a small wooden plant marker to cover the seed with a little of the mix. Just push some soil from the top of the block over the dimple that contains the seed. Some seeds require light to germinate and should not be covered. Always be sure to label the seedlings clearly. Some plants, like onions, do extremely well when several seeds are planted in the same block. This saves space indoors and does not harm the growth of the plants. For example, if four onion seeds are sown in one soil block, when transplanted outdoors the bulbs will grow

and push away from each other. The result will be four onions ready to harvest at once. The proximity will not cause deformed bulbs, but when planting out the blocks should be placed further apart in the hexagonal pattern than if each block contained only one seedling.

SOWING SEED IN POTS AND TRAYS

There are other methods of starting seeds: in pots or cells. The best kinds of planting cells are made of UV-stabilized plastic that are heavy and will last many years. Choose a type fitted with a tray to keep them together; this also makes them easier to water from the bottom.

Many gardeners like to use the styrofoam trays that are set up with a water reservoir and capillary matting. This makes watering easier, but has several drawbacks: the roots of the plants tend to grow into the matting; the roots often become damaged when you remove the plants for potting up or transplanting outdoors; the

Starting out Seed trays come in a variety of shapes and materials. Choose trays that are strong, rigid, reusable, and easy to water.

capillary matting has to be replaced every year; and the production of styrofoam damages the environment. Both plastic pots and styrofoam trays allow seedlings to become rootbound, while soil blocks do not.

SOWING PROBLEMS

The two most common problems that occur when starting seeds indoors are damping off and leggy seedlings. Damping off is a fungal disease that is promoted by excessive watering, over-fertilizing, or lack of sun or air circulation (see p. 176). The best way to prevent damping off is to water the seedlings from the bottom. This also encourages deep roots to develop more quickly because they reach down through the soil in search of water.

Leggy seedlings are usually the result of inadequate light. If you are using an artificial light source, like full-spectrum fluorescent bulbs, it is likely that the seedlings are placed too far away from the lamp. For the best results, position the light bulbs no further than 2in/5cm from the seedling foliage. If the seedlings are on a windowsill or in a sunny spot, the seedlings are receiving too much indirect light. Place the seedlings in the sunniest window, or supplement them with artificial light. Turn the trays often to get even lighting. Brush the seedlings with your hand or blow on them to imitate the wind. This helps to harden off and prevent leggy seedlings.

WATERING SEEDS

Seeds sown in soil blocks can be easily watered from the bottom. Gently pour water into the tray and the blocks will absorb and wick it up quickly. Be sure to put enough in so that the blocks in the middle of the tray get moisture too. If you are growing seedlings in pots, take the entire pot and sit it in a saucer of water, about ½in/1.5cm deep. The water will be wicked up into the soil very quickly. Stand watered pots in

Container vegetables *Cucumbers and summer squash grow well in a confined space. Sow seeds directly in the tub once all threat of frost has passed.*

a tray that has a ridged base to allow excessive moisture to drain out of the holes at the bottom of the pots. If placed on a flat tray, the soil in the pots may become waterlogged.

POTTING ON

If seedlings become too large for the 2in/5cm soil blocks, move them into 4in/10cm pots; square pots provide much more soil and growing space than round ones. Line the bottom with a 2in/5cm layer of moistened mix. Using a kitchen spatula, lift up the entire soil block and place it gently in the pot. Fill around the block with mix. Make sure that the seedling is no deeper than the top of the soil block, unless the seedling is a plant that needs deeper planting.

Working with Vegetables

Once a bed is planted, it needs only minimal care. Watering, weeding, and mulching are most commonly needed. Occasionally a crop will need a liquid organic feed to give it a boost. When harvesting, replant the area soon to another crop to prevent erosion and nutrient loss.

WATERING

The goal of the organic gardener should be to minimize the use of water. Reducing or eliminating watering saves time and labor; it is also good for the environment. Salt water covers most of the Earth, while fresh water accounts for

Wilting plants *All plants can wilt a little in the hot summer sun, especially at midday. Water them if they fail to recover when the day cools down.*

just 2 per cent of available water. The rain and water in ponds and streams is known as surface water, while water from deep wells is called ground water. When we draw ground water, we deplete the underground storage supply of fresh water – usually converting it to waste water.

For this reason, we should try to limit our consumption of this precious supply of fresh water to surface sources. I am fortunate enough to live in a home supplied with surface water from a spring. In all but the worst of droughts, the water supply is more than sufficient. If your water supply is from a deep well, as is the case in most cities, it is especially important for you to conserve water. To this end, consider installing a rainwater collection system in your garden. These devices attach to the gutters and downspouts from your home, diverting rainwater into a storage tank where it can be kept until needed for garden watering.

Plants use water continuously. The best way to reduce the need for constant watering is to prevent moisture loss in the soil by mulching – mulch all of your vegetable and perennial beds with a thick layer of organic matter to conserve moisture – close plant spacing, and working in plenty of compost to improve water retention in the soil. Heavy soils are less prone to drying out than light soils, except in arid locations.

DRIP IRRIGATION

When you do need to water the garden, be as economical as possible by watering only where it is needed. In this respect, the use of an overhead sprinkler is not advisable because it is unable to direct water to specific plants. The best way to conserve water is to use a drip irrigation system. Many gardeners never consider using this equipment, but simple models are very

RULES FOR WATERING

- Water less frequently, but water deeply enough to soak the soil.
- Water plants only when the soil is dry, but before the plants begin to suffer drought.
- Watering fruits that are nearly ready for harvest can cause fungus problems.
- Water newly transplanted plants, unless you have timed the planting to be followed by rain.
- If a hard crust forms on the top of the soil, cultivate it before watering. This will allow the water to penetrate and reach the roots.
- Do not water during the sunniest part of the day – much of the water will evaporate. Do not water in the evening – cool nights can encourage mold and fungus. Water plants in the early to mid-morning.

- Water plants slowly, allowing water to soak into the soil and reach the roots rather than run off.
- Watering fruits right before harvest dilutes the flavor – dry conditions at harvest time make fruits sweeter.

- Watering frequently in small amounts results in a shallow root system that can be very sensitive to minor droughts.
- If overhead watering is used, set out a bucket to measure how much water has been applied.

inexpensive and invariably pay for themselves many times over in the savings that you make on your water bill.

When considering a drip irrigation system, look for the simplest model. It needs to have a filter and a pressure-reducing valve from which a purpose-made hose is run around the garden. It is best to run a line close to the house and around the perimeter, avoiding the central areas of lawn where it may be damaged. Make sure that the hose is not left exposed where it may be mowed accidentally or trip someone up. Pierce small holes in the hose so that water emitters may be inserted. Use standard emitters for flat gardens and pressure-compensating emitters for hilly terrain or steeply terraced gardens. Emitters are rated at 2qt/2l, 4qt/3.8l, or 8qt/7.6l per hour.

If you need to put an emitter at a distance from the main hose, use a smaller-size tube to branch off. Some emitters act like tiny sprinklers and can be useful for watering delicate plants. Very often a timer is used to turn the water on and off once or twice a week. This allows you to control how much water the plants receive. Soaker hoses are sometimes used in combination with drip irrigation systems, but they are prone to clogging up with sediment from the water. Look for a special hose with premade holes spaced about 1in/2.5cm apart; this is useful for garden beds and can be used like a soaker hose, but will not clog.

You should only use your irrigation system when watering is necessary; the exception to this is when starting fruit trees (see p. 158).

RULES FOR WEEDING

- Remove weeds when they are quite small – this will make your workload much easier.
- Remove perennial weeds, roots and all.
- Always remove weeds before they go to seed.
- If you weed on a hot sunny day, most hoed weeds can be left in the bed as mulch. The sun will dry them out and kill the roots.
- Perennial weeds can be killed by frequent cultivation of the soil, which keeps these weeds from ever sending out shoots to the surface where they can thrive in the sunlight.

WEEDING

Hoeing is the most common method of weeding in organic gardening. You will have very little to do if you have prepared your beds well and mulched them well. Two types of hoe are necessary in the garden: the collinear hoe and the three-tine cultivator (see p. 273). Both have long handles that allow you to work from a standing position. Use the collinear hoe to cut off small weeds just below the surface, and tackle larger weeds with a three-tine cultivator.

If you are weeding around small delicate plants, such as strawberries or seedlings, kneel down and pull the weeds out by hand or use a handtool version of a three-tine cultivator to avoid damaging plants.

In certain circumstances, weeding is more easily accomplished with a flame weeder or a string trimmer. Grass and weeds that grow up between flagstones in a patio or paving bricks can be easily removed with a flame weeder. Flame weeders are particularly useful on hard gravel paths. When using a flame weeder, direct the flame onto the weed just long enough for the foliage to change color; do not let it burn completely. The singed foliage will die and decompose. String trimmers can be turned at an angle and are used for the same purpose.

MULCHING

There are four purposes to mulching:
- To prevent evaporation of moisture.
- To discourage weed growth.
- To stop erosion.
- To add organic matter to the soil.

Mulching is the practice of covering garden beds with a thick layer of organic material. Many types of organic matter may be used as mulch (see pp. 40–3 and below). In nature, the leaves of plants drop to the ground during the fall and become mulch; try to imitate this process in the garden. Mulching has been practised for thousands of years. For example, there is a long tradition of using straw to mulch

Collinear hoe Hold this hoe in both hands with your thumbs pointing upward; keep your back straight and the blade of the hoe parallel to the ground.

strawberries, which have very shallow roots that are easily damaged by weeding and cultivation. The straw mulch forms a protective layer that keeps weeds at bay and saves you from having to weed frequently.

Organic mulches retain a lot of moisture and provide an excellent barrier to soil evaporation. A thick mulch keeps the soil cool in the heat and bright sun of summer. If the sun cannot reach the soil, evaporation will be slowed. Another benefit is that weed seeds are discouraged from germinating. When annual weed seeds are buried beneath a layer of organic matter, they most often die before the foliage reaches the surface. Occasionally, well-established perennial weeds are able to send out shoots that penetrate the surface. If you notice emerging weed shoots, pull them out by hand immediately.

In areas with cold winters, apply mulch to the garden beds after the soil has warmed. Most

Straw mulch *Mulch strawberries with a thick layer of straw to keep weeds at bay and to protect the fruits from being soiled.*

gardeners plant the bed and wait for the seedlings to emerge before adding the mulch, but some seeds can grow right through the mulch. However, if you are transplanting seedlings, let them become established for a week or so before applying a mulch. If any weeds have germinated, remove them and compost them.

During the gardening year, a mulch will begin to decompose and provide nutrients to the soil. At the end of the growing season, many can be turned under and incorporated in the soil. This addition of organic matter is a great benefit to the soil. If you wait until spring to turn under the mulch, its decomposition may rob the soil of nitrogen and make renovating the beds more difficult.

MULCHING MATERIALS

Pine needles A 4–6in/10–15cm layer provides a good mulch around acid-loving plants.

Grass clippings Use as mulch around young seedlings. Follow with a thicker mulch of leaf mold or straw.

Leaf mold A 4in/10cm layer provides a good barrier against weeds. When leaf mold is incorporated in the fall, add lots of organic matter to build good soil structure. Leaf mold provides an excellent habitat for worms and insects that aerate and loosen the soil (see Making leaf mold, p. 49).

Compost A 3–5in/8–13cm layer makes an excellent mulch. If compost is too fine, it may be washed away by rain.

Straw Excellent for use around strawberries as it contains few weed seeds. Use a 6–8in/15–20cm layer to prevent light reaching the soil.

Hay First-cutting hay tends to contain weed seeds, so try to use second-cutting hay instead. A 4–8in/10–20cm layer will provide a good mulch. Spoiled hay that is unfit for animals is often available free and makes a fine mulch.

Shredded bark A very common decorative mulch for perennial beds. A 2–4in/5–10cm layer will give good results. However, as it decomposes, it robs the soil of nitrogen. Do not turn the bark under in the fall. If you purchase shredded bark, be sure it was not treated with any chemicals to make it decompose faster.

Sawdust and wood shavings Let the shavings mature well before use to prevent nitrogen depletion. Do not turn them under in the fall. Use a 1–2in/2.5–5cm layer.

Cocoa shells A 3–6in/8–15cm layer provides a decorative mulch for perennial beds. They are alkaline and should not be used near acid-loving plants. When the shells decay, which may take several years, work them into the soil. Peanut shells, rice hulls, buckwheat hulls, and nut shells also make good mulches.

Black plastic Avoid using black plastic because it may leach chemicals, especially DEHA, into the soil. Plastic also prevents rain from soaking into the garden beds and does absolutely nothing

Hay mulch Mulch vegetables in the garden with a thick layer of organic matter. A 4in/10cm layer of second-cutting hay makes a good mulch around potatoes.

Well-mulched plant *A thick layer of organic matter will suppress weeds and help to retain moisture, encouraging strong growth in a plant.*

to enrich the soil. Plant roots require oxygen and may even be harmed because the plastic discourages oxygen from entering the soil.

Newspapers Avoid using these unless you are certain that the ink and dyes are not synthetic.

SUPPLEMENTAL FEEDING

When watering the garden, you may notice that some plants need a nutrient boost. Many vegetables are annuals that require lots of nutrients to produce an abundant harvest. For instructions on how to make and use liquid feeds, see pages 50–3. Be sure to dilute these feeds carefully or the plants may be burned. Any commercial liquid organic feed should be diluted

exactly according to the manufacturer's directions. For other additives, see pages 54–6.

Bulbs Potassium supplements are often needed to ensure good flowering in bulbs. Apply soil amendments and mulch the plants after the foliage dies back, during the growing season, but not in spring before they bloom.

Bush and tree fruits/Vegetables Many plants, bushes, and trees will benefit from a side-dressing of solid feeds. Add compost, well-rotted manure, and soil amendments as a mulch, then gently mix them into the top 2in/5cm of garden soil.

Container plants Potted plants need more feed than those grown in the ground. Liquid organic feeds are the best source of nutrients for container plants, and should be applied every two to four weeks in the growing season. Top-dress perennials in containers with compost once a year. Slow-release organic fertilizers can be mixed into the soil when planting in a container.

Perennials Beds of perennials will benefit greatly from a mulch of seaweed every three to five years to add trace elements and organic matter. Apply fresh mulch every year and add soil amendments at the same time if necessary. Testing the soil will indicate which amendments are needed. Sprinkle high-phosphorus feeds, such as bone meal, and high-nitrogen feeds, such as blood meal, on the bed before mulching in the spring.

CONTROLLING EROSION

When rain falls on bare soil, each drop hits with great force. Soil particles are dislodged and washed away with the water that runs off the bed. The force of the rain hitting the ground compacts the soil, preventing moisture absorption and causing the water to wash away more of the soil on the surface. A thick, loose mulch absorbs the force of the rain and lets the water trickle down to reach the soil. Any dislodged soil particles are caught by the mulch and retained in the bed.

Choosing Fruit

Fresh organic fruit from the garden is a wonderful treat. Nothing compares in flavor and freshness to the first apple of the season or a succulent strawberry still warm from the afternoon sun. Store-bought fruits are shipped many miles and rarely retain their fresh-picked taste and texture.

Heirloom varieties

Fruit trees make excellent specimen trees in the garden and provide beautiful flowers during spring. Along with cane fruits and bushes, trees provide structure in the garden. Their placement can frame a beautiful view or obstruct an unsightly one.

One of the biggest concerns about growing fruit organically is the prevalence of pests and diseases. As with vegetables, choosing resistant varieties provides a good defense. Old heirloom fruits are often quite resistant to diseases but it can be difficult to find suppliers that stock them (see pp. 280–1). Even by choosing resistant varieties, you may experience problems with pests and diseases, but there are several effective, organic methods of control available (see pp. 168–72).

Obtaining benchgrafts

Some nurseries are dedicated to preserving heirloom varieties of fruit trees and bushes. They raise a wide selection of heirloom plants in their nurseries and will graft a variety of your choice onto your preferred rootstock. These types of plant are called "benchgrafts" (see pp. 154–5). Since the upper part of the plant, or scionwood, has just been grafted onto a rootstock, it will need special care until the graft heals.

Benchgrafts and delicate or weak plants should first be planted in pots in a rich compost, where they will receive tender loving care and daily attention. They can be planted out in their permanent locations in the fall. Fruit trees, bushes, and canes that are large, hardy, and vigorous should be planted directly in the ground in their permanent locations. When buying fruits, avoid being tempted to over-order, otherwise you will find yourself with more bushes than you are able to plant – they will not survive for long out of the ground. Planting trees and bushes is hard work; fortunately this task needs to be done only once, but the benefits will last for decades.

Olives *Although they are not cold hardy, olives can be grown under glass in cool climates. When grown outdoors, olive trees reach up to 30ft/9m in height.*

Blueberries *Consider nutrition when planning your planting. Blueberries are a good source of beneficial phytochemicals and many vitamins and minerals. Their colorful fruit are a tasty treat.*

A common problem encountered when establishing new fruit trees, bushes, and canes is working with poor-quality stock. Therefore, when purchasing your fruitstock, select from a reputable nursery and arrange for delivery in late winter or early in the spring, when the weather is still cool. (Alternatively, in warmer climates, have plants delivered in early winter and plant straightaway.) Shipping in warm weather often results in plant damage caused by excessive heat.

One important point to remember when growing fruit trees is that many bear fruits biennially, not every year, and most trees will not produce in the first few years after they have been planted.

CHOOSING THE RIGHT SITE

When planning the fruit garden, you need to consider climate (see box, left) as well as the topography of the land. The site may be sloped and provide frost pockets in low areas. Make use of features such as a brick wall or the side of a house to provide shelter for tender plants. You can create a microclimate on the sunny side of the house by protecting fruits from the wind. This will allow you to grow some fruits, such as figs, in climates that are usually too cold for them to bear fruit.

MAKING YOUR SELECTION

When choosing plants, it is important to consider the nutrient content they offer, as some fruits have higher nutritional value than others (see pp. 86–9). Select young trees wherever possible

 ## PREFERRED CLIMATES

Consider your climate carefully when deciding which fruits to grow. Choose varieties based on their cold hardiness, heat tolerance, and required winter-chilling periods, as well as disease resistance and flavor. Some fruits can only be grown in cool climates and others only in warm climates; a few plants perform well in both.

Cool climates Apples, cherries, plums, pears, blueberries, raspberries, blackberries.

Warm climates Oranges, lemons, limes, olives.

Cool/warm climates Grapes, currants, quinces.

as older trees often suffer shock from transplanting and take longer to bear fruit. A one- to two-year-old tree is a better choice than a large three- to four-year-old tree – a small tree involves less work when planting too.

Buy healthy, disease-free plants from a reputable nursery. The plants should be dormant when shipped so that they suffer less shock when transplanted. Plants that are shipped from the nursery are most often bare-rooted. This simply means that they were harvested when dormant and the soil was removed from their roots. If they heat up or dry out during shipment they may die. When they arrive at your home, it is imperative that you tend to them immediately.

The selection and quality from mail-order nurseries tends to be much better than that from most local nurseries. Local nurseries often sell fruit trees and bushes after they break dormancy which, in fact, is the worst time to transplant them. It is usually much more frugal to purchase bare-root plants in winter and arrange for delivery at the proper planting time in spring.

Remember to check the expected full-grown height of the plant. For example, an apple variety can be grafted onto many different rootstocks, which determine its mature size. One rootstock may permit the tree to reach full size (about 35ft/10.5m) while another may dwarf the tree so that it only reaches 8ft/2.5m.

ROOTSTOCKS FOR FRUIT TREES
Another consideration is the compatibility of the rootstock with your soil type. Some rootstocks grow well in clay soils while others prefer sandy soils. For example, the apple rootstock 'Antonovka' is the best rootstock for heavy clay soils, but it produces a standard-sized apple tree.

Irresistible trap Hang a bottle part-filled with sugar water near your apples, to lure sweet-toothed pests away from your crop and into the bottle trap.

The rootstock 'Poland 22' is a mini-dwarf tree but dislikes clay soils. If you have heavy clay soil but want a dwarf tree, the solution is to have 'Poland 22' grafted onto 'Antonovka' rootstock, which is then called an interstem. The variety is then grafted onto the interstem, which results in a dwarf apple tree that tolerates clay soils.

Some rootstocks also provide disease resistance to soil-borne diseases, so be sure to plant the trees with the grafts above the soil level. In Chapter 5, rootstocks are recommended for each tree fruit if appropriate (see pp. 251–6).

SELECTING FOR POLLINATION
There are many different varieties of almost every type of fruit. Some varieties store well, others are best eaten fresh; some are sweet and others tart. Some bear fruits early, others bear late. In order to have an extended harvest, it is a good idea to choose several different varieties. By doing so, you will have fruit to pick throughout the season, and the different varieties will cross-pollinate each other.

Pollination is essential for most plants to set fruit. It is primarily accomplished by insects in fruit trees, and by wind in nut trees. Many fruits are self-sterile and need the pollen of other varieties in order to produce fruit. This can pose a challenge in small gardens, if there is not enough room for two varieties of the same fruit. The easy solution is for one rootstock to have two or more varieties grafted onto it, so that different branches bear differing varieties of the same fruit. Many nurseries sell trees grafted in this way with popular varieties, or you can graft your own combinations at home – scionwood or budwood can be bought for this purpose (see pp. 162–3).

Equally, you may not need to have more than one variety of a fruit in your garden if other varieties of that fruit exist in a nearby garden. Visiting insects will cross-pollinate your tree.

PLANTING FRUIT

When your fruitstock arrive, they are in a state of shock from being dug up and transported. They need to receive immediate care if they are to survive their ordeal. Submerge their roots in water straightaway and heel them in. Pot them up, or plant them as soon as possible.

BARE-ROOT CARE

When fruitstock are dug up at the nursery, they are bound to lose some roots. During delivery, the wet packing material in which they are shipped begins to dry out, leaving them subject to drought. For this reason, soak the roots in water before planting. It is even important to wrap them in wet burlap before carrying them to the planting site. Keep the plants in a shady spot until they can go in the ground; if you are unable to plant them in their permanent spot within a day or two of delivery, pot them up or heel them in.

To heel plants into the garden, dig a trench and lay each plant down at an angle of 45° with its roots in the hole. Cover the roots with a mound of garden soil and keep them very moist with regular watering. Remember to provide shade for the exposed parts of the plant.

If the ground is frozen, pot up bare-root plants in compost. Keep them moist and place the containers in an outbuilding to protect them from extreme temperatures. During the daytime, open the door to provide the plants with necessary sunlight.

PLANTING BENCHGRAFTS

Benchgrafts are trees that have been grafted specifically at the gardener's request. The tree may have been grafted just days before being mailed and so it will still be in a very delicate

Benchgraft *A benchgrafted tree is created from the topgrowth of one plant and the rootstock of another. Note the V-shaped graft on the apple tree above.*

state when it is delivered to you. Like most delicate or weak plants, benchgrafts need extra care to get off to a good start. Pot them in pure compost until they are well established. Keep a close eye on their progress and supplement the compost with liquid organic feed as necessary. They may be planted out in their permanent locations during the fall after the growing season.

The grafts are generally covered with wax or a rubberband, so you will need to unpack your plants carefully to avoid damaging them. Prune off any obviously dead roots and soak the plant in water for about 12 hours. Place the tree or bush in a pot of appropriate size – it is acceptable to bend the roots to make them fit. If any specific soil amendments are required, mix them with the compost, then add the mixture to the pot and press down firmly with your fists. It is essential to have good contact between the compost and the roots. Add more of the mixture and press down again, more gently this time. Water the plant thoroughly and label it.

As benchgrafts grow, buds may form on the rootstock or interstem. These must be removed or energy will be diverted away from the grafted variety that you wish to grow. Remove any suckers that emerge. Container. plants do not overwinter well and should be planted in their permanent location in the fall.

PRUNING

Unless it has already been done by the nursery, it is essential that you prune back the top of the fruit tree once it is in the ground. This will concentrate the energy of growth into developing a healthy root system. The aim is to compensate for the roots that the plant lost when it was harvested by the nursery. Pruning back the tops after planting creates a balance between the top of the plant and its roots. A good rule of thumb is to remove half of every side branch of a tree or half the height of a multi-stemmed plant. For more information on pruning, refer to pages 164–7.

Bold and bright A selection of fresh fruits to be eaten raw, served in pies, or preserved as jellies or jams, are a welcome harvest at the kitchen table in summer.

PLANTING OUT

Soak bare-root plants in water for 12 hours before planting; plants in containers should be watered and moist, but not waterlogged. If you are not planting the tree in a cultivated bed it is important to dig a large hole and loosen the soil deeply. Without good drainage, the plant's roots will become waterlogged. Choose a fertile site and collect any soil amendments that will be necessary to provide for the specific requirements of the plant.

Prepare the site by digging a hole twice the size needed for the rootball of the plant. This is important to provide the best conditions for growth. Add bone meal to the bottom of the hole to encourage root development. Coco peat or lime can be used to change the pH depending on the plant's requirements. Avoid incorporating high-nitrogen amendments because they will encourage too much tender growth in the fall. Mix any required soil amendments with the compost and some of the excavated earth in a wheelbarrow.

Remove the bare-root plant from the water and prune off any dead roots. Wrap the roots in wet burlap and carry the plant to the prepared site. If the plant was in a container it can be transplanted when not dormant. Remove the plant from the container carefully, keeping as much of the soil with the roots as possible. If the plant is balled and burlapped, remove any metal cage or ties before planting the tree. Cut the burlap tied around the trunk and tuck it back under the rootball. Check to see whether the plant has become rootbound, and use pruners or a knife to slice into the spiralling roots. This will encourage new growth and help the plant to become established.

Place the plant in the hole and adjust the mound of soil beneath its roots until the plant is at the same depth as it was before being dug by the nursery. Use a stake across the planting hole to assess the correct soil level. Dig the hole deeper if necessary or add some of the soil mix beneath the roots to raise its height. Make sure that the trunk is perpendicular to the ground.

PLANTING A BARE-ROOT FRUIT TREE

1 Dig a hole twice the size of the root system. Loosen the soil deeply to ensure good drainage. Mix the excavated soil with compost and any soil amendments.

2 Prune off any dead roots and gently loosen the rootball. Place the tree in the hole and backfill with soil so that it is vertical and at the same planting depth as before.

3 Firm the soil to ensure good contact with the roots. Use the leftover sod to form a berm at the base of the tree to retain water. Water the tree thoroughly.

Staking trees Stake tall trees after planting, to give them additional support during strong winds. Smaller trees and bushes rarely need staking.

Fill the soil mix around the roots and press firmly by treading down the soil with the heel of your boot to ensure good contact between the roots and the soil. This eliminates any air pockets. Add more soil on top and firm again gently. The sod may be used to form a mound, or berm, around the base of the tree to retain water. If you use sod instead of soil to make the berm, place it upside down to discourage competition for nutrients from the grass.

Water the plant thoroughly, being careful not to cause erosion of the berm or the soil around the roots. Put a permanent label on the plant; plastic ones often fade after one season, so use a metal label that can be written on by making an impression with a ballpoint pen.

STAKING AND PROTECTION

If you have planted a tall tree, make sure that it is well staked to protect it from damage in strong winds and gales. Bushes and small trees rarely need staking.

Pound three wooden stakes into the ground outside of the berm, spacing them evenly around the tree. Using twine, tie the tree to each stake. Be sure to wrap the trunk with a soft cloth so that the twine does not injure the bark. Do not tie the tree too tightly or it may be damaged. As an alternative to twine, use a purpose-made rubber tree tie that can be adjusted as the tree grows.

In areas where damage from mice, voles, rabbits, or gophers is likely, you will need to protect the base of the tree with wire. Girdling by mice (see p. 159) is one common reason for failure of a newly planted fruit tree or bush.

Wrap a length of ¼in/0.5cm wire mesh or metal window screening (not fiberglass) around the base of the tree and secure it with twine. Remember that the wind can rock the tree and cause it to rub against the wire and so damage the bark. Sink the screening into the soil to prevent rodents from burrowing underneath.

WORKING WITH FRUIT

Once fruit trees, bushes and cane fruit are planted, they require regular care. Watering, weeding, mulching, and feeding are required as well as protecting fruits from birds and other pests. It is essential to protect the bark of newly planted trees and bushes from rodents.

WATERING

Correct watering is essential to producing great fruit. Some plants produce fruit best in dry conditions, while others need copious amounts of water to produce fruit. Consult Chapter 5 to ascertain the watering needs of specific fruits (see pp. 248–67). When establishing plants they often need significantly more supplemental water than they will need when mature. Most fruit trees will bear fruits a year or two sooner if they receive consistent thorough watering during their first two to four years of life. The best way to accomplish this is with a drip irrigation system (see pp. 144–5). Start with a small emitter that has a watering rate of 1gal/3.8l per hour and gradually add additional emitters on a side tube as the tree grows.

Young trees are often planted with a berm of earth around the base to retain water. Older and established trees have a large mulched area around their base to prevent competition from grass. Bushes should also be planted with berms of earth around them to retain water. As with watering vegetables, it is important to water less frequently but water deeply to soak the soil (see Rules for watering, p. 145).

The lack of water stresses trees and many bushes long before the signs of wilt are evident. A good way to test is to dig down 5–10in/13–25cm below the surface to see whether the soil is dry. If so, it is time to water.

Apply water slowly so that it can penetrate the surface and be absorbed, rather than run off. Keep watering until it has soaked deeply into the soil. Avoid watering your fruitstock immediately before harvesting, except in a drought. Excessive watering makes the fruits swell with juice that dilutes the flavor. Some of the best-tasting fruit is grown in semi-drought conditions.

MULCHING

Fruit plants should be mulched to conserve moisture. As the mulch decomposes, it adds organic matter and nutrients to the soil. Using

Preventing water loss *Apply a thick mulch around the base of newly planted trees and bushes to help retain moisture in the soil.*

Fruit protection Throw soft netting over your fruit crops as they near maturity to ensure that you rather than greedy birds get to enjoy the fruits of your labor.

mulch also prevents the growth of grass around the base of a fruit tree. Young fruit trees have many shallow, quick-growing roots that enable the tree to become established. The growth of these shallow roots can be retarded by a substance released from grass roots. When mulch is used, be sure to pull it away from the trunk of the plant in winter or it will encourage mice and voles to chew on the bark and girdle the plant.

UNWELCOME VISITORS

Fruit trees and bushes can be damaged by rodents and rabbits chewing on their bark. When a plant has had its bark removed all the way around the trunk, it is called girdling. Fruit trees and bushes must be protected from this kind of damage. Even mature trees that are 30ft/9m tall can be killed by voles after just a few days of chewing. Girdling most often occurs in winter

when there is little food for animals to eat. Each fall, clear away any grass or other vegetative growth from around the base of the plant to discourage rodents from choosing it as their winter home. Metal window screening is usually sufficient to discourage girdling; some gardeners prefer ¼in/0.5cm wire mesh, but in this case the top of the mesh should be covered with cloth to prevent damage to the bark.

In cool weather climates, consider the height of the snow in winter. The screen or wire mesh should extend above that level or rabbits may chew on the tree when standing on the snow. If using screen, fold it in half and keep the smooth edge at the top; push the rough edges into the soil. Wrap the screen loosely around the base of the tree and tie it with twine. Push the base of the screen into the soil to prevent rodents from going under the barrier.

PROTECTING FROM BIRDS

All soft fruits and some tree fruits are susceptible to damage and theft by birds when the fruits near maturity. There are two techniques for saving fruits. One is to plant a tree to lure them away from the crops. For example, a fruiting mulberry will attract birds away from your soft fruits. A second is to use nets. Soft netting can be thrown over bushes and trees as the fruits near maturity. Plants that cannot withstand the weight of the netting will need to be supported by stakes, but it is rarely necessary to build elaborate cages to exclude birds. Do not cover plants with nets during the growing season because this prevents birds from eating the pests. Plants only need to be covered as the fruits become ready for harvest.

FEEDING

One of the most effective ways of feeding fruit plants is to side-dress the plants with well-rotted manure. The manure can even be used as a mulch. If soil tests indicate deficiencies, sprinkle soil amendments on the soil before adding a mulch. Remember that the root system of a plant is as extensive as its topgrowth. Therefore, when feeding trees around their trunks, you need to cover an area that extends as far as the drip line of the tree.

If the soil is deficient in trace elements, apply a seaweed mulch every three to four years. A sprinkling of blood meal and bone meal every year will be a benefit to most fruits. If you choose to surround your fruits with sod, usea dibble or rod to make holes and fill them with soil amendments. In this way, the fruit trees and bushes rather than the grass will receive the amendments.

Another option for feeding fruits is to plant a cover crop. This will discourage the growth of weeds and sod, and when turned under it will provide organic matter to the fruit trees and bushes (see pp. 57–61).

Sweet almonds Almond trees produce delicate pink or white blossom in spring, followed by a harvest of tasty nuts (right) in fall.

Peaches nearing harvest Support drooping fruit-laden branches (left) to prevent damage to the tree. After harvest, the supports should be removed.

GRAFTING

Grafting is so easy and fun that every gardener should try it. The technique has been commonplace for more than 2,000 years and is an inexpensive way to propagate existing trees and bushes. It provides you with the opportunity to add new fruit varieties to your garden.

GRAFTING

Most cultivated fruits and nuts do not come true from seed and are propagated by grafting a bud or piece of wood onto a compatible rootstock. This may mean grafting a different variety of apple onto one branch of an apple tree in your garden or it may mean grafting a variety directly onto a rootstock.

Finding a compatible rootstock is very easy. If you have a fruit-bearing plant in your garden, the rootstock is likely to have sent out a sucker. This sucker can be dug up and grown in a pot (or elsewhere in the garden) and used for grafting. Very often an orchard or neighbor will let you take a small cutting from one of their trees to use as scionwood. Rootstocks can be purchased from nurseries, generally at a fraction of the price of a cultivated variety.

Grafting should take place in the early spring, when the plants are still dormant. The technique is most commonly used for propagating fruit trees, nuts, and a few flowering bushes such as roses. There are two basic methods: bud grafting and whip grafting.

BUD GRAFTING

Budding, or bud grafting, is often done during late summer instead of early spring. Though this method is most often used for roses and some bushes, it is appropriate whenever the size of the scionwood is different from the size of the rootstock. Using a sharp knife, make small cuts

BUD GRAFTING

 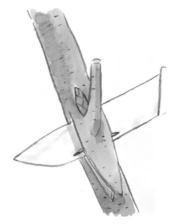 

1 *Using a sharp knife, make small cuts into the bark of the rootstock to form a T-shape. Gently ease back the flaps of the bark on either side of the cut.*

2 *Select a healthy bud on the scionwood. Cut from the base toward the tip, taking a slice of the bark and green cambium layer beneath.*

3 *Place the bud inside the T-cut so the two cambium layers are in contact. If necessary, cut off the top of the bud wood to make it fit. Wrap with tape.*

into the bark of the rootstock to form a T-shape. Try not to damage the greenish cambium layer under the bark. Using pruners, remove some scionwood from the tree you wish to propagate, or you may utilize scionwood obtained from a friend or nursery. If you are grafting in late summer, remove each leaf about 1in/2.5cm from the stem. At the base of each leaf is a bud that will produce growth in the next growing season. Cut from the base toward the tip. Be careful not to damage the bud. You should take a slice of bark and the green cambium layer beneath. Do not worry if you take a little of the wood by accident. Place the bud inside the T-cut that you made on the rootstock, making sure the cambium layer of the bud stays in contact with the cambium layer under the bark on the rootstock.

Gently fold back the flaps to cover the bark attached to the bud, being careful to leave the bud (and leaf stem, if there is one) exposed. Using a rubberband or grafting tape, secure the flaps. Remove the rubberband or grafting tape after about a month. Prune off the topgrowth of the rootstock in late spring after the bud has developed and grown a little.

WHIP GRAFTING

Whip grafting is used when the scionwood and the rootstock are of approximately equal size. Rootstock in this case can also mean a branch on which the scionwood is to be grafted. Using pruners, cut the rootstock horizontally 5–10in/13–25cm above the ground, then make a fresh cut on the scionwood. Using a very sharp knife, cut a V-shape in the rootstock. Make a matching point at the bottom of the scionwood, leaving space below the bottom bud.

Put the two pieces together. If they are not exactly the same diameter, ensure that on one side the bark of the rootstock fits flush with the bark of the scionwood (even if it does not line

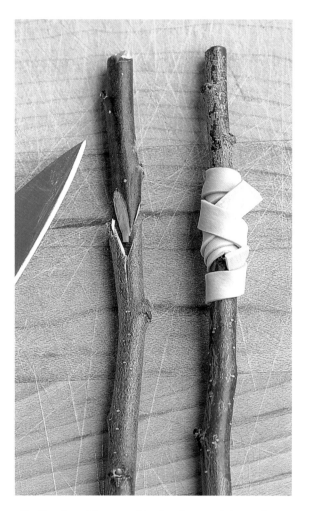

Graft union Wrap a rubberband around the graft union to hold it together until plant growth heals over the wound. You may also cover it with grafting wax.

up on the other side). Wrap a wide rubberband around the graft, starting below the graft union and working your way upward. Cover the whole graft union with the band.

The rubberband will hold the graft together until plant growth heals over the wound and binds into one piece. Tuck the end of the band under the last time around and pull it tight to secure the end. Grafting wax can be used over the tip of the scionwood and even over the graft – but it is not mandatory. Be sure to remove the rubberband after about six weeks.

PRUNING

Pruning is an art. When you prune fruit trees and bushes, you selectively remove parts of the plant to eliminate dead or diseased wood, promote the production of fruit and flowers, and improve the shape of the plant. Pruning keeps a plant healthy and vigorous.

MAINTAINING THE BALANCE

Pruning is necessary to balance the top of the plant with its roots when transplanting has taken place. When plants are dug up at nurseries for resale, their roots are inevitably damaged. Some roots are lost and so the tops need to be pruned to compensate for the smaller root system.

Many plants will not set much fruit if their branches are crowding one another. By thinning out the plant, more high-quality fruit will be produced. When pruning, it is possible to shape the plants into different forms for various locations. In a small garden, a fruit tree may be pruned into a flat fan shape against a fence or wall to save space. In a larger garden, a fruit tree may be allowed to mature into a fine pyramidal specimen tree. Or a fruit tree can be pruned and trained into a stepover, with just two branches held horizontally 12in/30cm above the ground, to border a vegetable garden. The possibilities are endless (see Training trees into shapes, p. 167).

RULES FOR PRUNING

- Do not injure the bark when making a cut. All trees, bushes, vines, and cane fruits rely on this thin layer of tissue to supply the water and nutrients. It provides the pathway from the leaves to the roots.
- Remove dead, diseased, and damaged portions of the plant as soon as they are discovered. Waiting may permit the disease to spread.
- Where branches rub against one another, remove one to prevent bark damage on both.
- Prune lightly every year instead of heavily every few years. This is easier work and promotes plant health and fruit production.

Correct cut *A clean, angled cut made about ¼in/0.5cm above a healthy bud.*

Too short *The tip of the bud is extending beyond the cut and will be vulnerable to damage.*

Too high *Cut is too far above the bud and will lead to stem dieback from the cut downward.*

Poor angle *Cut slopes toward the bud and will allow rainfall to run directly onto the bud.*

- When a limb is removed or a branch is headed back, a callus forms over the exposed wood to protect it from decay. Do not hinder callus formation with paint or tar.
- Most trees are best pruned during the late winter or early spring when the plant is dormant. Do not carry out pruning when the weather is extremely cold. Pruning in fall often promotes new growth that is tender and likely to be damaged during the winter.
- Remove unwanted suckers as soon as they appear. If left to be pruned later, they will unnecessarily utilize the plant's nutrients and resources.
- A branch that is headed back will grow in the direction of the last bud, so prune at a bud facing away from the center of the plant to discourage crowding.
- Before pruning, have a structure in mind and understand the reasons for pruning the plant in that particular way.

TYPES OF PRUNING CUT

When pruning a tree there are two basic cuts that can be made, each with a different purpose:

- Heading back is the process of pruning off parts of branches in order to improve the shape of the tree, to increase fruit production or to remove dead or diseased wood. When heading back a branch, leave one strong bud at the end to ensure the branch survives. The new growth will follow the direction of the bud.
- Thinning out is the process of removing branches to improve the structure of the tree and prevent overcrowding. The goal is to ensure good air circulation and that light reaches the center of the tree.

REMOVING LARGE BRANCHES

When removing a branch it is important to avoid leaving a stub which will cause decay and leave the tree vulnerable to insect damage. Cut back large branches in three stages to prevent damage

Heading back *Cut out dead, diseased, or damaged portions of branches. This eliminates crossing branches and often increases fruit production.*

Thinning out *Remove entire branches to improve the structure of the tree. This ensures good air circulation and prevents overcrowding.*

Open-centered tree The crown of the tree has been trained to create an open center that allows sunlight to reach the lower branches.

to the bark and to ensure a smooth finished cut. First make a cut from the bottom of the branch upward, about 1–2in/2.5–5cm away from the trunk of the tree. Make the second cut from the top of the branch downward, slightly further away from the trunk than the first cut. This will detach the branch from the tree. Make the final cut close to the trunk, but not so close that the saw damages the bark on the trunk.

TRAINING FOR BETTER FRUIT TREES

Several standard methods of pruning fruit trees ensure that sunlight reaches the center of the tree and that crowding does not occur:

- By creating a central leader, the tree has a clear vertical line, running from the trunk through the crown of branches. Trees shaped in this way are strong and able to resist damage from wind and ice.
- By heading back the main leader, the side branches become nearly as large as the new leader. This type of structure is known as a modified leader.
- An open center structure allows for air circulation and plenty of light to reach the center of the tree. This is used for stone fruits.

166

Early pruning of a tree will determine its shape at maturity. After the initial thinning out, the main branches should not need altering. Removing secondary branches and heading back is the only pruning that should be done. If heavy pruning is performed on an older tree, its yields will be temporarily reduced. However, pruning can also generate new growth in mature trees.

A fruiting spur often forms on one- or two-year-old wood on most types of fruit trees. Every time fruit is set, a new shoot forms on the other side of the spur. Fruiting spurs are therefore often zigzags of growth. As a tree gets older, its production of fruiting shoots and spurs decreases. By removing some of the older wood, new vigorous growth is stimulated, resulting in improved yields of fruit.

TRAINING TREES INTO SHAPES

Espalier Espaliering is an ancient art whereby a fruit tree is planted against a wall or fence and each year two horizontal branches are allowed to grow and all the others are removed. The espalier becomes taller with the addition of two more branches until it reaches three to six laterals. It is then kept at this level with regular pruning of any unwanted stems. Espaliered trees take up little space and produce a good harvest.

Fan Fanning is the process of growing a fruit tree or bush against a wall. The lateral shoots are pruned to be generally symmetrical. Once the fan is formed, prune regularly to maintain its shape.

Festooned A festooned tree is most often grown as a specimen tree. Instead of heading back the branches, they are bent down and tied to the trunk; this restricts the sap flow and encourages the production of fruits. Be careful not to break the branches when bending them down, or to damage the bark when tying down the branches. Prune back any fruiting spurs to 3in/8cm. Remove the ties after a few years, when the branches are permanently bent.

Stepover A stepover is an espaliered tree that has only one lateral at 12in/30cm above the soil level. Often used as a border around vegetable gardens.

Fanned out Ideal for stone fruits such as plums and peaches. Fanned trees are trained against a wall with the main branches spread out from the trunk.

Espalier Most commonly used for apple and pear varieties. Espaliered trees are evenly balanced with pairs of lateral fruit-bearing branches.

PESTS & DISEASES

The best way of dealing with pests and diseases is to avoid them by creating healthy plants in a healthy environment. Thriving plants are less likely to get diseases. A healthy environment filled with a diversity of plants encourages beneficial insects that keep pests under control.

PREVENTION AND CONTROL

Conventional thinking on pests and diseases is to find chemicals that kill or control them. Many organic gardeners have taken this same approach by finding organic pesticides and fungicides that perform the same job. This is flawed thinking because healthy plants grow vigorously and almost never require chemical protection against pests and diseases.

Studies show that deficiencies or excesses of nutrients cause imbalances in plants, which make them more susceptible to pests and diseases. Other studies show that plants grown in well-prepared beds, with good soil structure, have superior root systems and are more resistant to pests. It is clear that soil testing (see pp. 33–4) is necessary in the organic garden to ensure a balanced supply of nutrients, and that good soil structure must be created by double digging beds (see pp. 129–31).

Pests and diseases attack weak plants. Healthy vigorous plants may be attacked but the negative effects are most often minimal. Only when growing conditions are not optimal, and plants are stressed, are opportunities created for pests and diseases to flourish.

Sometimes weather or climate conditions cause stress to plants. For example, excessive rainfall can provide optimal conditions for fungal diseases but there is little that you can do to counteract this kind of stress, and your only option is to control pests and diseases.

Since the best method of pest and disease control is prevention, choose resistant varieties and practice crop rotation. Even in a small garden, rotating crops will discourage pests and diseases (see Crop rotation, pp. 78–81). By planting a diversity of crops in the garden and by avoiding planting large areas to a single crop, pests are unlikely to get out of hand. Pests that affect a particular crop will not reproduce ceaselessly without an endless supply of food. A variety of plantings, which include habitats for beneficials, will encourage insects, birds, and other animals to live in the garden and eat

Leaf damage Slugs and caterpillars can damage lush green foliage, leaving behind these tell-tale, crinkle-edged holes.

pests (see Beneficial wildlife, pp. 121–5).

There are also many biological controls that can be used. Parasitic wasps can be introduced into your greenhouse (see p. 172). These insects feed avidly on whiteflies. Good garden tool hygiene will help to prevent the spread of disease (see p. 270).

Beneficial insects and natural predators are a better means of pest control than pesticides. They create a natural balance in the garden. There will always be some pests, and there will always be some predators, but neither will have large populations that get out of control.

BARRIERS AND TRAPS

Sometimes pests cannot be controlled by the above methods, and you will need to take further action. One strategy is to create a barrier. Floating row covers can be placed over plants and secured at the edges or the material can be fitted over a frame just like building a polytunnel.

Another strategy is to set traps. Sticky cards can be placed in the garden or greenhouse to catch pests. Although some beneficial insects may be caught in these traps, troublesome pests will be ensnared too. This method can be very helpful in identifying an unknown, unseen pest, so that a specific control can be chosen. Some traps are set with a bait that attracts specific insects.

A further strategy of pest control is simply to remove the pests from the plants. Pick them off and squash them, or wash them away with a hose – whatever works!

USING ORGANIC PESTICIDES

The use of simple organic pesticides and fungicides can be an acceptable form of organic gardening, but try to regard them as a last resort. Pesticides and fungicides do not cure the underlying problem. When using them, try to search out the cause of the problem and take

Blackfly *These aphids typically gather together around stems or on the undersides of leaves, and suck the sap from healthy plants.*

the necessary steps to prevent it from occurring again in the future. (Note too that some organic certifying organizations forbid the use of certain organic pesticides and fungicides.)

To make a simple organic pesticide, mix half a teaspoon of liquid soap (not laundry detergent) with one tablespoon of olive oil in ½gal/2l of water and spray it on pest-infected plants.

I try never to use any organic pesticides or fungicides unless it is absolutely necessary. When Colorado potato beetles attacked my potatoes one year, spraying with a soap solution barely deterred them, so I harvested the crop as new potatoes instead of full-sized ones. I noted that one variety of potato was unaffected by the beetles and planted more of that variety in the following year.

Sole operator *A single snail can cause immense damage to a plant, leaving large holes and a silvery slime trail across plant foliage.*

PESTICIDES AND FUNGICIDES

A poison is a poison is a poison. Every time we use pesticides and fungicides we attack the garden with a form of chemical warfare. Organic pesticides and fungicides can be just as poisonous as their synthetic, agribusiness-produced counterparts. Therefore, great care must be taken in their handling and use. Nature can make chemicals that are as dangerous as those made by a chemist in the laboratory; the primary difference is that most of nature's chemicals are biodegradable. Listed below are some commonly acceptable organic pesticides and fungicides, but be sure to check with your local organic certifying agency before using them.

Diatomaceous earth The fossilized shell remains of algae have microscopic sharp edges that cut soft-bodied insects. The pests die from dehydration. Controls caterpillars, slugs, aphids, and other soft-bodied insects.

Garlic Make a spray by finely chopping an entire head of garlic and steeping it in mineral or olive oil overnight. Strain the oil and mix with a little soap and an equal amount of water. Spray on plants to temporarily deter pests.

Chili pepper Make a spray by finely chopping a chili pepper and mixing with water. Spray on plants to deter groundhogs, squirrels, and other large pests. A dusting of cayenne pepper on foliage is sometimes enough to deter a mammal.

Neem oil Extracted from the neem tree (*Azadirachta indica*). Although toxic, this liquid is only moderately more effective against pests than soap. Use only to control fungal diseases.

Pyrethrum An extract from *Tanacetum cinerariifolium*, pyrethrum is sprayed for immediate effect. Controls aphids and most other insects; kills beneficial insects. Use with caution.

Copper fungicide This product is used to control mildews and blights. It is commercially available in liquids or powders that are mixed with water.

Soap Plain dish soap (not laundry detergent) can be mixed with water and sprayed on plant foliage to kill a wide range of pests. Often a few drops of oil are added to the water as a spreader. Insecticidal soap contains a potassium salt to increase effectiveness. Controls: aphids, whitefly, mealy bugs, red spider mites, and others. Kills some beneficial insects.

Stinging nettle Make a spray by chopping nettle foliage and steeping it in water. Spray the solution on plants to deter pests.

Sulfur Use against powdery mildew and scab. May not be permitted by some organic certifiers.

Hot deterrent *Thinly sliced chili peppers, mixed in water, make an effective organic control against many garden pests that attack your crops.*

BIOLOGICAL CONTROL

Some biological controls, such as *Bacillus thuringiensis* (Bt), can be used in outdoor gardens, but they are most often used in greenhouses. Biological control is the importation of specific natural predators to control pests. One method even controls a disease (see *Trichoderma* below).

Aphidius matricariae A parasitic wasp that is used to control aphids in greenhouses.

Bacillus thuringiensis (Bt) This is a bacterium that prevents caterpillars from eating – which effectively kills them – yet is relatively harmless to animals, humans, and most insects. Sadly, Bt is quickly becoming ineffective because of its widespread use in the commercial production of genetically modified corn (see p. 70). Resistant varieties of pests have developed rapidly in recent years, but it may still be a useful biological control for reducing the caterpillar population in your garden.

Encarsia formosa A parasitic wasp that is used to control whiteflies in greenhouses. They are introduced by the gardener by bringing in several purchased wasp pupae. The wasps lay their eggs in the scales of the whitefly.

Heterorhabditis megidis A nematode that controls vine weevils, outdoors or under glass.

Phasmarhabditis hermaphrodita A nematode that is used to control slugs. However, a more effective method is to bury a steep-sided dish filled with beer in areas with slug damage. The slugs will be attracted to the beer and drown. Empty the dish and refill it with beer every day until the slugs are eliminated.

Phytoseiulus persimilis A predatory mite used to control red spider mites in greenhouses or outdoors.

Trichoderma A fungus that is used as a wound paint. It repels other fungi and can be used to control silver leaf *(Chondrostereum purpureum)* on fruit trees.

Hurting beneficials
Organic pesticides will usually kill beneficial insects, like this monarch butterfly caterpillar, along with the pests. Any pesticide or fungicide, even if organic, may have the negative side-effect of killing microorganisms in the soil.

PEST OR BENEFICIAL?

It is important to be able to visually identify the insects and animals that visit your garden so that you know what actions, if any, to take. Some of them will be unwanted pests while others are welcome beneficials that can be encouraged to stay in the garden (see pp. 121–5).

BENEFICIALS

Assassin bugs These eat many different types of bugs, especially the larvae.

Bats These reduce the number of insects in and around the garden.

Bees Bees are responsible for the pollination of more than one-third of the fruits and vegetables that we eat.

Centipedes Centipedes eat a wide range of soil-dwelling pests.

Domestic fowl Chickens and ducks eat insects and slugs.

Frogs and toads Frogs and toads feed on insects, snails, and worms. They are also an excellent form of slug control.

Ground beetles These prefer to live in areas with ground-cover plants. They eat cutworms, caterpillars, slugs, and snails.

Hoverflies The adults, like parasitic wasps, lay their eggs in pests. Their larvae help to control aphids.

Lacewings These will reduce the number of aphids, whiteflies, larvae, mites, and thrips.

Ladybugs Also known as ladybirds and ladybeetles. The adults eat aphids, mealybugs, and scale. In their immature form, the larvae eat mites.

Spiders Spiders build delicate but deceptively strong webs that catch many pests.

Wasps Parasitic wasps lay their eggs in pests. When the eggs hatch, the pest is destroyed.

Common toad *A pond-lover in spring, the toad roams on land for most of the year feeding on many pests in the garden.*

PESTS / BENEFICIALS

Ants Ants aerate the soil and clean up weed seeds and other debris. They also eat the sticky substance created by aphids, and in the process transport pests to other plants. If aphids are controlled, ants will not cause problems.

Birds Birds can be the gardener's best friend. They control many pests. However, sometimes they attack a crop before harvest. Place floating row covers over plants before fruits mature. Another tactic is to plant a tree such as a mulberry that attracts birds away from crops for the table.

Nematodes Nematodes are microscopic. Some are pests and others are beneficial. Those that feed on insects are often useful in controlling pests. Root knot nematodes, stem and bulb nematodes, and potato cyst nematodes are only a few examples of the many types that are pests in the garden. Crop rotation is an effective control of some of these pests (but not cyst nematodes). Destroy any affected plants.

PESTS

Aphids Aphids are also known as greenfly and come in many colors. They affect virtually all plants, bushes, and trees, making the leaves sticky or blistered. Aphids tend to spread viral diseases to legumes. Control them with ladybugs and other beneficial insects, or spray aphids off plants with a blast of water. If a pesticide must be used, a garlic or soap spray works best.

Beetles and weevils Weevils are a type of beetle. Predatory wasps, ladybugs, and birds are the primary natural predators of all beetles and weevils. Flea beetles are notable because they jump when the plant is touched. If flea beetles are a problem, clear plant debris out of the garden in the fall to discourage recurrence. Protect plants with floating row covers or apply parasitic nematodes to the soil.

Japanese beetles, and their larvae (known as white grubs), attack seedlings and flowering plants. The beetles eat the flowers and leaves; the grubs feed on the roots and kill the plant. Shake plants to remove beetles and cover them with floating row covers. Set out baited traps.

Asparagus beetles only affect asparagus. Pick them off by hand. Mexican bean beetles are quite destructive. They look like large beige ladybugs. Remove beetles by hand and install floating row covers. Pollen beetles attack many plants, especially brassica seedlings. There is no effective method of control except for applying floating row covers before a problem occurs.

Borers Squash vine borers are the most common type of borer. They attack melons, cucumbers, and squashes. They are the larvae of a moth and eat a hole in the stem that causes plants to wilt and die. The stem may be opened with a knife and the borer removed. Bury the wound under soil to help it heal.

Caterpillars and worms Caterpillars are the larvae of moths and butterflies. Most eat plant foliage and fruit; however, some attack the roots.

Gardener's friend Ladybugs are welcome visitors to the garden as they feed on the gardener's enemies, such as aphids, scale insects, and mealy bugs.

Pick caterpillars off and destroy. Look for eggs left behind on foliage and remove. *Bt* may be used as a biological control.

Earwigs Earwigs eat the tips of buds just before they flower. They also eat young leaves. Set an earwig trap by stuffing hay or dried grass into a pot and support upside down on a stick near affected plants. The earwigs are nocturnal and will occupy the trap during the day. Empty the trap daily and destroy pests.

Flies and maggots Whiteflies lay eggs on the undersides of leaves. When the eggs hatch, the maggots eat the foliage. They are very common in greenhouses; control with parasitic wasps (*Encarsia formosa*). They can be discouraged in the garden by planting marigolds. Carrot root flies lay eggs that hatch into maggots that eat into root crops. Cabbage root maggots (larvae of the cabbage fly) eat and tunnel into roots. Good hygiene is the best defense, so destroy the roots of the previous year's brassicas every spring. Parasitic nematodes or diatomaceous earth may be applied to the soil around the roots of each plant. Apple maggots and the larvae of fruit flies eat into fruits. Good hygiene is essential, so clean up dropped fruit to discourage them.

If onion maggots are a problem, practice companion planting or create several small patches in different areas of the garden. If one patch of onions is damaged by onion maggots, it is less likely that others will also be damaged.

Celery flies and other leaf miners are controlled by removing damaged plants or branches and destroying them. Control corn rootworms by rotating crops.

Grasshoppers These pests completely defoliate plants. The most effective organic control are guinea fowl, which feed avidly on this insect.

Leafhoppers Most leafhoppers spread diseases, especially viral diseases. The tops of leaves get

Vole damage *The trunk of this tree was damaged by voles during the winter. If more bark had been stripped away, the tree might have died.*

pale spots. Control them by encouraging beneficials into the garden.

Mammals Racoons, deer, and groundhogs are only excluded from the garden by effective fences. Electric fences work best. Mice girdle trees in winter, so protect your trees with screen or woven wire around their bases.

Mealybugs These small pests have a fluffy white foam attached to their bodies. Control them with mealybug destroyers – a type of ladybug. In greenhouses, clean off with insecticidal soap.

Millipedes Distinguishable from centipedes by their two pairs of legs per body segment instead of one. Millipedes damage potatoes and eat seedlings and soft growth on fruits. They flourish in soils that are high in organic matter. Control with crop rotation, regular cultivation, and good hygiene. Leave infested areas of the garden unplanted for a year or two.

Scale A collection of species that suck on plant leaves and stems. They look like tiny bumps. Remove infested plants (or portions of plants) and destroy. A soap and oil spray is effective against many scales when in the crawler stage.

Slugs Slugs and snails eat leaves and seedlings. You may notice a slime trail. Cultivate the soil to kill eggs, and set a slug trap (see p.172). Encourage predators like birds and frogs.

Spider mites Mites produce tiny webs in plants. They rarely kill trees and bushes but can affect annuals. Use the predatory mite *Phytoseiulus persimilis* to control them. Apply a soap spray to cut down on their numbers. In hot dry climates, keeping plants wet can help.

Thrips Thrips are sap-sucking insects that leave behind a white-colored deposit on the leaf. They feed on the upper leaf surface rather than the underside. They may also affect petals of flowers and prevent them from opening. Predatory mites are an effective control in greenhouses. Since they thrive in dry conditions, water affected plants regularly. They may be treated with pyrethrum.

DISEASES AND AILMENTS

NAME	SYMPTOMS	NAME	SYMPTOMS
Bacteria			yellow blotches. To control the problem, avoid overhead watering and ensure good air circulation.
Wilt	There are many types of bacterial wilt. Each is specific to a single plant or a group of plants in the same family. Often the plants get a gray, fuzzy growth that looks like botrytis.	Botrytis	Also known as gray mold. It may attack seedlings in damp weather. Plants with soft leaves are at risk. Dead, discolored patches develop on stems, causing the plant to die. The best cure is prevention – remove dead plant debris from the garden regularly. Ensure good air circulation and avoid overhead watering.
Canker	Affect many fruit trees, causing sunken spots on the stems which release thick, colored liquid. Remove affected branches and destroy. Clean tools well after pruning.		
Blackleg	Affects plant cuttings and potatoes. The stems collapse at soil level and the plant dies. It is caused by poor garden hygiene. Destroy affected plants. Only buy "double certified" seed potatoes.	Fusarium wilt	Affects most plants, causing black patches on the stems and leaves. Crop rotation is the most effective method of control. Remove diseased plants and soil from around their roots and destroy. Plant resistant varieties.
Molds/mildews			
Damping off	Affects seedlings. The stem rots at soil level, killing the plant. The only solution is good air circulation and bottom-watering.	Verticillium wilt	Affects plants in the garden and greenhouse, creating long brown stripes on the stems. Remove diseased plants and soil from around their roots and destroy.
Rust	Small bright orange or brown spots on leaves, caused by mold spores.	Crown rot	A soilborne fungal disease that is prevented by good drainage. Keep mulch away from the stem.
Fungal leaf spot	Round blotches of fungus on leaves or fruits.	Foot/Root rot	Affects a wide range of plants. This fungus causes the stem to discolor, wilt and die. Crop rotation and good drainage are the best prevention.
Blackspot	A fungal disease that attacks roses.		
Powdery mildew	Affects most plants. A white powder-like mold appears on the upperside of leaves. Avoid dry conditions to discourage the problem.	Tomato/Potato blight	Causes brown discoloration on the tips of leaves. Control by avoiding overhead watering and ensuring good air circulation. Choose resistant varieties of vegetables.
Downy mildew	Affects most plants. White fluffy fungal growth develops on the underside of leaves. The upperside develops		

DISEASES AND AILMENTS

NAME	SYMPTOMS	NAME	SYMPTOMS
Onion white rot	A fungal disease that affects alliums by causing a white fungus on the bulbs. Crop rotation is the only effective method of prevention. If you develop a problem with onion white rot, do not grow any alliums in that location for a decade.		potassium levels inhibit the plant's uptake of magnesium.
		Nitrogen deficiency	Causes pale green leaves with a yellow tint.
		Potassium deficiency	Causes leaves with a bright yellow or reddish edge.
Southern blight	Similar to damping off but affects older plants like crown rot. Do not grow plants in contaminated areas. Do not save seeds from affected plants.	Phosphate deficiency	Slows plant growth and the leaves may appear to be yellow.
		Boron deficiency	Can cause cankers, discoloration, and bad taste and texture. Fruit can be small and disfigured.
Scab	Affects many fruit trees, causing dark brown patches on the leaves and fruit. Plant resistant cultivars. Remove any affected branches immediately and destroy. Consider an open-center tree shape to encourage air circulation and allow sunlight to reach the center of the tree.	Calcium deficiency	Affects fruits and causes blossom end rot. Causes bitter flesh and pitted skin.
		Other problems	
		Speckle leaf	A disorder that causes dark spots on the leaves of many plants and is reported to be caused by high ozone levels in the air. If this problem occurs, choose a resistant variety.
Clubroot	Causes swollen and disfigured roots which stunt plants. Remove and destroy infected plants.		
		Drought	Causes the foliage to wilt, dry, discolor, and fall off. Plants may be stunted or may die.
Viruses			
Mosaic virus/Cucumber mosaic virus	Viruses cause disfigured flowers and foliage. Can affect all plants. Most viruses are brought into your garden by insects. Good hygiene is essential. Clean tools well after pruning infected plants. Buy plants that are certified virus-free. If you have infected plants, destroy them immediately.	Excessive watering	Turns leaves yellow and the plants may wilt.
		Irregular watering	Causes distorted leaves and flowers.
		Transplant shock	Causes leaves to wilt, turn yellow and drop. Harden off seedlings before transplanting.
Deficiencies			
Magnesium deficiency	Very common in potted plants. Leaves show yellow or red discoloration. Acid soils and heavy watering decrease magnesium levels. High	Frost or low temperatures	Cause many plants to defoliate and die back or die.

CHAPTER 5

DIRECTORY OF FRUITS, & HERBS

VEGETABLES,

GUIDE TO DIRECTORY

When grouping vegetables for crop rotation, it is important to consider their botanical family. Members of the same plant family are often susceptible to the same diseases and should not be grown in a bed where another member of that family was grown the previous year.

HOW TO USE THE DIRECTORY

In this directory, the plants have been separated into botanical families (see panel opposite). Each entry provides advice on how to choose the most appropriate site for the crop and indicates any specific soil preferences or needs. It discusses the

Garden variety With so many varieties to choose from, the hardest part of planning a garden can often be deciding which ones to leave out of your planting.

NUTRITION RATINGS

Excellent source 40–100+% of recommended daily allowance (RDA) per serving.
Good source 25–39% of RDA per serving.
Significant source 10–24% of RDA per serving.
Source Less than 10% or lack of quantitative data.
Phytochemicals Only vegetables that are very high in phytochemicals are listed as excellent sources; all other vegetables are sources of phytochemicals.

best sowing or planting techniques for that plant as well as routine care and maintenance needed during the growing stage. Key pests and diseases that may pose a threat to your crop are identified too. A selection of recommended varieties highlight some of the most popular varieties grown as well as some with unusual features.

VEGETABLES, FRUITS, & HERBS

The vegetables, fruits, and herbs described in this directory are grouped according to their family to help you when drawing up a crop-rotation plan.

Beets and Swiss Chard *Beta vulgaris*

Plant type Biennial

Nutrition Significant source of vitamin C and folic acid. Source of potassium.

Uses Beets are grown both for their root and for their greens. Some are used for animal fodder, others to make sugar, and most to eat fresh, cooked, or pickled.

SITE AND SOIL

Choose a deeply cultivated site enriched with compost. Light soils are preferred to clay soils. Make sure the soil is not deficient in boron. A pH of above 6.0 and cool temperatures produce the best color. Good drainage is essential.

SOWING

To speed up germination, soak seeds in warm water for 15 minutes. Start seeds indoors in early spring for an early crop or sow direct outdoors when the soil has warmed after the spring thaw. Sow ½in/1cm deep, about 2in/5cm apart in a bed, every two weeks until early summer.

CARE AND MAINTENANCE

Weed regularly, taking care not to damage roots. Thin to 3in/8cm. Do not overwater, but keep the soil moist. Add high-nitrogen compost in summer.

Pests and diseases Boron deficiency. Excessive wet may lead to fungal leaf spots in mature plants or damping off in seedlings.

HARVEST

Using a garden fork, lift large beets from the soil in the fall. Small beets can be pulled by the tops. Use the greens; they are ideal in salads. Store roots at cool temperatures (32°F/0°C) at high humidity through the winter. Before storing, twist off the leaves well above the root: cutting tends to make

In areas with mild climates, beets, such as 'Pronto' (above), can be left in the ground throughout the winter to produce the first spring greens of the season.

the stems ooze juice. Storing the roots in the garden over winter is possible in warm climates, but cold tends to make them rather woody.

VARIETIES

Chioggia Popular candy-striped root.

Colossal Long Red Mangel Use for making sugar.

Crosbys One of the best-tasting storage beets.

Detroit Dark Red Good flavor and stores well.

Pronto Can be harvested in spring as small beets or in the autumn as a main crop.

SWISS CHARD

Chard (*Beta vulgaris* var. *cicla*) is grown for its leaves and stems, which are braised, or used lightly cooked in salads. Growing conditions are similar to beets. Chard is quite cold hardy.

Bright Lights Stems in a range of different colors.

Fordhook Giant Very cold hardy.

Rhubarb Chard Has delicious ruby-red stems.

Spinach *Spinacia oleracea*

Plant type Annual

Nutrition Excellent source of phytochemicals and vitamin A. Good source of vitamin C and folic acid. Significant source of iron and magnesium. Source of potassium, B2, B6, calcium, and protein.

Uses Smooth or textured spinach leaves are used fresh in salads or cooked as vegetables.

PEST CONTROL

Spinach leaves are eaten by spotted cucumber beetles and caterpillars. Regularly check the leaves for damage. Remove pests by hand and destroy.

SITE AND SOIL

Spinach is fast growing and tolerates a wide range of soils. It is quite cold hardy, but at high temperatures tends to bolt. It also tolerates partial shade, which it prefers during the heat of summer. Spinach grows best in a soil pH of 6.5 to 7.5.

SOWING

Sow seeds directly in the garden, starting as soon as the soil can be worked in early spring. Continue sowing at three-week intervals for a continuous harvest throughout the spring, summer, and fall. Germination tends to be erratic where soil temperatures exceed 85°F/29°C. Space the seeds at intervals of 1–2in/2.5–5cm, sowing them ½in/1cm deep. Sow them in rows 12in/30cm apart.

CARE AND MAINTENANCE

Water and weed as necessary. If the plants start to bolt, harvest them immediately.

Pests and diseases Caterpillars and spotted cucumber beetles. Spinach blight is spread by aphids: destroy any affected plants.

HARVEST

An entire plant or just several leaves at a time may be harvested. Thin out as necessary, by harvesting young plants and serving them fresh in salads. Try to use them as soon as possible after picking. Perfect unblemished leaves may be frozen.

VARIETIES

Bloomsdale Longstanding Tasty variety.

Nobel An old thick-leaved variety.

Strawberry Spinach *(Chenopodium capitatum)* An unusual mild-flavored variety.

The small, strawberry-like fruits borne on the stems of the strawberry spinach can be eaten or left to provide ornamental interest in the vegetable garden.

Endive *Cichorium endivia*

Plant type Annual or biennial

Nutrition Significant source of vitamin A and folic acid. Source of calcium, iron, and fiber.

Uses This leafy vegetable is sometimes cooked but best served fresh as a salad vegetable. Blanching increases sweetness.

SITE AND SOIL

Choose a site with light shade to protect from bitterness and bolting. Endive is a cool-season crop that likes a moisture-retentive rich soil.

SOWING

Sow early varieties in late spring for a summer crop; sow in summer for a fall crop. Sow directly outdoors at 2in/5cm intervals and thin to 8in/20cm; close spacing helps self-blanching.

CARE AND MAINTENANCE

Endive is fast growing. Water as necessary. For five days prior to harvest, place a 4–6in/10–15cm cardboard disc on top of the plant or place a bucket or clay pot over the entire plant. Blanch nearly mature plants one at a time. Eat them straightaway because blanched plants tend to spoil quickly.

Pests and diseases Slugs and aphids cause the most problems.

HARVEST

Between seven and thirteen weeks after sowing, harvest blanched plants by cutting across the crown. The plant may resprout and produce another crop. Leaves may be individually harvested as needed. Endive does not store well.

VARIETIES

Fijne Krul Groen (Moss Curled) Very hardy.

Indivia Riccia Romanesca da Taglio A tall variety.

Nummer Vijf 2 (Batavian Broad-leaved) Crumpled leaves that are tasty in salads.

Pink Star Drought-resistant plant that tastes like looseleaf lettuce.

Endive can have curly, serrated leaves (like those of 'Fijne Krul Groen', left) or long, broad leaves. It has a slightly bitter taste and is best mixed with other greens in salads.

Chicory *Cichorium intybus*

Plant type Biennial

Nutrition Source of vitamin A, folic acid, calcium, iron, and fiber.

Uses Sometimes cooked, these slightly bitter greens are best in salads. The roots of Belgian endive and some radicchios are forced in winter.

SITE AND SOIL

Chicory requires a long growing season to harvest the roots for forcing. It is cold tolerant, and does not require nitrogen-rich soil.

SOWING

Sow seed outdoors in spring. Italian dandelion may be sown very early, or started indoors for the earliest harvest. Thin to 8in/20cm apart.

CARE AND MAINTENANCE

Weed regularly and keep watered during drought.
Pests and diseases Slugs and aphids.

HARVEST

Some chicories are eaten fresh while others are forced for winter greens. Dig the roots in the late fall and cut off the leaves; save only thick roots. These may be stored in sand, like carrots, for later forcing. Belgian endive may be forced in the garden in areas with mild winters. Cut off the greens and cover the crowns with soil about 6in/15cm high. New tops will grow in four to twelve weeks, depending on temperature. To force plants indoors, trim the root tips and any sideshoots, leaving a carrot-like root about 8in/20cm long. Plant the roots in moist potting compost in a deep pot. Leave space between the roots and the edge of the pot, and leave the crowns exposed. Cover with another pot (opaque) and keep at 50–65°F/10–18°C for three to five weeks. Harvest the resulting regrowth by cutting just above the crowns. Compost the root. Radicchio may be harvested directly from the garden or forced.

VARIETIES

Sugar loaf chicory produces a romaine lettuce-like head; radicchio or red chicory produces a reddish green head with a tight heart. Italian dandelion leaves can be harvested just twenty-eight days after planting. Belgian endive produces yellow-tinged heads when forced in the winter.

Palla di Fuoco Rossa Popular red radicchio.
Selvatica da Campo Italian dandelion variety.
Variegata di Castelfranco Red chicory variety.
Witloof and **Aksenta** Belgian endive varieties.

Some radicchios, such as 'Palla di Fuoco Rossa', above, are harvested in the fall and stored. The roots are forced in winter to provide a leafy salad.

Artichokes *Cynara cardunculus* Scolymus Group

Plant type Perennial (annual in cool climates)
Nutrition Excellent source of phytochemicals.
Significant source of vitamin C, folic acid, and
magnesium. Source of potassium and fiber.
Uses Sepals are served with melted butter or
mayonnaise. Mature globes used as cut flowers.
The hearts may be pickled or used in salads.

SITE AND SOIL

Artichokes need a sunny, sheltered site with
a soil pH of 6.5. They tolerate light frost.
Remember that they may grow to 5ft/1.5m tall
with a 36in/90cm spread. Enrich the soil with
compost or well-rotted manure.

SOWING

Sow indoors eight weeks before the last of the
spring frosts in moist compost in 2in/5cm soil
blocks. Germinate at 70–80°F/21–27°C. Once
seedlings emerge, grow at 60–70°F/16–21°C.
Transplant six- to eight-week-old plants to the
garden so that they receive ten days of
temperatures below 50°F/10°C. Space 36in/90cm
apart. In areas where temperatures do not fall
below 18°F/-8°C in winter, seeds may be sown in
fall for a spring harvest, adding about twenty days
to maturity than if transplanted.

CARE AND MAINTENANCE

Protect plants from heavy frosts. Weed regularly
and mulch heavily to prevent the roots from
drying out. Ensure the plants have plenty of water.
Pests and diseases Slugs, aphids, and earwigs
may cause problems.

HARVEST

Harvest after 85–110 days depending on variety.
In late summer to mid-fall, cut mature buds before
they begin to open. In warm climates, shoots can
sometimes be purchased or divided from existing
plants in the garden. To do this, use a sharp knife,
or a spade, and divide an established plant in the
garden so that each half has two or more shoots
and a good root system. Do this in the spring and
replant both halves about 36in/90cm apart.

VARIETIES

Green Globe Needs a long growing season and
mild winters.
Purple Globe A variety with attractive color and
good flavor.

*The globes of artichokes (such as 'Purple Globe',
shown here) are actually flowerbuds, which are
prized for the tender flesh on their sepals.*

Sunflowers *Helianthus annuus*

Plant type Annual

Nutrition Excellent source of vitamin B1. Source of vitamins B2 and B3, calcium, iron, potassium, and fiber.

Uses Good source of organic vegetable oil for cooking in the kitchen. Seeds can be eaten whole, served in baked goods, or used as bird food. Large flowerheads bring height, color, and ornamental interest to the garden.

Site and soil

Sunflowers tolerate a wide range of soils. Choose a site where the height of these plants will not shade other vegetables.

Sowing

Sow directly in the garden after all chance of frost has passed. Sow them ½in/1cm deep and 6–12in/15–30cm apart depending on variety. Germination takes two to ten days at 70°F/21°C.

Care and maintenance

A mulch may be helpful in retaining moisture. Weed as necessary until plants become tall. Keep soil evenly moist for a large harvest.

Pests and diseases Raccoons and birds attack the crop before harvest.

Harvest

When the heads of the sunflowers begin to droop, it is time to begin harvesting. Using pruners, cut the stem 1in/2.5cm below the flowerhead and hang to dry in a warm place. The heads may become moldy but this will not affect the seeds. For birdseed, the heads may be hung outdoors as they are. Typically seeds are removed by rubbing the heads against a coarse screen, or against another flowerhead. Store the seeds in a cool dry place. To eat, soak for 12 hours in warm water, then spread the seeds on a cookie sheet and bake them in a warm oven until they are crisp. Oil is produced by cracking the seeds with a mill and pressing. Filter the resulting oil through cheesecloth.

Varieties

Black Oil Good variety for feeding to birds.

Mammoth Russian Large head with delicious seeds that are good for oil.

Velvet Queen Best grown for its deep red flowers as the seeds are not worth eating or pressing.

Bright yellow sunflowers are easy to grow and are useful as well as attractive. Their seeds are a nutritious food for humans as well as for birds.

Sunchokes *Helianthus tuberosus*

Plant type Perennial

Nutrition Significant source of vitamin B1 and iron. Source of vitamins B2 and B3, calcium, potassium, and fiber.

Uses Sunchoke roots have a sweet flavor and are very nutritious. Their tall yellow flowers are useful for adding height in the garden.

SITE AND SOIL

Sunchokes tolerate a wide range of soils. They can easily take over the entire garden, so grow them by themselves surrounded by grass. Mow around them regularly; if they overwhelm the site, simply mow them down and return the bed to lawn.

PLANTING

Cut large tubers into smaller pieces before planting. Plant 5in/12cm deep, 12in/30cm apart as soon as the ground can be worked in early spring. Cover and gently firm the soil.

CARE AND MAINTENANCE

If the plants do not appear extremely vigorous, soil may be hilled up around the bases. Water during dry periods in the first year. Depending on the variety, the tops may range in height from 5–20ft/1.5–6m. They may be trimmed back to 5ft/1.5m in mid- to late summer if desired.

Pests and diseases Few pests or diseases bother sunchokes and rarely affect the harvest.

HARVEST

Lift as needed for the table with a garden fork. They store well in the ground, but may be harvested and stored in a very moist and cool location for winter use in colder climates. Be sure to leave some in the ground to grow in future years.

VARIETIES

Fuseau Bears long, smooth tubers.

Red Excellent flavor.

The roots of sunchokes (also known as Jerusalem artichokes) are starch free and therefore especially valuable in the diet of diabetics. They are very easy to grow, but can easily take over the entire garden if not controlled.

Lettuce *Lactuca sativa*

Plant types Annual

Nutrition Excellent source of phytochemicals. Source of vitamins A, B, and C, calcium, fiber, and potassium. Romaine is a significant source of folic acid and a good source of vitamins A and C.

Uses Ideal for salads. Look effective when grown in ornamental beds.

SITE AND SOIL

The key to growing good lettuces is quick growth under ideal conditions. Lettuce is a cool-season crop, so grow lettuces to be harvested in summer in partially shaded spots. Spring and fall crops should be grown in full sun. Winter crops can be grown in a cold frame. Lettuces need very fertile soil with lots of nitrogen. Ensure soil is not deficient in boron. Working rich compost into the soil will help retain moisture. Rotate their location from year to year to deter pests and diseases.

SOWING

While it is perfectly acceptable to sow seeds directly in the garden, starting them indoors three to five weeks before transplanting will provide optimum conditions for germination. Transplant outside as soon as the soil can be worked in the spring. Every two or three weeks, start more seedlings indoors. Each time a lettuce plant is harvested from the garden, replace it with a seedling started inside. As spring turns to summer, begin sowing varieties that can tolerate more heat. For example, a garden plot planted with cos and leaf lettuce in the spring might have iceberg and a heat-tolerant leaf lettuce in the summer, and a butterhead and cos in the fall. Lettuce may vary in size from 4–12in/10–30cm. Set transplants in the garden spaced appropriately for the variety. Start seedlings indoors in 2in/5cm soil blocks and

germinate between 50–68°F/10–20°C. A basement may be suitably cool for germination. After seeds germinate, move to a sunny location. When transplanting be sure to match the soil level; planting too deeply can be a problem. Water thoroughly after transplanting.

CARE AND MAINTENANCE

Keep weed free and add a little compost when replacing a harvested plant. During a drought, water regularly, 1–2in/2.5–5cm a week. In adverse conditions, plants may bolt. Watch for the heads becoming soft on icebergs, or cos and leaf lettuce suddenly growing tall. Taste a leaf for bitterness. Pinching back the top of a cos or leaf lettuce may

Iceberg lettuce, also known as crisphead lettuce, has crispy leaves that form a large solid heart which is cabbage-like in appearance.

PEST PREVENTION

A ring of sharp objects such as crushed eggshells placed around each plant will protect young lettuce leaves from being eaten by slugs.

help prevent bolting, but it is best to harvest the plant early and transplant a new seedling to replace it. In warmer weather, choose varieties resistant to bolt and tolerant of heat. Romaine gets bitter quickly if the soil dries out.

As winter approaches, the most cold-tolerant varieties should be planted in the garden. Before frost damages the crop, cloches or cold frames should be put over the plants. The plants will not grow much after frost, but will remain fresh well into winter in the cold frames. A simple preservation method is to surround a bed with hay bales, and then place old storm windows over the tops of the bales, creating a large, inexpensive cold frame. If very cold weather threatens, bales may be placed over the glass for more insulation.

Pests and diseases Greenfly, aphids, slugs, snails, and most chewing insects are common pests (see Pest prevention, above). Cutworms, downy mildew, and mosaic virus may also affect plants. Botrytis, also known as gray mold, may attack seedlings in damp weather. Remove and dispose of afflicted plants. Row covers can be used to shade the plants, which discourages bolting.

HARVEST

Lettuce is best harvested in the morning, when it is most crisp. Its flavor, quality, and nutrition are at their peak just after picking. Head lettuce should be harvested when the head is firm. To harvest, remove the entire plant and compost the

roots and outer leaves. Some lettuces, especially leaf lettuces, can be harvested by picking the outer leaves, leaving the inner leaves to mature. Lettuce loses most of its nutrients in storage. It may be refrigerated for up to a week in a sealed container (to retain moisture), but is best eaten fresh.

LEAF VARIETIES

Leaf lettuce tolerates much warmer conditions than most head lettuces. They hold their leaves up and out in a very loose and open fashion.

Black-seeded Simpson An early variety with tasty curly leaves.

Blushed Butter Oak Oak-leaf type with pink-veined leaves.

Bronze Arrow Flavorsome oak-leaf type.

Chicken Lettuce Heat-tolerant variety.

The slender, crisp leaves of cos or romaine lettuce are noted for their good flavor. The striking white stems look and taste rather like fresh celery.

Deer Tongue Tasty, loose triangular leaves.

Fanfare Unusual leaves.

French Red Popular red-leafed lettuce.

Lau Round Leaf Very hardy variety with an unusual flavor.

Red Curl Lollo rossa type, with frilly leaves.

Red Salad Bowl Leaves rarely turn bitter. Lasts well if leaves are harvested at regular intervals.

Red Sails A tasty variety that matures to purple.

CRISPHEAD VARIETIES

This type of lettuce is also known as iceberg, when its outer leaves are removed. It has a cabbage-like appearance, with crispy leaves that form a large solid heart. Although crisphead is the least nutritious of the lettuces, it is the most common type found on sale in stores because it ships well and tolerates warm weather.

All the Year Round A hardy variety with a slightly looser head. It can be grown under low light conditions in a greenhouse.

Beatrice Worth considering for its flavor.

Iceberg Long-lasting variety grown for its crunchy leaves.

BUTTERHEAD VARIETIES

Also known as Boston lettuce, butterheads form small rounded heads of smooth soft leaves. The outer leaves are green, and the inner leaves are yellow to white. Butterhead lettuces are particularly high in vitamins, but they only grow successfully in cool weather climates and need a very rich soil.

Audran Forms a large head that has a creamy texture and lime-green leaves.

Blonde du Cazard Mid-green leaves.

Buttercrunch Does not form tight heads like most butterhead varieties.

Juliette Tender green leaves with a touch of burgundy coloring.

Randolph Olive-green outer leaves with a purple sheen, and tender light-green inner leaves.

Leaf lettuces, especially the frilly and red-splashed varieties, such as 'Red Curl' (above), add a decorative element to the vegetable plot.

ROMAINE VARIETIES

Also known as cos, romaine lettuces have long broad leaves with thick juicy stems. They hold their leaves upright in a tight bunch. Romaine lettuces usually take longer to mature than other types of lettuce.

Ballon Tolerates cold weather.

Erthel Tender and bolt resistant.

Jericho Heat tolerant.

Parris Island Cos Noted for its taste.

Rouge d'Hiver A red-leaved variety that is tolerant of cold weather.

Forellenschluss An Austrian heirloom with maroon splotches on green leaves and tasty stems. It is very resistant to bolt.

Stoke Noted for its small crisp leaves.

Sweet Potatoes *Ipomoea batatas*

Plant type Perennial

Nutrition Excellent source of phytochemicals and vitamins A and C. Significant source of vitamins B2 and B6, and copper. Source of calcium, magnesium, iron, potassium, fiber, and protein.

Uses Grown as annuals for their delicious roots, attractive flowers, and colorful leaves. The young leaves are often picked and used like spinach.

SITE AND SOIL

Sweet potatoes grow best in soils with good drainage and a high level of nitrogen. Sandy fertile soil is best, with a pH level between 5.5 and 6.5. Choose an open, sunny site that is shielded from wind. Sweet potatoes prefer high temperatures. To create the best conditions, grow them in tubs or in raised mounds of compost above soil level.

PLANTING

Sweet potatoes are usually grown from roots harvested in the previous year. Six weeks before transplanting into the garden, place a few of the roots in moist soil and keep them at a temperature of 75°F/24°C. When the shoots reach 8–10in/ 20–25cm long, cut them off with some roots and plant into 6in/15cm pots. Transplant into the garden in late spring after all danger of frost has passed. Alternatively, shoots may be purchased and planted directly in the garden. Ensure that the date the shoots are shipped corresponds with your expected planting date.

CARE AND MAINTENANCE

Keep sweet potatoes well watered and weed regularly. Make sure that tub-grown crops are not allowed to dry out. A thick mulch will help retain moisture. An application of organic liquid fertilizer may help to produce larger tubers. Deter vines from rooting by gently lifting them. If the vines are allowed to root, a very large quantity of small tubers will be produced instead of fewer decent-sized tubers.

Pests and diseases Sweet potato weevils, aphids, caterpillars, and root knot nematodes may prove to be a problem. Fungal leaf spots, fusarium wilt, and southern blight affect sweet potatoes growing in hot humid climates.

HARVEST

Depending on variety, sweet potatoes mature about 90–150 days after planting; yellowing foliage indicates maturity. Using a garden fork, lift the roots gently, trying not to damage their fragile skins. To store the roots, cure them at 80°F/27°C and 80–90 per cent humidity for one week, then store them in a cool (50°F/10°C) place with high humidity.

VARIETIES

Centennial A good short-season variety.
Jewel (Golden Jewel) High-yielding variety with deep orange flesh.

Popular in cooked dishes, sweet potatoes are also often grown in a tub on a patio or front lawn for their attractive foliage.

Kales *Brassica oleracea* var. *acephala*

Plant type Annual or biennial

Nutrition Excellent source of phytochemicals and vitamins A and C. Significant source of calcium and copper. Source of potassium and fiber.

Uses Young leaves of broad-leaved types are used raw in salads; the older leaves are cooked like spinach or added to soups.

SITE AND SOIL

Kales prefer a fertile well-drained soil that has been deeply cultivated. They prefer medium rather than high levels of nitrogen, so work in well-rotted compost only.

SOWING

Sow directly in the garden about three months before the first expected fall frost. Sow at intervals of 3in/8cm; thin seedlings to 9in/23cm spacing. Kales can also be started indoors for an earlier crop. Transplant seedlings to the garden four weeks after sowing to 9in/23cm spacing. Seeds germinate best at 75°F/24°C.

CARE AND MAINTENANCE

Water frequently (once a week during drought) and keep free of weeds. Mulching will help to retain moisture.

Pests and diseases Flea beetles, slugs, cabbage loopers, cabbage root maggots, and aphids.

HARVEST

Starting two months after planting, and continuing into winter, harvest individual leaves by cutting with pruners. After overwintering kales in the garden, pick new leaves at 4in/10cm long in the spring. Kales store well by freezing. In severe winter climates, hardy dwarf varieties can be grown under cloches for a continuous harvest.

VARIETIES

Kales survive 5°F/–15°C and surprisingly some varieties also survive heat. Many flowering kales are grown as ornamentals or as garnishes. These flowers are actually showy leaves, not real flowers. Some American kales are known as collards. These generally have broad, flat, rounded leaves that extend down the stems.

Champion A popular collard variety.

Greenpeace A hardy variety that is able to survive temperatures of 20°F/–7°C.

Hanover Salad Use as a mesclun green.

Long Standing A hardy variety that is tolerant of heat.

Russian Red Purple-veined gray-green leaves that are very tender. Great for salads and stir-frying.

Kales are among the most nutritious vegetables in the garden. They are also the hardiest of all the brassicas, and their flavor increases noticeably after a frost.

Cauliflowers *Brassica oleracea* var. *botrytis*

Plant type Biennial

Nutrition Excellent source of vitamin C and other beneficial phytochemicals. Significant source of vitamin B6, folic acid, and pantothenic acid. Source of fiber and potassium.

Uses Most cauliflowers have a white head that tastes best after a frost. Young leaves surrounding the head are cooked or eaten fresh in salads.

SITE AND SOIL

As with all brassicas, crop rotation is very important to discourage soilborne diseases. Plant in a fertile, humus-rich soil that retains moisture. Cauliflowers that are going to be overwintered need a protected site. Do not plant them in high-nitrogen soils or they will become soft. Cauliflowers have a spread of up to 36in/90cm and a height of up to 24in/60cm, so allow enough space between each plant for it to develop fully.

SOWING

Success depends on planting the correct variety at the appropriate time and in the right location. Dunking the seeds briefly in hot water before sowing indoors may help to prevent disease. Start seeds indoors five weeks before transplanting outside. Germinate at 70°F/21°C and then reduce the temperature to 60°F/16°C. Plant outside at the appropriate time for the variety being grown.

CARE AND MAINTENANCE

Water regularly during the growing season. Do not let the soil dry out. Apply a high-nitrogen liquid feed to overwintered cauliflowers in the spring to encourage them to set seed which can be saved for future planting. Blanch the heads to keep them white. Wrap the leaves around the head and bind them with soft twine or pin them together with a toothpick. This prevents discoloration caused by the sun. Heirloom varieties may need more careful attention to prevent discoloration. Weed regularly after planting until the leaves are large enough to shade out the weeds.

Pests and diseases Pollen beetles, flea beetles, cabbage loopers, cabbage root maggots and aphids. Cutworms attack the stems, causing the plant to wilt and die (see Pest prevention box, opposite). Ensure all seed-starting equipment and trays have been sterilized.

HARVEST

Refer to the table below to establish the correct time to harvest your crop. Using pruners or a

CAULIFLOWER TYPES			
TYPE	WHEN TO SOW	WHEN TO PLANT	WHEN TO HARVEST
Winter (no frost)	Late spring	Summer	Winter and early spring
Winter	Late spring	Mid-summer	Early spring
Early summer	Late winter	Mid-spring	Early to mid-summer
Summer/Fall	Late spring	Early summer	Late summer to late fall

knife, cut just below the head when it is still firm and tight. Summer/fall varieties mature in about fifteen weeks; winter varieties in about forty weeks. After harvest, remove the entire plant to deter soilborne diseases, and add to the compost.

WINTER VARIETIES
Snow's Overwintering Has many small sprouts.
Snowball Produces perfect 8in/20cm white heads and is quite disease resistant.

EARLY SUMMER VARIETIES
Snowball Early Produces 6in/15cm white heads.

SUMMER/FALL VARIETIES
Snowball Self-Blanching Produces a 6in/15cm head in the fall. The outer leaves growing up around the head to reduce the need for binding.

PEST PREVENTION
Plant brassica seedlings inside a small collar of heavy paper or cardboard to protect the plant from damage by cutworms.

NON-WHITE VARIETIES
Orange Bouquet Colorful Fı hybrid.
Verde di Macerata An Italian variety with medium-sized soft green head.
Violet Queen Violet-colored Fı hybrid variety.
Violetto di Sicilia A variety planted mid-summer and harvested in late fall or early winter.

Most cauliflowers produce a white broccoli-like flowerhead similar to the one shown here. There are also attractive purple and green varieties.

Cabbages *Brassica oleracea* var. *capitata*

Plant types Biennial

Nutrition Excellent source of phytochemicals and vitamin C. Significant source of vitamin B6. Source of calcium, fiber, and potassium.

Uses Can be eaten fresh or cooked. Many varieties have a sweet juicy flavor. One of the easiest vegetables to store.

SITE AND SOIL

Cabbage needs fertile, humus-rich soil that holds moisture. The soil should be rich in nitrogen and have a pH level above 6.0. Discourage disease by planting in a location where brassicas have not been grown for three years.

SOWING AND PLANTING

Sow seeds indoors five weeks before transplanting. Germinate at 75°F/24°C, then, once seedlings have germinated, reduce the temperature to 60°F/17°C. Transplant outside in the fall at 8in/20cm spacing for early varieties, or at 10–12in/25–30cm in the early spring (for mid-season varieties) or the late spring (for late and storage varieties). In cold climates, early varieties do better when sown directly under a cold frame in late winter or very early spring.

CARE AND MAINTENANCE

Hill up soil around winter cabbages for stability as they grow. Keep the soil moist. Use row covers if necessary to protect from pests. Feed with high-nitrogen compost once during the growing season. Splitting is a problem with early varieties, caused by rapid new growth after heavy rain or irrigation after a dry period. Deep cultivation near the roots may deter plants from splitting.

Pests and diseases Flea beetles, slugs, cabbage loopers, cabbage root maggots, and aphids.

HARVEST

Remove entire plant from garden when the head has matured and feels firm. Cut off the root and compost it to help eliminate soilborne diseases. In areas with cold climates, harvest storage cabbages and place them in a root cellar with high humidity at 32°F/0°C.

VARIETIES

Cabbages are often grouped by their time of maturity. Early varieties are planted in the fall or late winter for a spring harvest, and often have small heads or loose leaves. Mid-season varieties are planted very early in the spring and may be harvested from early summer to fall. They typically have large round heads. Late varieties are sown in the late spring and harvested in early winter, usually for storage in a root cellar.

Early Jersey Wakefield Matures in 75 days.

January King A well-flavored late variety.

Kissendrup A mild-flavored mid-season variety.

Premium Late Flat Dutch A good winter keeper.

ORIENTAL BRASSICA VARIETIES

These Asian specialities have a mustardy flavor and lettuce-like leaves. They may be stirfried or used as greens in salads.

Bok Choi (Pak Choi) *Brassica rapa* var. *chinensis*

Chinese Broccoli *Brassica rapa* var. *alboglabra*

Chinese Cabbage *Brassica rapa* var. *pekinensis*

Oriental Mustards (Yukina Savoy) *Brassica juncea*

Mibuna (Mizuna Greens) *Brassica rapa* var. *nipposinica*

Tatsoi *Brassica rapa* var. *narinosa*

The hardy variety 'January King' needs fertile soil and a high level of nitrogen to produce healthy heads of large, purple-green leaves.

Brussels Sprouts *Brassica oleracea* var. *gemmifera*

Plant type Biennial

Nutrition Excellent source of phytochemicals and vitamin C. Significant source of vitamins A and B6, and folic acid. Source of fiber and potassium.

Uses Brussels sprouts taste best when quickly blanched. They are eaten cooked.

SITE AND SOIL

Brussels sprouts prefer a moisture-retentive soil. A pH between 6.5 and 7.0 produces the best crop. For tight, firm sprouts, do not grow in beds that have recently had rich compost or manure added.

SOWING

While seeds can be sown in the garden, for best results start seeds indoors four to six weeks before transplanting. For an extended harvest, choose less hardy early types as well as the more hardy late-season ones. Transplant in mid- to late spring 18in/45cm apart, and plant deeply to provide extra stability. Do not let transplants dry out.

CARE AND MAINTENANCE

Keep well watered and weeded. A thick mulch keeps plants from drying out during summer.

Pests and diseases Cabbage loopers, mealybugs, and mildew may affect the sprouts.

HARVEST

Most of the old open-pollinated varieties tend to produce poorly, and Fı hybrids generally do better in the garden. However, there are a few open-pollinated varieties, including 'Early Half Tall', 'Hamlet', and 'Paris Market', which produce a good crop. Most varieties are ready to harvest in 120 days, after the first frost. Pick the lowest sprouts first by cutting them near the stem. The upper sprouts will continue to grow in size.

'Early Half Tall' is a very early variety which produces a heavy crop all along the stalk, from the top to the bottom.

Harvest throughout the fall and winter. If there is no snow cover in winter, protect the sprouts with hay or harvest the entire plant and hang it in a moist cool location. After harvest, remove the entire plants from the garden to deter soilborne diseases, and add them to the compost. Smashing the stem will speed up decomposition.

VARIETIES

Early Half Tall Open-pollinated early variety.

Hamlet Productive open-pollinated variety.

Paris Market Open-pollinated; matures quickly.

Rubine Decorative red-leaved variety.

Trafalgar High-quality hybrid.

Kohlrabi *Brassica oleracea* var. *gongylodes*

Plant types Annual

Nutrition Excellent source of vitamin C. Source of potassium.

Uses The swollen stem or bulb is very nutritious when eaten raw, but is often served cooked.

SITE AND SOIL

Kohlrabi prefers light soils that are well drained. Working in compost will provide nutrients for this cool-season crop. Crop rotation is the best defense against diseases.

SOWING

Start sowing outdoors in spring, spaced 8in/20cm apart, or sow indoors two weeks before transplanting. Sow purple varieties directly in the garden in mid-summer.

CARE AND MAINTENANCE

Kohlrabi is quite drought tolerant. Water occasionally and keep the bed weed free.

Pests and diseases Clubroot, flea beetles, and cabbage root maggots.

HARVEST

Kohlrabi is ready for harvest in as little as forty days. If the diameter exceeds 3in/8cm the inside may be woody. Leave purple varieties in the soil until frost threatens. They can be stored in moist sand with some leaves attached.

VARIETIES

Erfordia An old variety with green bulbs.

Gigante Bears 10lb/4.5kg bulbs.

Logo An early variety that is best eaten small.

White Vienna Overwinters well.

Kohlrabi is grown for its swollen stems, called bulbs. The flesh is white and the skin may be pale green or purple.

Broccoli *Brassica oleracea* var. *italica*

MUSTARD
BRASSICACEAE

Plant type Annual or biennial
Nutrition Excellent source of phytochemicals
and vitamin C. Good source of folic acid.
Significant source of vitamins A, B2, and B6, and
phosphorous. Source of fiber, calcium, and iron.
Uses Broccoli is best eaten raw or quickly
blanched in boiling water.

SITE AND SOIL

Broccoli needs soil with moisture-holding ability.
Improve sandy soils by incorporating lots of
compost. Plants can tolerate frost, and often grow
most vigorously after a fall frost.

SOWING

Sow every two weeks starting in early spring in the
garden, or start indoors four to six weeks before
transplanting. If starting indoors, keep soil
temperature above 75°F/24°C to speed up
germination, then reduce the temperature to
60°F/16°C. Plant outside at 12in/30cm spacing.
If sowing outdoors, plant three per 12in/30cm and
thin to one per 12in/30cm. Sprouting broccolis
need to be planted deeply and may need to be
staked in the fall. Plants survive temperatures of
10°F/–12°C. Space plants 24in/60cm apart.

CARE AND MAINTENANCE

Water frequently and keep free of weeds. Broccoli
needs about 1in/2.5cm of water every two weeks.
Pests and diseases Black rot, cutworms, cabbage
loopers, cabbage root maggots, and flea beetles.
Use row covers to keep pests at bay.

HARVEST

Cut main heads when they are tight, before the
flowerbuds begin to open. Add compost after the
first harvest to encourage sideshoots to form. Chill

*Closely related to cauliflowers and cabbages, broccoli
is a cool-weather plant, best harvested in spring or fall.
Calabrese (above) are large-headed varieties.*

the cut heads as soon as possible. Cut the
sideshoots when they are about 4in/10cm long,
before the buds begin to open. To harvest seeds,
allow a plant with a central head to bloom, and
collect the seeds when they mature.

VARIETIES

Broccoli Raab Grown for its mustard-like leaves
and small florets used in salads.
Calabrese Varieties with large heads measuring
about 8in/20cm in diameter.
De Cicco Produces a small main head, followed by
sideshoots that can be harvested over a long time.
Purple Sprouting One of the hardiest winter
vegetables. The shoots freeze well.
Romanesco Varieties with light green heads,
suited to areas with long cool summers or warm
winters, as they take 75–100 days to mature.
Waltham A flavorful open-pollinated variety.

Rutabagas *Brassica napus* var. *napobrassica*

Plant type Biennial

Nutrition Good source of vitamin C. Source of potassium.

Uses Grown for their sweet, yellow-fleshed roots used in soups and stews, or mashed as a side dish. Young roots are grated for sprinkling on salads and the greens can be cooked like kales.

SITE AND SOIL

Rutabagas are a cool-season crop and prefer a well-drained soil with low levels of nitrogen. Test the soil to check that it is not deficient in boron. Choose an open site with light, fertile soil. Heavy soils do not produce a good crop.

SOWING

Sow seeds directly in the garden in early to mid-spring. Sow them ½in/1cm deep, spaced at intervals of 3in/8cm. Thin young plants to 9in/23cm spacing, utilizing the greens or any small roots for the table.

PEST PREVENTION

To protect crops from flea beetles, place cloches or floating row covers over the plants. Secure the covers to the ground at the edges.

CARE AND MAINTENANCE

Keep the bed free of weeds and water 1in/2.5cm per week if there is not sufficient rain. Mulching will preserve moisture and discourage weeds.

Pests and diseases Downy mildew, powdery mildew, and flea beetles. Consider choosing a mildew-resistant variety.

HARVEST

Begin harvest in about twenty-six weeks. To lift roots, use a garden fork or pull by the tops. They may be left in the ground until needed, but overwintering in the garden may result in woody roots. It is better to harvest the unused portion of the crop before winter and store in a root cellar, in dry sand, or in a rutabaga clamp outdoors.

VARIETIES

American Purple Top Matures within ninety days.

Eastham Turnip Excellent flavor.

Gilfeather Sweet-tasting, easy-to-grow variety.

Krasnoselskaya/Krasnoje Selskoje A variety that is good for storage.

Sharpe's Yellow Garden Good garden variety.

Rutabagas are grown for their sweet-tasting roots. The skin of the root is usually purple and buff, as in 'American Purple Top' (left).

Turnips *Brassica rapa* var. *rapifera*

Plant type Biennial

Nutrition Roots are a significant source of vitamin C. Greens are an excellent source of vitamin C, a good source of vitamin A and folic acid, and a significant source of calcium.

Uses Roots have a yellow or white flesh that is cooked. The leaves are used in salads or are cooked like spinach.

SITE AND SOIL

Moist soil is essential, because turnips bolt in dry conditions. Work plenty of compost into the soil and apply a mulch to retain moisture. Choose a sunny location and test for boron deficiency.

SOWING

Sow directly in the garden three weeks before the last frosts in early spring. Sow seeds ¼in/0.5cm deep, spacing them 3–4in/8–10cm apart. Seeds germinate when the soil reaches 40°F/4°C. For a second harvest, sow a second crop in mid-summer, about two months before the first frosts are expected.

CARE AND MAINTENANCE

Ensure that the turnips do not dry out. This will cause them to bolt. Apply mulch to ensure consistent moisture. Water at a rate of 1–2in/2.5–5cm a week during dry periods.

Pests and diseases Watch out for flea beetles and mildew.

HARVEST

Do not leave turnips in the ground too long otherwise they will become woody or bolt. Harvest them after about five weeks by pulling them by the stems. Leaves may be harvested during the growing season, but leave enough on each plant to keep the roots healthy and to ensure that the plant keeps growing. Pull summer-sown turnips after the first fall frost. Store in a root cellar or in an outdoor clamp, like rutabagas.

VARIETIES

Gilfeather A sweet-tasting turnip.

Purple Top White Globe A traditional variety producing a reliable crop.

Seven Top Grown only for its greens.

Shogoin Produces wonderful tops as well as a large white root.

Grow hardy turnips for eating fresh during summer and keep some in storage in a root cellar, for use throughout the winter.

Radishes *Raphanus sativus*

Plant type Annual or biennial
Nutrition Good source of vitamin C. Source of potassium and fiber.
Uses Immature seed pods and young leaves of radishes are often used in salads. The roots are used fresh in salads or are cooked in soups.

SITE AND SOIL

Radishes are generally a cool-season crop. Grow in full sun in a light, well-drained soil. Radishes grow best in low nitrogen conditions.

SOWING

Start sowing radishes in the garden in early spring and continue throughout the growing season at two-week intervals. In summer, sow the seeds in partial shade. 'Daikon' is best sown in late summer to discourage bolting. Sow seed ½in/1cm apart and harvest some young plants to make room for the others to mature. Radishes germinate and mature so quickly that they can be sown alongside slow-germinating crops, such as parsnips, to act as handy row-markers.

CARE AND MAINTENANCE

Radishes are very fast growing and usually crowd out any weeds. Water the plants regularly during dry conditions.
Pests and diseases Slugs, flea beetles, and cabbage root maggots may attack radishes.

HARVEST

Start harvesting radishes three weeks after sowing. Large varieties may need as much as ten weeks to reach full size. Harvest small early radishes promptly, before they become woody. 'Daikon' and overwintering radishes may be left in the ground longer without any risk of them becoming

Tangy crisp-rooted radishes come in a variety of colors and forms. They are quick to germinate and are ready for harvest in as little as twenty-one days.

woody. After harvesting, the roots may be stored like carrots in buckets of sand. Moisten the sand a little to keep the radishes from drying out.

VARIETIES

Black Round Rammanas Tasty black variety.
Black Spanish Round Edible seed pods. Suitable for overwintering.
Chinese Green Meat Attractive green flesh.
Daikon Suitable for eating fresh or pickling.
Easter Egg Small round radishes in pastel colors.
Eighteen Days Fast-maturing variety.
Long White Icicle Crisp tasting. Stores well.
Miyashige High quality fall-harvested radish.
Slobolt Good for storage.
Small French Breakfast Great-tasting variety.

Watermelons *Citrullus lanatus* var. *lanatus*

Plant type Annual

Nutrition The only food plant commonly grown in gardens which is a significant source of pantothenic acid. It is higher in vitamins B1 and B6 than any other commonly grown plant. Excellent source of vitamin C. Good source of vitamin A. Significant source of magnesium. Source of potassium and fiber.

Uses Eat fresh or use in blended drinks.

SITE AND SOIL

Watermelons are heat-loving and grow best in long-summer areas. In temperate climates, only quick-maturing varieties can grow. They need at least 75 frost-free days, or must be grown in a greenhouse. Well-drained sandy soils are best. See site, soil, and sowing advice for melons, page 205.

CARE, MAINTENANCE AND HARVEST

Mulch well to conserve moisture, and water regularly during dry periods. They take 75–110 days to mature. Ripe watermelons sound hollow when tapped. Cut the stem about 1in/2.5cm from the fruit. They can be stored for two to three weeks at 45°F/7°C.

Pests and diseases High humidity levels cause powdery mildew and mosaic virus. Watch for aphids and fruit flies.

VARIETIES

Georgia Rattlesnake A popular variety with light and dark green striped skin and sweet pink flesh.

Moon and Stars A popular heirloom variety with patches of yellow and small round "stars."

Sugar Baby Matures within eighty days.

Yellow Baby A large yellow-fleshed variety.

Heat-loving watermelons, such as 'Georgia Rattlesnake' (left), grow best in long-summer areas. They are valued for their large, round or oblong fruits, packed with pink or yellow flesh.

Melons *Cucumis melo*

Plant type Annual
Nutrition Source of fiber. Cantaloupes are an excellent source of vitamins A and C, and a significant source of folic acid. Honeydews are an excellent source of vitamin C, a significant source of vitamin B6, and a source of potassium.
Uses Served as a starter or refreshing dessert.

SITE AND SOIL

Choose a site with good exposure to the sun, because the soil will warm up sooner in the winter and the growing season will be extended. Prepare a garden bed in the usual way (see pp. 128–133), then dig holes 12in/30cm across and 12in/30cm deep, spaced about 4ft/1.2m apart. Mix the soil you have removed with an equal amount of rotted manure, then return it to the hole leaving a mound above the level of the soil.

Melons require a temperature above 64°F/18°C to germinate and prefer a temperature above 70°F/21°C during the growing season. It may be necessary to build a cold frame over the bed, or to grow melons in a greenhouse in cool climates – winter melons and cantaloupes are the most successful under glass. Melons need a soil with a pH of 6.5 to 7.0.

SOWING

In warm areas, sow three seeds directly in each prepared mound after all chance of frost has passed. In cool climates, it is best to start seeds indoors in 4in/10cm pots. Three weeks after germination, long before the seedlings become rootbound, transplant three seedlings to each prepared hill outside. Be sure all danger of frost has passed and harden off seedlings before transplanting. If the site is exposed to wind, you may need to protect seedlings with cloches until

Melons, such as the honeydew 'Helios Yellow' (above), are heavy feeders. To produce the best fruits they need lots of water and plenty of sunshine.

they are established. If the seedlings experience cold weather, they may never bear fruit.

CARE AND MAINTENANCE

Melons rarely require weeding after they are established because the foliage usually shades out the weeds. Melons usually need watering; use a simple drip irrigation system with a timer to ensure consistent moisture. Add a thick mulch to help retain moisture and keep the melons clean. Mulch after the vines reach 12in/30cm long. Some varieties produce long vines that can overrun the garden; train these back towards the hill, taking care not to damage the vines. After five leaves have developed on a vine, pinch the tip to encourage sideshoots.

Fruiting takes place on sideshoots, and male flowers are on the main vine. Melons are insect pollinated, so be sure not to use row covers when flowering. If they are grown in a greenhouse, you will need to pollinate by hand. Use a small paintbrush to lift pollen from male flowers and brush it onto female flowers on sideshoots. Cross-pollination is possible and the resulting seeds, if saved, may produce nearly inedible fruit. Each vine will produce only three to four melons. In mid- or late summer, pinch off all small fruit and any flowers, leaving just a few large melons to mature. A high-nitrogen liquid organic feed may be applied halfway through the growing season. If growing melons in a cold frame, remove the glass during the day and replace at night if necessary. For greenhouse melons, keep the plants small by pinching the tips regularly. Pinch the main vine at 6ft/1.8m, and laterals after the fifth leaf. In a greenhouse, maintaining a minimum temperature of 75°F/24°C at night will help to produce a good crop of fruits.

Pests and diseases Cucumber beetles, aphids, spider mites, whiteflies, and vine borers are the most common pests. Powdery mildew and verticillium wilt may cause problems.

Harvest

All the work during the growing season pays off at harvest time. Muskmelons are sweet smelling when mature. The stems may also crack. By simply lifting the fruit the stems will usually separate from the melon. Winter melons are ready a little later, when the temperature falls.

Cantaloupe varieties

Cantaloupes typically have orange flesh with a rough, textured skin. The flesh is very sweet, and the skin is grey to green, with deep grooves.

Collective Farm Woman Yellow to white, sweet-tasting flesh.

Hybrid St. Nick Grows well in the north.

Jenny Lind A small fruit with unequaled flavor.

Mango Melon A mango-flavored variety.

Melba Earliest-producing melon with small fruit and pale orange flesh.

Muskmelon varieties

Muskmelons are usually smaller than cantaloupes and have smooth, greenish skin with intricate brown or beige markings. Their flesh color ranges from green to nearly pink.

Amish Grown for its sweet, juicy flesh.

Banana Grown for its sweet banana flavor and orange flesh.

Blenheim Orange An orange-fleshed variety that grows well in short seasons.

Crème de la Crème A delicious hybrid.

Haogen Grows well in northern climates. It has green flesh and yellow skin.

Honeydew varieties

Honeydews generally have green flesh and light-green smooth skin that is rather thin.

Golden Honeydew Orange-fleshed variety.

Golden Honeymoon Green-fleshed variety with an orange rind.

Helios Yellow A popular North American variety.

Winter melon varieties

This group includes casaba melons and crenshaws, which have dark green skins. Winter melons are more prone to disease than other melon groups. They tend to have less fragrant flesh and keep better when stored. Store in a cool place for up to eight weeks.

Crenshaw Best started indoors because of its long growing season.

Golden Beauty Casaba A good keeper.

Hasan Bey Casaba Noted for its snow-white flesh, this variety needs a long, hot growing season for a succesful crop of fruits.

Sungold Casaba Has a short maturity period of just ninety days. Suitable for storage.

Turkish Striped Noted for its mild sweet flavor.

A green-fleshed honeydew (back) and an orange-fleshed canteloupe (front) ready for the table. In the last days before harvest, the sugar content rises significantly.

Cucumbers *Cucumis sativus*

Plant type Annual

Nutrition Source of vitamins A and C, and potassium.

Uses Harvested as young fruits and eaten raw or pickled. Occasionally used in soups.

SITE AND SOIL

Select a sheltered site, and prepare holes about 12in/30cm in diameter and 12in/30cm deep. Space the holes 24in/60cm apart, measuring from the center. Fill the holes with compost with a pH of 6.0, and mound the soil slightly.

SOWING

Cucumbers do not transplant well, so plant seed in prepared mounds after the soil has warmed and all danger of frost has passed. The soil temperature should be 70°F/21°C. In short-season areas, you may need to start seeds indoors four weeks before transplanting. Use cloches to protect young plants.

CARE AND MAINTENANCE

Use trellis or stakes to support the plant, and tie in tendrils as they grow. Bush varieties do not need support. Cut the tip of the plant after five leaves have formed to encourage stronger new growth. Cut the tips again when they reach the top of the support. Feed with a high-potassium organic liquid feed to produce a high yield. Regular watering is essential.

Pests and diseases Slugs and cucumber beetles are the worst pests. Watch also for aphids, mildew, cutworms, and spider mites. Cucumber mosaic virus causes undersized distorted leaves.

HARVEST

Start to harvest about twelve weeks after sowing, and continue until the first frost.

VARIETIES

Boston Pickling A very productive old variety.

Early Cluster Ready for harvest in fifty-two days.

Lemon A yellow fruit that is almost round.

Longfellow Slender variety, best eaten fresh.

Striped Armenian Unusual S-shaped fruit, with superb flavor. It has alternating light and dark green stripes.

Vert de Massy Prized for making pickles.

West India Gherkin A sweet-tasting cucumber.

White Wonder Old variety with ivory-white fruits that are good for pickling or eating fresh.

The cucumber 'West India Gherkin', shown here, yields a large crop of small oval fruits. They should be picked when young and tender and eaten fresh or pickled.

Summer Squash *Cucurbita pepo*

Plant type Annual
Nutrition Significant source of vitamin C.
Source of vitamin A, calcium, iron, and fiber.
Uses Range of fruits, from zucchini to scallop,
that are best harvested young and small.

SITE AND SOIL

Pick a sheltered site, and prepare holes about
12in/30cm in diameter and 12in/30cm deep.
Measuring from the center, space the holes
36in/90cm apart for bush types, 6ft/1.8m apart for
vines. Fill the holes with compost with a pH of
6.0, and mound the soil slightly. Summer squash
does not require high nitrogen levels.

SOWING

Summer squash does not transplant well, so plant
seed in prepared mounds after the soil has warmed
and when all danger of frost has passed. Usually
one week after the last frost is a good time to
plant. The soil temperature should be 60°F/16°C.
Start seeds indoors four weeks before
transplanting. If planted out too early, cover the
plants with cloches. A thick mulch added after
planting will preserve moisture and keep the fruits
from touching the ground where they will become
soiled and be exposed to insects and diseases.

CARE AND MAINTENANCE

Regular watering is essential for summer squash.
Feed the plants with a high-potassium organic
liquid feed to produce a higher yield. Bush types
require no staking, whereas vine types may be
trained to grow up a trellis or allowed to grow
along the ground. If the plants are not supported
by trellis or stakes, gently train the vines clear of
any paths so that they do not become damaged.
If too many fruits are being produced, leave one or

two squashes on the plant past maturity. These
will not be edible, but will slow down the
production of new squashes to an acceptable rate.

Summer squash is insect pollinated. If row
covers are needed to protect from pests or if no
fruits are setting, you may need to hand-pollinate.
First identify the difference between male and
female flowers. The female flower has a tiny bump
or thickened section of stem just beneath the
flower; the male flower is slightly smaller and
lacks this bump. Pick a male flower, remove its
petals, and brush it against the centers of the

*Summer squash is easy to grow and bears plenty
of fruits. 'De Nice à Fruit Rond' (above) bears
round fruit with a good flavor.*

female flowers. Do not damage the female flowers.
Pests and diseases   Squash vine borers are the worst enemy of summer squash. Watch also for slugs, cucumber beetles, and cucumber mosaic virus. Keep a regular check on the undersides of leaves as this is where bugs commonly lay eggs.

HARVEST

Start harvesting about fifty days after sowing. Cut or twist off the young fruits. The flower may still be attached to the fruit. Zucchini are at their best when harvested about 4–5in/10–12cm long; yellow squashes can be cut when they reach about 5–6in/13–15cm; harvest scallop types when they are about 3in/8cm in diameter. Continue harvesting until the first frosts. Before the frosts arrive, pinch out the tips of plant stems to encourage the remaining small fruits to mature quickly. The male flowers are often harvested to be sautéed or stuffed, or used to decorate dishes.

VARIETIES

For spaghetti squash, see Winter squash, p. 211.
Benning's Green Tint   Tasty scallop squash.
Cousa   A sweet nutty-tasting variety that is often stuffed.
De Nice à Fruit Rond   Perfectly round fruit with a good flavor. Harvest when no larger than 5in/13cm.
Giant Early Prolific Straightneck   Very productive varieties.
Golden Bush Scallop   Golden version of 'White Bush Scallop' with pale green flesh.
Verte Non Coureuse d'Italie (Cocozelle) The finest-tasting summer squash. Be sure to pick when young to enjoy the best flavor.
White Bush Scallop   Flat, round pancake-like fruits that are as attractive as they are tasty. Suitable for the decorative garden.
Yellow Crookneck (Early Summer Crookneck) Very tasty fruit with a highly textured skin. Harvest young to retain the flavor.

The unusual shapes and bold colors of some summer squash, such as 'Yellow Crookneck', make a striking display in the vegetable plot.

ZUCCHINI VARIETIES

Black Zucchini   Matures in only forty-four days.
Burpee Hybrid   Produces a large harvest.
Costates Romanesco   A good-tasting dark and light green-striped squash.
Dark Green Zucchini   Large producer of shiny green fruits.
Gold Rush (F1)   Bears uniform yellow fruits.
Grey Zucchini   Mid-green, speckled varieties.
Nimba   A cold hardy variety with speckled skin.

Winter Squash *Cucurbita* spp.

Plant type Annual

Nutrition Excellent source of phytochemicals. Source of potassium and fiber.

Acorn squashes are a good source of vitamin C, and a significant source of vitamin B1 and magnesium. Pumpkins are a good source of vitamin A, and a significant source of vitamin C. Hubbards are an excellent source of vitamin A, and a significant source of vitamin C. Butternuts are an excellent source of vitamins A and C, and a significant source of vitamin B6 and magnesium.

Uses Can be boiled, baked, or made into pies. Some are grown only for ornamental value.

SITE AND SOIL

Pick a site that is sheltered from the cold and one where the long vines of winter squash will have ample room to grow. Prepare holes about 12in/30cm in diameter and 18in/45cm deep with centers spaced 36in–6ft/90cm–1.8m apart or more, depending on the variety. Fill with compost or well-rotted manure with a pH of 6.0. Mound soil slightly. High nitrogen levels are necessary for a good harvest.

SOWING

Seeds may be soaked in water for a few hours to aid in germination. Seeds may be sown directly in the garden, but since some varieties require a long season to produce mature fruit, starting seeds indoors typically produces a better harvest. If sowing outdoors, plant six seeds in each prepared hill, and thin to three seedlings per hill. For sowing indoors, it is essential that roots are not damaged during transplanting. To ensure this, avoid sowing them in pots because removing them for transplanting disturbs the roots. Instead, use

2in/5cm soil blocks, which work much better (unless they are started too early and the roots spread into neighboring soil blocks). Lift the soil blocks with a spatula or other flat device and transplant gently. Sow one seed per soil block, two to three weeks before transplanting in late spring. Harden off plants for a week before planting them outside, two to three seedlings per hill.

CARE AND MAINTENANCE

Regular watering is essential. Feed the plants with a high-potassium organic liquid feed to produce a higher yield. Vines may be trained up a trellis if the

This group of fruit ranges from inedible ornamental pumpkins to tasty squashes. The fruits may be as small as a softball, or too big to carry.

plant is a variety that produces small fruit; however, vines are typically grown on the ground, and trained so that they are kept clear of nearby paths and do not get trodden on or knocked by passing traffic. Mulch well to preserve moisture and to protect the fruit from insects and diseases in the soil. If not trained, the vines may grow into undesired locations. Do not allow them to grow out of the beds and into the lawn, where they are more likely to be attacked by squash vine borers, the primary enemy of all squashes.

Squash is insect pollinated. If row covers are being used, or if no fruits are setting, it may be neccessary to hand pollinate (see Summer squash, Care and maintenance, pp. 209–10).

Kabocha squash are small fruits with deep-ribbed skins and yellow flesh. The skin is typically dark green but some varieties may range to gold in color.

Pests and diseases   Squash vine borers are the worst problem. Butternuts are generally not bothered by borers. Watch out also for slugs, cucumber beetles, and cucumber mosaic virus. Check for bugs laying eggs on the back of the leaves; cucumber beetles can carry bacterial wilt. Black rot may be found on fruits in storage.

HARVEST

In fall, cut the leaves away from the fruit. This will help them to ripen. Light frosts will kill leaves and make harvest easier, however it may damage the fruit and shorten the time it can be stored. Before a heavy frost, cut the stems with a knife or pruners about 1in/2.5cm from the fruit. The stem will be drying and the skin of the fruit hardening. Handle the fruits gently, especially butternuts. Let the squash cure or dry in sunlight for a few days to a week, depending on the type. If frost is expected, cover them with a blanket at night. Store in a low humidity location with plenty of air circulation between the fruits. Store squash at a temperature of about 55°F/13°C.

ACORN VARIETIES

Table Gold   Produces a bright orange fruit that may need sweetening when cooking.
Table Queen   A dark green variety that keeps well.

BUTTERNUT VARIETIES

Baby Butternut   Produces tasty dark-orange fleshed fruits that store extremely well.
Long Island Cheese   Often grown as a pumpkin, the fruit is round in shape and ribbed.
Waltham   Produces uniform fruits with rich orange flesh.

CUSHAW VARIETIES

Golden Cushaw   Crook-necked variety.
Green Striped Cushaw   Good garden variety.
Hopi   Striped variety grown for its fleshy neck.
Orange Cushaw   Good garden variety.

Pumpkins typically have red-orange skin. Most have seeds that are a delicacy when toasted, and some pumpkins make wonderful pies. 'Dill's Atlantic Giant' (left) produces massive fruits.

DELICATA VARIETIES
Delicata Small orange-fleshed fruits.
Sweet Dumpling A round-fruit variety.

HUBBARD VARIETIES
Baby Blue Hubbard Bears 5–7lb/2.2–3.2kg fruits.
Blue Hubbard Produces large oblong fruits that store well.
Boston Marrow The best-tasting squash available.
True Green Hubbard Pointed at both ends, the fruit has very sweet flesh.

KABOCHA VARIETIES
Black Forest An old variety that produces small fruits with deep orange flesh.
Buttercup This dark green variety has a small button on the flower end of the fruit.

SPAGHETTI VARIETIES
Vegetable Spaghetti Produces long strands of flesh. Best harvested when 8–10in/20–25cm long.
Tivoli Fruit is borne on a bush rather than a vine.

PUMPKIN VARIETIES
Dill's Atlantic Giant Produces 200lb/90kg fruits.
Jarrahdale Good for boiling or baking.
New England Pie A classic dark orange color and small rounded shape.
Rouge Vif d'Etampes (Cinderella) Bold red fruits.
Valenciano A white-skinned pumpkin.

OTHER VARIETIES
Pink Banana Jumbo Produces 30in/75cm long fruits that truly look like a pink banana. This pumpkin tastes great when baked.

Wheat *Triticum aestivum*

Plant type Annual

Nutrition Source of vitamin E and folic acid. Whole wheat is a source of fiber.

Uses Grain can be used for breadmaking. Sow as a cover crop (see pp. 57–61)

Most gardeners do not consider growing wheat because they think of it as a field crop only grown on large acreages. What most do not realize is that with an area of 5ft/1.5m x 4ft/1.2m area, enough grain for two loaves of bread can be produced. How many loaves of bread are consumed in a typical household in a year? Between 52 and 100? To supply the typical household, a bed measuring between 20ft/6m x 25ft/7.5m and 20ft/6m x 50ft/15m is all that is needed to supply enough wheat for a family for a year.

Additionally, winter wheat can be sown in the fall for a mid- to late spring harvest (or early to mid-summer in areas with long winters) leaving space in the garden available just in time for planting tomatoes, melons, eggplants, and peppers. In order to grow wheat for this kind of harvest, it needs to be grown intensively, with rich soil and close spacing. To ensure a good crop, get off to a good start by sowing seeds in flats and transplanting the seedlings.

SITE AND SOIL

Choose a site that will not be needed in early spring by other crops. Many gardeners prefer to spread plantings across different areas of the garden instead of planting wheat in one large block. Cultivate the bed just before planting.

SOWING

Seeds may be sown directly in the garden, or started in flats and transplanted out with 5in/12cm spacing. Start seeds in flats three weeks before transplanting. If sowing directly in the garden, broadcast seeds at the rate of 4lb per 1,000sq. ft/2kg per 100 sq. m in the fall. Soil should be very well prepared for an early harvest. Work lots of compost into the soil. If the soil is not extremely fertile, harvest may be delayed until mid-summer.

CARE AND MAINTENANCE

Weed in early winter, as the tops die back. Weed once in early spring. Water regularly, especially just before harvest.

Pests and diseases In certain arid areas grasshoppers may be a problem. In very wet climates molds and fungi may affect the crop. It is essential to have enough sunny weather prior to harvest to dry the crop.

HARVEST

It takes approximately forty days from when the wheat sets heads until harvest. Cut off the heads and place them on a flat surface. Walk across them with hard-soled shoes. Separate the seeds from the chaff by tossing up into the air in a light breeze. The chaff will blow away leaving behind the seeds for collection.

VARIETIES

The variety of wheat to grow in your location will depend on your climate and growing conditions. Pick a variety that grows well in your area and be sure to avoid GMO seeds.

Hard Red Recommended garden variety.

Early Stone Age Fast regaining popularity.

If you have a generous-sized garden, you might consider growing a crop of wheat to provide you with sufficient grain for a weekly loaf of bread.

Corn *Zea mays*

Plant type Annual

Nutrition Significant source of vitamin B1.
Source of potassium.

Uses Eaten on the cob when freshly harvested.
Less sweet varieties are best left to dry to become
popcorn or to grind for use in cooking as
cornmeal or corn flour.

SITE AND SOIL

Time the planting carefully because a cold soil
temperature is the most common cause of crop
failure. Morning soil temperature should be
65°F/18°C before sowing, so a southern
orientation is essential for an early crop. Choose a
location where the 36in–7ft/90cm–2m high plants
will not throw shade over other areas of the
garden. Corn is shallow rooted and grows best on
well-drained soil with a lot of nitrogen.

SOWING

Start sowing directly in the garden when the soil is
warm. If there is a late frost after sowing,
replanting may be needed. Corn requires
pollination by wind. The tassels are male and the
ears female. The wind blows pollen from the
tassels onto the silk of the ear, and the pollen
travels down the silk into the ear to pollinate it.

It is best to plant seeds in a pattern of at least
four rows wide with rows spaced 12in/30cm
apart. Seeds should be sown about 12in/30cm
apart in the rows, 1in/2.5cm deep. Sweet and
Super-sweet varieties need warmer temperatures
to germinate. If growing more than one variety of
corn, it is essential to prevent cross-pollination.
Plant blocks of corn at least one week apart, or
separate them by 15ft/4.5m or more. Varieties
that have different maturation dates may be
planted at the same time.

CARE AND MAINTENANCE

Weed regularly until the corn is established.
Watering is unnecessary except in severe drought.

Pests and diseases Deer, raccoons, and
groundhogs are the main pests. An effective
protection against these is an electric fence with a
good charge. A fence is easy to install and to
remove, but if you have any doubts about your
skills, you should, for safety reasons, employ a
professional electrician. Wires should be spaced at
4in/10cm near the bottom, and and the spacing
should gradually be increased to 9in/23cm. To
protect crops from deer, ensure the top wire is
18ft/2.4m above the ground. Corn borers, spotted
cucumber beetle larvae, asparagus beetles,

*When sweet corn is ready for harvest, the plump
yellow kernels will emit a milky-white fluid when
pressed gently.*

cutworms, and corn rootworms may attack the corn. A drop of mineral oil on the silk is the traditional way to repel borers. If worm problems occur, remove the entire plant after harvest and add to the compost. Cultivate the soil before replanting the bed.

HARVEST

Pick sweet corn just before cooking to retain maximum flavor. Sweet corn can only be stored successfully by freezing or removing the kernels and canning them. Popcorn and grinding corns are best left to mature in the garden, unless there is a very wet fall (in which case, harvest early and hang entire plants upside down in a sheltered location). When the leaves have died, harvest the corn, shuck and dry it in a warm location before storing. After drying, popcorn may be popped right on the ear. Grinding corn should be removed from the cob and stored at room temperature.

DENT CORN VARIETIES

Dent corn is a little softer than flint corn, and forms a slight depression at the tip of the kernel as it dries. Dent corns grow best in warmer climates and are used to make a fine flour.
Hickory King Popular garden variety.
Reid's Yellow Dent Popular garden variety.
Trucker's Favorite White Best suited to southern areas. Ideal for roasting.

FLINT CORN VARIETIES

Flint corns grow best in cold areas and are used to produce a coarse cornmeal.
Hopi Blue Flint Tolerates very high ground.
Longfellow Probably the most popular variety.
Mandan Bride Multicolored corn, traditionally used by Native Americans for flour corn.
Vermont Yellow Flint Suits northern climates.

SWEET CORN VARIETIES

Butter and Sugar Sweet yellow and white kernels.

To enjoy sweet corn (in this case, 'Butter and Sugar') at its sweetest, eat as soon as possible after harvest; otherwise the sugars quickly convert to starch.

Golden Bantam An all-yellow variety of great quality. Able to germinate in cool soil well.
Shoe Peg Disease-resistant variety, with kernels that grow in a haphazard pattern on the cob.

SUPER-SWEET VARIETIES

Super-sweet varieties were introduced during the 1980s. After harvest, they retain their crisp texture for several days and their sweetness tends to increase slightly. They freeze particularly well.
Jumpstart Earliest bicolor variety.
Northern Earliest yellow super sweet variety.

POPCORN VARIETIES

Miniature Blue Has thin cobs only 2–4in/5–10cm long that are very attractive dried.
Strawberry A small plant that creates beautiful miniature ears. Produces the most tasty popcorn.

217

Beans (Various)

Plant type Annual

Nutrition Excellent source of phytochemicals. Source of vitamins A, B1, B8, and C, calcium, phosphorus, and iron.

Snap beans are a significant source of vitamin C. Dried beans are a source of vitamins B1 and B2, calcium, sulfur, and iron.

Lima beans are a source of vitamin A, B1, and C, folic acid, potassium, phosphorus, fiber and some vitamin B8, magnesium, calcium, and iron.

Uses The seed pods of snap beans are used fresh or preserved by freezing or canning. Other beans are grown for their seeds, which are harvested dry or in the shell-bean stage. Winged beans are grown for their tuberous roots.

SITE AND SOIL

Beans do not require a high nitrogen soil. Like all legumes, they collect atmospheric nitrogen and fix it into nodules on the roots that slowly release nitrogen into the soil. This is the nitrogen source for the plant. Choose a site with well-cultivated soil that has good drainage. It is essential to rotate crops to prevent diseases and to utilize the bed for a nitrogen-loving crop in a future year.

SOWING

In order to create nitrogen-releasing nodules, legumes have a symbiotic relationship with bacteria in the soil. If beans have been grown in the garden before, it is very likely that the correct type of bacteria already exists in the soil. If not, or if planting them in a different area of the garden where legumes have not been grown, it is best to inoculate the seeds before planting. This simply involves buying a packet of the appropriate type of bacteria (there are several) in dry form and dusting the seeds with them before planting.

Beans will germinate above 55°F/13°C (except fava beans which are frost tolerant). Most types are self-pollinating. Sow outside after all chance of frost has passed. Sow seeds 2in/5cm deep. For bush varieties, space 4–8in/10–20cm apart. For pole varieties, prepare a tripod made of branches or bamboo that is 6–8ft/1.8–2.5m tall. Tie the tops with twine. Plant two or three seeds at the bottom of each of the legs of the tripod. For runner varieties, it is essential to create a very tall support. Typically this is done by stringing twine between a brick placed on the ground and a hook placed in the wall on the side of a building. Provide ample height for the plants; 12–14ft/3.6–4.2m should be sufficient. Plant two

For pole beans, construct a framework of canes or horizontal and vertical twines along which the stems can be trained and supported.

Runner beans, such as 'Scarlet Runner' (left), prefer a cool climate and grow on vines that can reach up to 14ft/4.2m. They can be harvested as snap, shell, and dry beans.

or three seeds at the base of each string. The flowers of runner beans look particularly attractive against a white or green background. Fava beans may be planted in late fall in areas where the temperature does not drop below 10°F/–12°C. This will result in a much earlier harvest the next year.

CARE AND MAINTENANCE

Consistent moisture is essential for a good harvest. Water regularly during dry periods at a rate of up to 2–3in/5–8cm per week. Weed as necessary, and consider applying a mulch around the plants to preserve moisture.

Pests and diseases Aphids tend to spread viral diseases to legumes. Watch for Mexican bean beetles, which look like large, beige ladybugs, as they are quite destructive. Also watch for slugs and, occasionally, Japanese beetles. Prevention is the best solution to diseases. Rotate crops every year and prevent aphids from spreading diseases by using row covers. Watch for ascochyta blight in all chickpeas.

HARVEST

Begin harvesting snap beans fifty days after sowing (sixty days for pole varieties). Regular harvesting will encourage new pods to form. Some pods may have strings that must be removed before cooking. To do this, snap off both ends of the pod and pull the attached string. To save seeds from snap beans, leave a plant to mature to the dry seed stage, and harvest the seeds as described below for dry beans.

Shell beans, also known as horticultural beans, may be harvested when the seeds in the pods swell and look plump. Remove the pod from the plant, open it up and remove the soft seeds. Regular harvesting every week or so will encourage the formation of new pods.

Dry beans are left to mature on the plant. When most of the leaves have fallen from the plant in the fall, harvest the entire plant by cutting it off just above soil level. It is usually necessary to complete drying indoors. Tie bunches of plants by their bases and hang them in a warm dry location. When they are completely dry, the pods may be

When trained on a teepee of canes, runner beans, such as 'Butler' (above), form a flowering pyramid that adds an attractive focal point to the vegetable plot.

opened by hand and the seeds removed. Alternatively, place the entire bunch of plants in a sack, seal it with a tie, and then beat it vigorously to extract the seeds from the pods. The seeds will be at the bottom of the bag, the leaves and stems above. Separate out the beans from the rest. If dried beans are left too long in the garden, the seeds may fall from the pods and be lost.

Winged types have pods that may be harvested as snap or dry beans. However, they are usually grown for their nutritious tuberous roots. To harvest these, cut the plant off just above the ground before the first frost. Lift the roots using a garden fork; they may be as far as 12in/30cm below the ground. Brush off dirt and break off any tiny roots. Store in the same way as potatoes.

Soybeans may be easily shelled by boiling them for a few minutes. Quickly cool them in water, then pop the seeds out of the pod back into the pot for further cooking. After they have been shelled, they may be preserved by freezing.

COMMON, BUSH, AND POLE BEANS

This category includes snap, shell, and dry beans depending on the variety. Many older varieties may be first harvested as a snap bean, then as a shell bean, and finally as a dry bean. There are both bush and climbing varieties. The snap varieties are known as green beans, French beans, and string beans. The pods are harvested young, and eaten fresh or lightly cooked. The pods vary in thickness and length. They may be colored green, yellow, green with red spots, or other colors. The dry varieties fit into many categories including kidney, navy, and pinto.

SNAP BEAN VARIETIES

Garden of Eden A pole variety.
Kentucky Wonder A green pole bean.
Maxibel French Filet A tasty snap bean whose long slender pods are best picked quite young.
Purple Peacock A pole bean that is also harvestable as a dry bean.
Rocdor Yellow Wax Tasty yellow bush bean.
Royalty (Royal Burgundy Purple Red) A stringless variety. Its purple pods turn green when cooked.
Triomphe de Farcy Bush type with slender pods.
Wren's Egg A pole bean that is harvested in its snap state or allowed to mature to a dry bean.

SHELL BEAN VARIETIES

Cannelli Typically used for minestrone soup.
Borlotto Lingua de Fuoco Use as a shell or dry bean.
French Horticultural Archetypal shell bean.
Vermont Cranberry Grown as a dry bean, but makes a wonderful shell bean.

Dry bean varieties

Black Coco Ideal for black bean soup.

Black Turtle Also used for black bean soup.

Indian Woman Yellow Dry Bush variety that has been grown for more than 1,000 years.

Jacob's Cattle Ready for harvest within just eighty-eight days.

Old Fashioned Soldier Used for baking.

Runner beans

Runner beans are perennials that are grown as annuals, and prefer a cooler climate. The vines grow to 14ft/4.2m. Consider growing them up a trellis on the side of the house. They also tolerate some shade. This type of bean may be harvested as a snap bean, then a shell bean, and finally a dry bean. If snap beans are not continually picked,

Although the pods of dry beans are too fibrous to eat, the seeds are delicious. The seeds store well and are often made into wonderful soups.

production will dwindle, and the remaining pods will quickly begin to mature. Runner beans are also admired for their attractive flowers, which are edible.

Butler Tasty green pods.

Désirée Recommended garden variety.

Jack in the Beanstalk Grows to 20ft/6m.

Painted Lady Beautifully colored seeds.

Scarlet Runner Grown for its attractive orange-red flowers which attract hummingbirds.

Streamline Recommended garden variety.

Adzuki bean varieties

This type of bean is very high in protein. The immature seedpods may be eaten as snap beans, but more typically they are harvested in the fall and dried. Adzuki bean is one of the most important dried bean crops in Japan. Elsewhere in the world, all varieties are simply called 'Adzuki' when offered for sale. Be sure to harvest this type of bean before the pods break open and the seeds are lost.

Chickpea varieties

Also known as garbanzo beans, this type of bean has been in continuous cultivation for more than 2,000 years. The bushes produce small round seeds that are harvested as a shell bean and used pickled or lightly cooked. Chickpeas are also the major component of hummus.

Desi A good variety that is easy to grow.

Kabuli Dislikes cool spring temperatures.

Cowpea varieties

This bush type is grown for its dried seeds. They are also known as field peas, black-eyed peas, and cream peas. They prefer long hot summers.

Colossus Crowder Larger and earlier than 'Mississippi Silver'.

Magnolia Blackeye/California Black Eye Pea A variety with good flavor.

Available in a range of colors, the pods of snap varieties, such as 'Royalty' (left, top) or 'Rocdor Yellow Wax' (left, bottom), are harvested young and are eaten fresh or lightly cooked.

Mississippi Silver Creamy flavor when cooked.
Texas Pinkeye Popular garden variety.
Zipper Cream A very sweet-tasting variety.

FAVA BEAN VARIETIES

Also known as broad beans, fava beans are almost always in bush form, with a height of 24in–5ft/24in–1.5m. This cool-season type produces bean pods that can be used fresh as well as harvested as dry and shell beans. Some varieties are very cold hardy and can tolerate frost.

Banner Suitable for growing in very warm climates, but needs 140 days to reach maturity.
Extra Precoce a Grano Blanco (Early White Seeded) Suits cool climate areas.

HYACINTH BEAN VARIETIES

This climbing perennial, treated as annual, may reach 20ft/6m, and has edible immature pods. The seeds are most often dried and cooked, or used for sprouting. Choosing a daylight-neutral type is important for this sub-tropical bean. Its attractive flowers add ornamental interest in the garden. These beans may produce two crops in a season if there are twenty weeks between the last spring frost and the first fall frost. After harvesting the first crop, cut off the plant at the ground and harvest the second crop before winter. Hyacinth beans may be started inside and transplanted. Dwarf bush and climbing varieties are available.

LENTIL VARIETIES

Lentils are high in protein, fiber, and complex carbohydrates. The small bushes have pods that contain only one or two lentils. Weed the crop well or competition will devastate it. Harvest when the plants are damp, or many of the lentils will drop from the pods and be lost.

Brewer Yellow-seeded variety.
Crimson Produces small red seeds. Tolerant of less rainfall.
Indianhead Produces small black seeds.
Redchief Most commonly grown variety, which matures in ninety-five days.

LIMA BEAN VARIETIES

This type of bean is particularly sensitive to cold weather. The plants may be bushes, reaching 12ft/3.6m. The young pods are sometimes eaten but more often they are harvested as shell or dry beans. They require temperatures of more than 65°F/18°C to germinate. Some varieties are daylight sensitive, and may not produce well.

Fordhook Tolerates a wide variety of climates.

MUNG AND URD BEAN VARIETIES

The small, yellow seeds of mung beans are often used for sprouting and served in salads and in sandwiches. They may also be eaten dried or as shell beans. The pods are edible but unappetizing. Outside of southeast Asia, available varieties are simply referred to as mung or urd beans.

SOYBEAN VARIETIES

Soybeans are often pressed for cooking oil or are grown as snap beans. They are also made into tofu. The young tender pods are often boiled and served as a delicious appetizer. They are high in protein and provide good yields. They can be stored or frozen in the pods or shelled.

Amish Green Pleasant-tasting variety.

Black Jet An heirloom grown for its dried seeds.

Butterbeans Bears light green to yellow beans.

Garnet Popular garden variety.

Pride Select Yellow Very productive variety.

Tammany Popular garden variety.

TEPARY BEAN VARIETIES

The tepary beans are produced on bushes or vines and are useful for their high protein levels. They are dry beans that are used in soups or ground into flour. All cultivated varieties are bush types. Try 'Blue', 'Brown', 'White', or 'Ivory'.

WINGED BEAN VARIETIES

This type of bean is from southeast Asia and is grown primarily for the tuberous roots produced by many varieties. Treated as a perennial, it is a pole bean variety that produces long pods that are 1in/2.5cm wide containing large beans that are harvested as a dry bean. There has been a lot of publicity about this type recently because both the tuberous roots and beans are very high in protein. While potatoes have only 7 per cent protein, these tuberous roots have 20 per cent. The roots can be eaten raw but are more often cooked like potatoes. Young pods may be harvested as snap beans. In the fall, before the first frost, lift the tuberous roots gently with a garden fork. Store in a root cellar with high humidity. Choose a variety that produces a tuberous root; a few do not.

YARD-LONG VARIETIES

This sub-tropical Asian type has long pods that sometimes reach 30in/75cm long. Be sure to pick a daylight-neutral variety or yields will be small in colder climate areas. The seed pods are harvested young and are blanched or stir fried.

Asparagus The only variety readily available outside of Asia.

Soybeans are pressed for cooking oil or grown as a snap bean. The seeds (those of 'Blackjet' are shown above) are high in protein and provide good yields.

Peas *Pisum sativum*

Plant type Annual

Nutrition Excellent source of phytochemicals and vitamin C. Significant source of vitamin B1 and folic acid. Source of vitamin K, potassium, and fiber.

Uses Peas can be eaten fresh or cooked. They are suitable for drying and are easy to freeze. Snow and snap peas also have edible seed pods. Some peas are grown for their edible greens.

SITE AND SOIL

Peas do not require a high-nitrogen soil. Like beans, they collect atmospheric nitrogen and fix it into nodules on the roots that slowly release nitrogen into the soil. If peas have been grown in the garden before, the correct type of bacteria probably exists in the soil. If not, you will need to inoculate the seeds (see p. 218). Peas are a cool-weather crop suitable for spring sowing. Summer harvests are generally not abundant in areas with hot summers. Choose a sunny site that has been deeply cultivated with a lot of low-nitrogen compost worked in. Peas will not tolerate wet soil, so good drainage is essential. As with beans, it is important to rotate peas every year. Prepare the site further by providing a fence or trellis for the peas to climb. Many gardeners use stakes, but a better solution is to build a simple frame of bamboo and tie twine across.

SOWING

At the foot of the trellis, sow in a wide band (twenty-four seeds per 12in/30cm). Plant seeds ¾in/2cm deep. Begin planting in early spring as soon as the soil can be cultivated. Germination

Some varieties of pea need to be shelled while others have edible pods. Like all legumes, peas fix nitrogen and store it in nodules on their roots.

will be poor until the soil has reached 50°F/10°C. Protect seeds and seedlings in case of frost. For a fall harvest sow seeds two months before frost.

CARE AND MAINTENANCE

Peas will not tolerate drought, so keep the soil well drained but moist. Water at a rate of 2–3in/5–8cm a week unless there is a lot of rain. Mulch plants as they mature to keep roots cool, retain moisture, and control weeds.

Pests and diseases   Prone to pea root rot, powdery mildew and molds. Slugs and earwigs can decimate shoots; use barriers.

HARVEST

Pea greens may be harvested from selected varieties as needed. Snow peas, snap peas, and shelling peas are all ready for harvest in about fifty-five days, depending on variety.   Harvest shelling types and open the pods to reveal lush green seeds, which may be used fresh or frozen. The entire plant may also be harvested and hung in a warm place to dry for dried peas. Snap peas are typically harvested fresh and used immediately. They may also be shelled. Snap peas can be frozen in the pods. Snow peas are used fresh or quickly sautéed; they do not keep well.

SHELLING PEA VARIETIES

The shelling type has inedible pods, and the small round green seeds are harvested for use fresh or dried. Peas are the easiest vegetable to freeze and retain almost all their nutrition.

Maestro   A very reliable crop of sweet peas.

Tall Telephone   Freezes particularly well.

Thomas Laxon   Produces large dark green peas.

SNAP PEA VARIETIES

A unique type with edible pods and big seeds. This variety is sometimes shelled, but more often eaten like a green snap bean. Remove strings before cooking. Snap peas must be cooked.

Snap peas are the easiest vegetable to freeze and they retain almost all their nutrition when frozen. 'Sugar Snap', shown here, is a stringless variety.

Amish Snap   Prolific, but less sweet variety.

Cascadia   A bush variety resistant to some viruses and powdery mildew.

Sugar Snap   High-yielding, even in hot weather.

SNOW PEA VARIETIES

Also known as sugar peas, these are harvested for their edible pods when the seeds are very small. Remove the strings before eating.

Dwarf Grey Sugar   A sugar pea variety that provides delicious greens and edible lavender flowers that provide color interest in the beds.

Giant Dwarf Sugar   Short variety grown for its large pods.

Mammoth Melting Sugar   Sweet-tasting variety. Grows well as a fall crop too.

Onions *Allium cepa*

Plant type Biennial

Nutrition Excellent source of phytochemicals. Significant source of vitamin C. Source of vitamin A, calcium, iron, potassium, and fiber. Shallots are an excellent source of phytochemicals, and source of vitamins A and C, calcium, and iron.

Uses Harvested early as scallions or grown for their large round bulbs, eaten raw or cooked.

SITE AND SOIL

Onions prefer a rich soil with lots of compost worked in, and a pH over 6.5. Choose an open sunny site that has good drainage. Onions have low nitrogen requirements so do not plant on freshly manured ground. Onions are daylight sensitive. Some varieties require long days for the bulbs to enlarge in size and mature; others need

Once they have been harvested, dry onions in the sun for about ten days, ensuring good ventilation by laying them on a raised wire screen.

shorter days. Choose a variety suited to the location of the garden. Generally long-day varieties should be grown except when gardening near the equator.

SOWING

Onions are a cool season crop that grows best below 75°F/24°C. They require a long growing season to produce large bulbs for storage, but some may be harvested as scallions or spring onions in an immature state. While sets are planted directly in the garden as soon as the soil can be worked, it is best to start sowing indoors to achieve good results with seed.

One method that works particularly well is to plant three or four seeds in each soil block. As the bulbs mature, they push each other aside gently without getting damaged. By this method, four times more onions can be started from seed indoors without taking up any more space or requiring any additional effort. All the onions planted together should be harvested together. Sow in late winter to early spring indoors, and transplant out as soon as the soil can be worked.

Plant the seedling groups 6in/15cm apart. In long-season areas, sow directly in the garden, ½in/1cm apart and ¼in/0.5cm deep, as soon as the soil can be worked. Thin to 3in/8cm spacing by harvesting some of the seedlings as scallions.

Some varieties grow best when sown in fall for an early harvest the next year. However, this is only possible in mild-wintered areas. Onions grown from sets are much more likely to have diseases, so if you grow both from seed and sets, plant them in different areas of the garden.

CARE AND MAINTENANCE

Water regularly. Onions have shallow roots and require well-drained soil. They need 1in/2.5cm of water per week, either by rain or irrigation. Keep them well weeded, especially immediately after transplanting.

Pests and diseases Onion maggots, downy mildew, thrips, and onion white rot are the most common pests. If onion maggots are a problem, practice companion planting (see pp. 118–19). (If you introduce a few onion plants randomly throughout the garden, they will also deter pests affecting other plants.)

HARVEST

Harvest scallions as needed. Bulbs will begin to mature in about eighty days. Start harvesting and use immediately as they mature. Storage varieties should be left in the ground until the leaves die in the fall. Pull or lift the onions using a garden fork. Dry in the sun for about ten days, ensuring good ventilation. Do not let dry onions come into contact with the ground. The outer skins must be dry and papery before storing. Store onions at 32–42°F/0–5°C at low humidity. A cool upstairs room or attic is a good choice. Check stored onions regularly for neck rot; compost or use affected onions immediately.

RED- AND PURPLE-SKINNED VARIETIES
Italian Blood Red Bottle Spicy, attractive variety, but not suitable for long-term storage.
Rose de Roscoff A medium daylength variety with pink coloring.
Stockton Red Popular red onion that is grown for its sweetness.

SUMMER ONION VARIETIES
Certain varieties do not store well but produce delicious mini onions during the summer.
Purplette A glossy rich-tasting bulb.

WHITE-SKINNED VARIETIES
Fresno White Popular variety.
White Portugal Tasty variety that stores well.

Onion tops are bent over in the fall to help cure them before harvest and storage. If stored properly, you can be ensured a year-round supply.

YELLOW- AND BROWN-SKINNED VARIETIES
New York Early A tasty variety that produces well and is suitable for storage. Highly dependable and easy to cultivate.
Walla Walla Sweet Yellow Mild-tasting when eaten raw.

PICKLING ONION VARIETIES
Some cultivars are best when harvested about 1in/2.5cm in diameter. These onions are not dried for storage, but usually preserved by freezing or pickling. Sow directly in the garden and harvest them in about eight weeks.
Snow Baby A variety worth trying.

CHIVE VARIETIES

These perennials are grown for their round hollow grass-like tops. They have pinkish-purple blossoms that also make them a good choice for the ornamental garden. Soil requirements are the same as for storage onions. Chives can be grown from seed or divided from an existing patch. Once planted, chives generally spread and produce an edible attraction in the garden. Chinese chives have decorative star-like flowers and garlic-tasting leaves.

EGYPTIAN TOP ONION VARIETIES

These perennial onions produce a small bulb at the tip of their stems, above ground, where a flower might typically form. They are typically sown in the fall directly in the garden. They also may be harvested as scallions in the spring, but starting in mid-summer and extending well into fall, bulbs can be harvested from the tips of these plants. Pick when the tops begin to dry. Store by freezing. Cultivate in the same way as onions.

SCALLION VARIETIES

Also known as spring onions, most of these are perennial bulb onions harvested in the spring for their greens. Bunching onions are a bulbless type only grown for their greens. Welsh bunching is a perennial that can even be used like leeks when mature. Cultivation is identical to onions above.

Deep Purple Produces red-based and green-topped scallions all summer long.

Evergreen Hardy White A very tasty variety that is winter hardy.

SHALLOTS

These garlic-flavored onions form bulbs like onions, but have several smaller odd-shaped bulbs within. They are eaten raw or cooked and add a distinctive flavor that is much milder and more delicate than that of standard onions. The greens may also be harvested as scallions for salads. Stored bulbs can be broken apart into the smaller bulbs and planted in the spring to produce next year's crop.

Shallots are eaten raw or used in cooking to add a distinctive garlic-onion flavor that is much milder than that of standard onions.

Leeks *Allium porrum*

Plant type Biennial

Nutrition Significant source of vitamin C.

Uses Leeks have a delicate onion flavor and are particularly good in soups where they create a creamy texture.

SITE AND SOIL

Choose an open site and work compost into the soil to increase its moisture-holding ability. A deeply cultivated soil, with high-nitrogen levels is required. Work fresh manure into the soil three weeks before transplanting. Do not let leeks dry out in high temperatures.

SOWING

Start seeds indoors in late winter, eight to twelve weeks before the last spring frost. Leek seeds can be sown directly but with less successful results. Sow two to four seeds in each 2in/5cm soil block, and space the blocks 2in/5cm apart. Transplant when the seedlings reach 8in/20cm high; allow 9in/23cm between transplanted soil blocks. Place each soil block in a 6in/15cm deep hole in the bed and gently fill soil around the stem leaving about 2in/5cm of the plant visible above the soil.

CARE AND MAINTENANCE

Water around the seedlings and firm the soil against them gently after transplanting outdoors. This will help to blanch the stems. Leeks need regular and thorough watering until they are well established. Do not let the soil dry out during summer droughts, and keep the bed free of weeds by weeding regularly. Mulch to discourage weeds and retain moisture.

Pests and diseases Stem and bulb nematodes, onion maggots and a range of soil-borne mildew and fungus diseases.

HARVEST

Leeks are easy to grow but hard to store. Unless severe weather is expected, it is best to leave them in the ground until needed.

VARIETIES

American Flag Stores well in the garden.

Bleu de Solaise French heirloom with blue leaves that stores well through the winter in the ground.

King Richard Large, long plant of superb quality.

Scotland Hardy variety that tolerates 15°F/–10°C.

Varna A tall slender leek with good flavor. Often harvested early at a very small size.

Leek stems can be blanched by planting the seedlings deeply and mounding up the soil during the growing season. The flavor is best after a light frost.

Garlic *Allium sativum*

Plant type Perennial

Nutrition Excellent source of phytochemicals. Source of vitamins A and C, calcium, and iron.

Uses Grown for its bulb-like root. The green chive-like stems are tasty eaten fresh.

SITE AND SOIL

Choose a site with full sun and dig in compost. Good drainage is essential. Garlic tolerates a wide range of temperatures, but requires a cool period below 50°F/10°C for at least two months.

SOWING

Separate the head into cloves. Plant only those that are more than ½in/1cm in diameter. During the late fall, plant cloves with the pointed end up, and the root end (flat base end) down. In the coldest areas it may be necessary to delay planting until the early spring. The roots need to start forming before the ground freezes. Plant cloves 6in/15cm apart and 2in/5cm deep.

CARE AND MAINTENANCE

Little attention is needed in the growing season. If stiffneck varieties attempt to flower, pinch off the shoot. Water during the bulb-forming stage. As the bulb grows, it will push upward and out of the ground. Weed the bed regularly.

Pests and diseases Garlic is very hardy with few diseases and pests. Watch for onion maggots, downy mildew and onion white rot.

HARVEST

When the leaves start to die back and turn brown, lift the bulbs with a garden fork. Be careful not to damage the outer wrapping around the cloves. You can leave the plants in the ground for longer to increase size, but do not let them start

sprouting. Dry bulbs well in a dark, dry place with good air circulation. Trim the roots after drying. The necks can be braided and hung for storage or decoration. Garlic stores best at 40–50°F/4°–10°C, and keeps for nearly a year.

VARIETIES

The stiffneck garlics tend to sprout in storage but have a better flavor. The softneck types store better but have many more small cloves. Elephant garlic is much larger but has a very mild flavor.

German Extra Hardy A stiffneck variety with tasty dark red cloves.

New York White/Polish White A softneck type that is very winter hardy and productive.

Russian Red A stiffneck type that is very hardy and flavorful. A favorite of garlic connoisseurs.

When you find a variety of garlic that you like (a softneck variety is shown above) and that grows well in your garden, separate the heads and replant the cloves.

Asparagus *Asparagus officinalis*

Plant type Perennial

Nutrition Excellent source of phytochemicals and folic acid. Significant source of vitamins B1, B6, and C. Source of potassium, fiber, calcium, and iron.

Uses Tasty, tender shoots are eaten cooked.

SITE AND SOIL

Choose a sunny or partially shaded spot with good drainage. Dig a trench 12–18in/30–45cm wide and 12in/30cm deep. Using a garden fork, loosen the soil at the bottom of the hole. Add 2–3in/5–8cm of compost, then 1–2in/2.5–5cm of the topsoil. Dust heavily with bone meal. Using a garden fork, mix the compost, topsoil, and bone meal. Then add another inch of compost and another inch of topsoil and mix again. Every 18in/45cm, mound up the soil 2in/5cm high.

SOWING AND PLANTING

Prune any damaged roots, and soak the crowns in warm (95°F/35°C) water. Place a crown on each mound of soil and spread the roots evenly around. Cover with 2–3in/5–8cm of compost and gently pack down. Fill in with some of the remaining soil. Leave the remainder piled next to the trench.

CARE AND MAINTENANCE

During the first year, weed carefully around the growing stems, but do not harvest any, so that the asparagus can develop its root system. As the shoots grow, fill around them carefully, using all the soil from the pile next to the trench, until the soil is slightly mounded. Water regularly and mulch well. Cut back the ferns in the fall.

Pests and Diseases Rust, slugs, and asparagus beetles. Crown rot, a soilborne fungal disease, is best prevented by good drainage.

Asparagus is treasured for the tender shoots that appear in spring. Male and female plants are available, but the male plants are more productive.

HARVEST

Starting in the second or third year, cut small shoots in mid- to late spring. Always leave a few shoots to mature, and do not overharvest in the first three years. To harvest, bend a spear until it snaps, or use an asparagus knife to cut off the shoot below soil level.

VARIETIES

Martha Washington and **Mary Washington** are hardy disease-resistant varieties.

Purple Passion An FI hybrid that has purple spears.

Buckwheat *Fagopyrum esculentum*

Plant type Annual

Uses Grain is cooked or ground. Good for use as a green manure. Buckwheat attracts bees and other beneficial insects to the garden.

To grow as a green manure (see pp. 57–61), turn the earth right before sowing. Doing this disturbs weed seeds so that they do not have a competitive advantage over the buckwheat. Sow the buckwheat on the surface of the soil during the spring, summer, and early fall.

Buckwheat will not tolerate frost and needs thirty days to reach a useful state for green manure. Sowing may be accomplished by hand or with a simple hand-powered broadcast seeder, depending on the size of the plot. Rake gently over the plot if it is small, or if large, drag a dead tree branch over it to slightly cover the seed. If there is no rain forecast for the next week, irrigate with about 1in/2.5cm of water from an overhead sprinkler. Otherwise, do not weed or water (unless absolutely necessary), simply watch it grow. After the white or pink flowers form, turn the greens under and cultivate the soil.

To grow for a crop of grain, follow the instructions given above, but rather than turn the greens into the soil let the flowers go to seed. The seed should be hard and dry, but not so dry that it falls off the plants when touched. Harvest the entire plant.

The grain may be thrashed with a flail in the traditional method, or small harvests may be placed in a pillowcase or sack and beaten to separate the chaff from the seed. Leave the seed in a warm place to finish drying. It may then be stored for a very long time at room temperature. Grind or cook buckwheat according to use.

Buckwheat matures so quickly that three successive crops can be grown in a season to increase soil fertility. It attracts bees and other beneficial insects to the garden.

Rhubarb *Rheum* x *hybridum*

Plant type Perennial
Nutrition Source of vitamin C, calcium, and fiber.
Uses The stems are eaten cooked.

Rhubarb is among the earliest of crops, and may be harvested from late winter through to summer. Its stems are boiled or baked in pies and tarts.

Site and soil

Choose a site that is sunny and has good drainage. It is essential to spend a lot of time preparing the soil so that the rhubarb will produce a good harvest for the next twenty to forty years. The extra effort spent now will pay off with many years of bountiful harvests. Dig holes 36in/90cm apart. The holes should be very large, up to 36in/90cm in diameter. This may seem excessive but it is worthwhile. The removed soil should be mixed with compost at a ratio of two parts soil to one part compost. Backfill the hole, leaving a 12in/30cm diameter hole that is 2in/5cm deep. Rhubarb is hard to grow in very warm climates.

Sowing

Instead of buying rhubarb seed, it is much better to purchase crowns. Plant one crown in each prepared hole and fill around it with soil. Press gently to ensure good contact between the soil and the roots. Water generously after planting.

Care and maintenance

After the plants begin growing, apply a thick mulch to conserve moisture and discourage weeds. Over the years, adding a little compost followed by mulch will continue to feed the rhubarb and ensure a good harvest. The soil must not dry out, even when the plants are dormant. When flower stalks appear, remove them before bloom to encourage leaf stalk production. If a plant should become crowded with many small stalks, dig up the plant and divide it into two or three plants and replant as described above.

Pests and diseases Rhubarb is usually free of pests and disease. Watch for European corn borers, cabbage worms, and rhubarb curculio (a beetle). Diseases that might affect rhubarb are verticillium wilt, and crown rot. If a disease should occur, destroy the entire patch and start with resistant varieties elsewhere in the garden.

Harvest

Starting the second year, harvest the stems from late winter through summer. Twist and pull the stems when the leaves are fully developed.

Varieties

Canada Red Popular variety.
Victoria Best available variety because the stems never get woody.

Peppers *Capsicum* spp.

Plant type Annual

Nutrition Sweet peppers are an excellent source of phytochemicals and vitamin C. Hot peppers are an excellent source of phytochemicals. Both types are sources of vitamin A, potassium, and iron.

Uses Hot peppers add spiciness to dishes; sweet peppers are eaten fresh or baked. Their colorful fruits add ornamental interest in the garden.

SITE AND SOIL

Choose a site with full sun. Do not rotate with other members of this family. Work a lot of compost into the soil and ensure good drainage.

SOWING

Start seeds indoors six to eight weeks before transplanting. Be sure not to start them too early otherwise the seedlings will be rootbound and leggy. Pepper seedlings are very sensitive to their roots being disturbed. They may also suffer from damping off; therefore it is best to bottom-water seedlings. Start seedlings in 2in/5cm soil blocks. Seeds germinate best at 75°F/24°C. Sow two seeds to each block and cut the stem of the weaker seedling when two leaves develop. Reduce the temperature to below 70°F/21°C after germination. Transfer the seedlings into 4in/10cm pots if necessary before transplanting. Harden them off when the soil temperature is 60°F/15°C, usually two to three weeks after the last frost. Space the plants 18–24in/45–60cm apart, depending on variety.

CARE AND MAINTENANCE

On exposed sites, make sure the plants are shielded from wind. Almost all peppers are bushes and do not need staking. Pinch the tips of pepper plants to promote lateral growth and to encourage the plants to set fruit. Consistent moisture is essential to produce good sweet peppers. Hot peppers generally require more water, but any dry spells will usually result in much a hotter flavor. Water at a rate of 1in/2.5cm per week if there is insufficient rainfall. Weed as necessary. Apply a medium-strength nitrogen organic liquid fertilizer if the plants show little growth.

Pests and diseases Aphids, whiteflies, caterpillars, and spider mites. If the site does not have good drainage, root rot may be a problem.

Available in a wide range of bold colors and shapes, the fruits of sweet peppers are grown for their crisp, mild-tasting flesh.

Calcium deficiency may result in blossom end rot. If cutworms are a problem, sink a cardboard ring into the soil around the base of the plant.

HARVEST

The time to first harvest is affected by many variables, including variety and personal preference (not to mention the weather). But you should be able to start harvesting ten weeks after transplanting, and continue until frost. Begin harvesting hot peppers fifteen weeks after transplanting. They may be stored by drying, or making them into a liquid sauce. They do not store well fresh. Sweet peppers are best used fresh but may be refrigerated for up to three weeks. They do not can or freeze well.

When saving seeds from peppers, be sure to pick seeds from plants that were not grown near other varieties because there is a danger of cross-pollination. Cross-pollination may result in a hotter flavor in the mild sweet peppers.

HOT AND CHILI PEPPER VARIETIES

The hot peppers make extremely decorative plants, earning their place in the garden for looks as well as flavor.

Boldog Hungarian Spice Paprika pepper.

Caribbean Red Heirloom hot pepper.

Cayenne Long Slim Best variety for drying and grinding into a red pepper powder.

Early Jalapeño Popular in Mexican dishes.

Habanero An ultra-hot pepper that dries well and is commonly used in Jamaican "jerk" sauces.

Hungarian Yellow Wax Hot Produces fairly hot yellow banana-shaped fruits.

Numex Twilight Good display of colorful fruits held above the foliage.

Prairie Fire Attractive fruits.

Red Peter Pepper Heirloom variety grown for its novelty shape rather than its flavor.

Tabasco An attractive plant. Best known for the hot sauce made from its fruits.

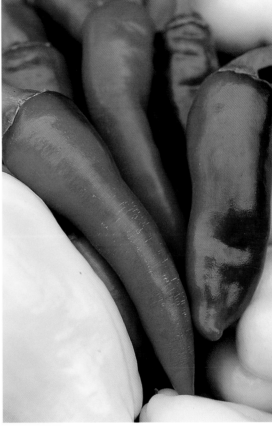

Hot peppers, such as 'Cayenne Long Slim' (above), are also ornamental, so even if you find them too hot for the table consider using them in the flower garden.

SWEET PEPPER VARIETIES

Albino Produces small cream fruit.

Antohi Romanian Bears long red fruits.

Aussie Red Bell-shaped pepper.

California Wonder Green-skinned variety that is popular for stuffing.

Chocolate Near brown-colored skin.

Giant White Cheese Non-bell-shaped variety.

Hungarian Slender, sweet-tasting fruits that mature from dark green to deep red.

Islander (F1) Excellent lavender pepper that grows well under adverse conditions.

Jupiter Very tasty variety.

Orange Sun Grown for its bold color.

Tomatoes *Lycopersicon esculentum*

Plant type Perennial grown as annual

Nutrition Excellent source of phytochemicals and vitamin C. Significant source of vitamin A. Source of potassium and iron.

Uses Fruits are eaten fresh in salads, or used for sauces, soups, and casseroles. Leaves are toxic.

SITE AND SOIL

Tomatoes prefer a very sunny site with rich fertile soil. I find that they are best grown in the same site every year, fed with a compost made mostly of tomato vines and leaves. Be sure not to plant tomatoes near any black walnut trees. The roots of these trees release a chemical into the soil that retards the growth of tomato plants.

SOWING

Sow seeds indoors no earlier than six to eight weeks before transplanting, otherwise the seedlings will be rootbound and leggy. They are also prone to damping off so water them from the bottom only. Using 2in/5cm soil blocks, sow two seeds to each block and cut the stem of the weaker seedling when they develop two leaves. Seeds germinate best at 80°F/27°C. After germination, reduce the temperature to below 70°F/21°C. Transfer the seedlings to 4in/10cm pots if necessary. Once the nights reach 45°F/7°C, harden off the seedlings. Space transplants 12–24in/30–60cm apart, depending on the variety. Plant them very deeply, leaving only 1–2in/2.5–5 cm of the plant visible above the soil. The buried stems will develop roots and help the seedlings to become established. Pinch off the leaves near the stem, if necessary. Shield plants from the wind and water them with a high-phosphate fertilizer after transplanting.

CARE AND MAINTENANCE

To avoid diseases, water the root area only and do not irrigate from above. In dry periods water each plant with about 2gal/7.6l a week. Apply a thick mulch to retain moisture and discourage weeds. Uneven watering – letting plants get very dry then watering heavily – can cause cracks that start at the stems of the fruit and extend down their sides. Stake non-bush plants to keep the fruit off the ground. A 5–7ft/1.5–2m tall stake will support the plant well. Some cherry tomatoes have very long vines: grow against a trellis or train up a twine.

You can prune tomatoes for a slightly larger

Tomatoes vary greatly in shape and color. This mixed basket includes 'Auriga', 'Sweet Million', golden cherry tomatoes, and green-striped 'Zebra'.

Tomatoes are perennials in very warm climates but are grown as annuals elsewhere. Varieties range from large beefsteak to the small cherry types shown here.

and earlier harvest. The fruits produced also tend to be slightly larger if the suckers growing between the main stem and the leaves are pinched out. The best time to prune is when the sucker is 2–3in/5–8cm long. In late summer, prune back the top of the main stem to a few leaves above the top fruits. This stops new growth and helps to mature any unripe fruit before cold weather arrives.

Pests and diseases These vary by area, so ask local gardeners for advice on what to look for. The tomato hornworm, aphids, leafhoppers, potato cyst nematodes, whiteflies, mosaic viruses, gray mold, foot rot, root rots, and blossom end rot may affect plants.

Harvest

Pick tomatoes as they ripen. Cherry tomatoes and some cold-season types are the first to bear fruit, whereas long-vine types take longer. Tomatoes do not refrigerate well. Use fresh or store them by drying or canning. In the fall, green tomatoes may be harvested for use straightaway, or the entire plant may be removed and hung in a warm place to encourage the green fruit to ripen.

Varieties

Aunt Ruby's German Green Bears green fruits.
Auriga Good-tasting variety, high in carotene.
Black Russian Grown for its excellent flavor.
Garden Peach Yellow soft-haired fruit.
Matt's Wild Cherry Great-tasting variety.
Micro Tom Suitable for growing in containers.
Principe Borghese Suitable for paste or drying.
Silvery Fir Tree Good ornamental display.
Sweet Million Productive climbing cherry variety.
Wonder Light Bears lemon-shaped fruit.
Zapotek Pleated Large, creased tomato.
Zebra Large, productive beefsteak variety with dramatic coloring but mild flavor.

Other varieties

Tomatilloes *(Physalis ixocarpa)* are small green (or orangeish) fruits that grow inside paper-like husks. To use, remove the husk and chop the fruit into small pieces.

De Milpa Suitable for storing.
Green Husk Ideal for making salsa.
Purple Prolific, flavorsome variety.
Toma Verde Produces small, pale green fruits.

'Black Russian' (back of picture) is as dramatic in appearance as it is superb in flavor. 'Wonder Light' (foreground) has curiously lemon-shaped fruit.

Eggplants *Solanum melongena*

Plant type Perennial grown as annual
Nutrition Source of vitamin C, iron, potassium, and fiber.
Uses Colorful fruits provide ornamental interest. Serve cooked.

SITE AND SOIL

Choose a site with full sun, and plant in a deeply cultivated bed that is well drained. Add lots of compost to the soil.

SOWING

Soak the seeds in water for 24 hours to encourage germination. Start seeds indoors in a slightly acidic compost (pH 6.0), six to eight weeks before planting them outside. Transplant to 3–4in/ 8–10cm pots when they get large. About a week before planting out, harden off the plants with cool 60°F/16°C water. After all danger of frost has passed in late spring, plant them outside spaced 18in/45cm apart.

CARE AND MAINTENANCE

Mulch and keep well watered. Weed as necessary until plants are established. For large fruits, limit the number of fruits to six per plant.
Pests and diseases Aphids are the worst enemy; however, verticilium wilt may cause problems.

HARVEST

Begin harvesting in late summer. Using pruners, remove fruit from the stem. Picking regularly will encourage production. Storage is possible for a few weeks at high humidity around 55°F/13°C.

VARIETIES

Black Beauty Grown for its taste and reliability.
Casper When small, fruits can be eaten unpeeled.
Diamond Bears slender, dark purple fruits.
Machiaw An Fı hybrid with long, thin fruits.
Rosa Bianca Purple-streaked fruits with a mild and sweet flavor.
Turkish Orange Small fruits with green veining.

Available in many colors and shapes, the white and light purple varieties of eggplant tend to be less bitter than the dark purple varieties.

Potatoes *Solanum tuberosum*

Plant type Perennial

Nutrition Excellent source of vitamin C. Significant source of vitamins B3 and B6, and iodine. Source of potassium and fiber. The only commonly available source of B3 and iodine.

Uses Cooked in a variety of ways, eaten hot or cold. Suitable for storing during winter.

SITE AND SOIL

Potatoes need fertile well-drained soil. Choose a sunny site and work plenty of compost into the soil. Potatoes will tolerate a wide range of soils but grow best where the soil is cultivated deeply and has a pH of 5.0–6.0. Potatoes are subject to soilborne diseases so it is essential to rotate this crop every year.

PLANTING

It is possible to grow potatoes from seed, but the results are most often unsatisfactory. The best way is to buy "double certified" seed potatoes. This means that they are certified to be organically grown as well as certified to be disease and virus free. After the first year's crop, save some in the root cellar to plant out the next spring.

Before planting seed potatoes, cut them into pieces about 1½in/3cm in diameter such that each portion has an eye. Let the pieces rest for a day for the cut sides to dry before planting. Small seed potatoes need not be cut. Potatoes tolerate mild frosts and cool soil. In early or mid-spring, plant the cut or whole seed potatoes so that their tops are 2–3in/5–8cm deep and are spaced about 12in/30cm apart. If the seed potatoes have already started to sprout, plant them with the sprouts pointing up. Firm the earth around the planted seed potatoes very gently. The sprouts will emerge from the ground in two to three weeks.

CARE AND MAINTENANCE

As the potatoes grow, weed as necessary. When the plants reach about 12in/30cm, hill up the soil around the bases of the plants to a height of 6in/15cm. Do this very gently so as not to disturb the roots or any tubers that may be forming. After hilling, apply a 1in/2.5cm mulch of straw or hay to deter weeds and conserve moisture. If the soil is not hilled around the bases of the plants, the potatoes may become visible and exposed to daylight. When this happens, the potatoes develop a greenish tinge; this area is toxic and should not be eaten. During dry spells, water at a rate of 2in/5cm a week. Check development of potatoes

Though most potatoes have white or yellow flesh, there are also red-, pink-, and even blue-fleshed cultivars. Combine several for a striking display at your table.

in early summer by digging up a small tuber. If they are too small in size or no tubers have developed, apply an organic liquid feed and check again in three or four weeks.

Pests and diseases Colorado potato beetles are the worst pest affecting potatoes. Row covers and hand picking are the best solution. There are many diseases that affect potatoes and prevention is the best solution. Ensure the bed has well-drained soil, plant only certified disease- and virus-free seed potatoes, and rotate the crop every year. Diseases to watch out for are blackleg, potato blight, ring rot, and scab. Insects that may affect potatoes are aphids, cutworms, flea beetles, and leafhoppers.

Hollow areas in tubers are caused by excessively rapid growth. To combat this, reduce watering and do not feed with any high nitrogen fertilizers. Speckle leaf is a disorder that causes dark spots on the leaves and is reported to be caused by high ozone levels in the air. If this problem occurs, choose a resistant variety.

Harvest

Young potatoes may be harvested as "new potatoes." They are ready for harvest during mid-summer. On rare occasions insects may attack a crop so vigorously that the best solution in that particular year is simply to harvest all the potatoes as new potatoes. Mature potatoes are ready for harvest when the leaves and stalks of the plants begin to turn brown and die back in the fall. Cut the stems off above the ground and let the potatoes remain in the soil for a week or two before lifting them with a garden fork. This will harden the skins of the potatoes and make it much easier for you to harvest them without damaging the skins. Harvest potatoes on a dry sunny day. Let them rest in the sun for an hour or two before storing them in a cool moist place. It is essential that they do not freeze while in storage otherwise they will spoil. New potatoes are best stored by

freezing, because they tend to spoil in a root cellar. Save some of the potatoes from the harvest to use in next year's planting.

Varieties

Alaskan Sweetheart A red-skinned variety with pink flesh. Best harvested as a new potato.

All Blue Purple-skinned variety with blue flesh. This variety stores very well in a root cellar throughout winter.

Dark Red Norland A red-skinned variety that stores better than most red potatoes.

Russet Nugget Popular variety that stores well.

Swedish Peanut A fingerling variety.

Yukon Gold An early maturing variety that keeps very well in storage.

Choose "double certified" seed potatoes, which are guaranteed to be both organic and free from viruses and diseases.

Celery *Apium graveolens*

Plant type Biennial

Nutrition Significant source of vitamin C and folic acid. Source of potassium and fiber.

Uses The stalks are usually eaten fresh or used in soups and stews. The leaves are typically used to flavor broth or are composted.

SITE AND SOIL

Choose a site that is not near parsnips as both crops may be attacked by celery flies. Rotating celery in the garden will discourage diseases and pests. Improve the soil's moisture-retaining ability by working in plenty of organic compost. Some varieties of celery need to be planted in trenches to blanch the stems. Prepare a trench measuring 11in/28cm deep and slightly more than 12in/30cm wide. Fill the bottom of the trench with a 2in/5cm layer of compost.

SOWING

Sow directly in the garden after all risk of frost has passed and thin to 9in/23cm spacing. Start sowing indoors ten weeks previous for an earlier crop, but check regularly for blistered leaves and other signs of disease. Do not plant too early because the plants are likely to bolt if temperatures drop below 50°F/10°C. To blanch traditional celery, either plant in trenches (see opposite), or wrap the stems loosely with heavy paper, such as corrugated cardboard or brown parcel paper, or use several layers of newspaper.

CARE AND MAINTENANCE

Celery requires consistent moisture. Water the plants regularly during drought at a rate of 1in/2.5cm per week. An organic liquid fertilizer applied one month after germination will be beneficial. Self-blanching varieties should be

Traditional celery has white, pink, or red stems that are blanched. Typical American varieties have green stems and are not blanched.

mulched with a thick layer of straw to help retain moisture in the soil.

Pests and diseases Celery flies and slugs may affect celery. Fungal leaf spots may occur in younger plants. Remove all infected leaves immediately, including those that are on the ground, and compost them. Boron deficiency and cabbage root maggots may also affect celery.

HARVEST

Using a garden fork, lift self-blanching varieties and paper-wrapped varieties before the first frosts. Plants are usually ready for harvest within fourteen weeks. Store in a high humidity location that is cool but protected from freezing. If the celery is planted in a trench, its harvest season is extended well into the winter. To store for harvest through the winter and spring, build a straw or hay bale house over the trenched plants. Put a bale at each end of the row, and bales along both sides. Fill the gap above the plants with loose hay or straw, cover with boards and sit bales on top of the boards. Celery may be stored in the refrigerator for five weeks if kept slightly moist.

TRENCH VARIETIES

Traditional celery has white, pink, or red stems that are blanched. The red stem varieties have the best taste and hardiness, but require blanching to ensure protection from sunlight. Planting in a trench works best, but is the most labor intensive. Tie together the stems loosely with twine and fill in the trench gradually as the plants grow. When the trench is filled, you may need to add a collar of paper, or better yet heap up the soil to form a mound around the growing plants.

Gewone Snij (Cutting Celery) Tolerates frost and overwinters well with hay bale protection.

Giant Pink Good soupmaking variety.

Groene Pascal Grown for its taste.

Pink Plume Suitable for use in soups.

Red Stalk Suitable for storing. It has a strong celery flavor and is as good fresh as it is in soups.

Tall Utah 52/70 Flavorsome variety.

Zwolse Krul Ideal for soupmaking.

SELF-BLANCHING VARIETIES

Typical North American varieties have green stems and are not blanched.

Galaxy Grown for its good flavor, this variety can be harvested over a long period.

Gigante Dorato 2 (Golden Self-blanching) Matures early and is popular with gardeners.

Latham (Latham Self-blanching) A wonderfully tasty variety with yellow stems.

HOW TO BLANCH CELERY

1 *Dig a trench one spade deep and 12in/30cm wide. Line the bottom with 2in/5cm of compost. Plant seedlings 9–12in/23–30cm apart, or sow seeds directly.*

2 *In mid-summer, bundle plants together, wrap with thick paper and fill soil around stalks. This is done to blanch most varieties. Fill to the bottom of the leaves.*

3 *As the plants grow, mound up the soil every few weeks. Always leave the foliage visible above the soil. Slope the soil away from the plants to drain off rain.*

Carrots *Daucus carota*

Plant type Biennial
Nutrition Excellent source of phytochemicals and vitamin A. Source of vitamins Bs, C, D, E and K, and potassium.
Uses Roots are eaten fresh in salads or cooked.

SITE AND SOIL

Carrots prefer deeply cultivated soil that is loose and sandy. Heavy soils may create oddly shaped roots that are more difficult to harvest.

SOWING

Directly sow in garden beds in closely spaced rows about 1in/2.5cm apart. As soon as the soil has warmed and is workable, begin sowing in early spring and continue through mid-summer for a continual harvest.

CARE AND MAINTENANCE

Weed regularly until the carrots are well established; the tops will discourage weed growth.

Do not overwater or let the soil become soggy.
Pests and diseases Carrot rust flies are attracted by the scent of the foliage, so be sure to compost harvested tops and thinnings. Like parsnips, boron deficiency may be a problem. To prevent blights, use a three-year crop rotation.

HARVEST

Once the carrots display a good bright color (about eleven weeks), they may be harvested by lifting with a fork or pulling by the tops. Store in buckets in sand with the tops removed or leave in the garden. Carrots store best in a cool dry conditions. Baby carrots may be harvested to thin the bed and they taste delicious.

VARIETIES

Chantenay Good for storage.
Oxheart Thick-rooted variety suitable for storage.
Purple Dragon Source of rare phytochemical.
Scarlet Nantes Smooth long-rooted variety.
Thumbelina Small, round apple-shaped roots.

The taste of organically grown carrots is notably superior to those not grown organically. 'Chantenay à Coeur Rouge 2' (left) stores well.

Parsnips *Pastinaca sativa*

Plant type Biennial

Nutrition Significant source of vitamin C and folic acid. Source of potassium and fiber.

Uses Roots are boiled or added to soups, stews, and casseroles.

SITE AND SOIL

Parsnips like a loose and deeply cultivated soil. Heavy soils should be mixed with liberal amounts of compost. Small and deformed roots are likely to occur in heavy soils.

SOWING

Sow seeds in early or mid-spring, spaced 1in/2.5cm apart, sown ½in/1cm deep in rows closely spaced (8–12in/20–30cm apart depending on variety). Mark the row well for easier weeding before germination. The seed is very slow to germinate, taking about three weeks. Ensure the seeds you sow are fresh because germination rates of seeds stored for more than a year are very low. Thin seedlings to 2–3in/5–8cm. Do not allow soil to dry out during the germination period.

CARE AND MAINTENANCE

Weed as necessary until established. Take care not to overwater the plants.

Pests and diseases Try to choose a canker-resistant variety, or plant a little later to minimize canker damage.

HARVEST

Depending on the variety, parsnips are ready to harvest about 105–120 days after planting. To harvest, lift with a garden fork. If harvesting in the fall, mow the tops first. Following a heavy frost in the fall, roots may be harvested and stored in a root cellar. They keep best near freezing with high humidity. Better yet, leave them in the garden over winter and harvest in early spring before any growth occurs. If growth begins the center of the root will be woody. To save seeds, leave a few parsnips in the ground during winter, and let them grow the next spring. Parsnips are pollinated by insects and the seeds can be harvested in the fall.

VARIETIES

Hollow Crown Smooth, slender root with white flesh that keeps its texture in stews.

HAMBURG/TURNIP-ROOTED PARSNIP

A variety of parsley that is grown for its roots, which are used just like parsnips in cooking. Its cultivation is the same as for parsnips.

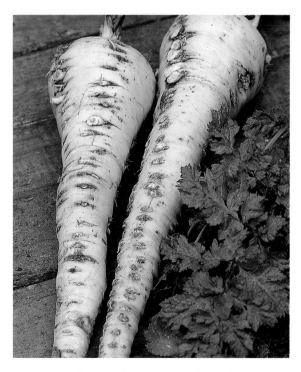

Parsnips, such as 'Hollow Crown' (above), become very sweet when stored in the ground during winter because sugars start to form as fuel for the spring growth.

Minor Salad Vegetables

Amaranthus (Amaranthus spp.) Grown for its light green oval leaves. Amaranthus is also known as Indian or African spinach because it can tolerate growing in warm conditions. This plant prefers to grow in high-humidity locations. Not cold hardy.

Orach (Atriplex hortensis) A colorful salad ingredient, which may have green, yellow-green or red leaves, depending on variety. Orach tolerates hot weather but suffers damage from frost. Direct seed 2in/5cm apart, thinning to 6in/15cm. Harvest in forty days when plants reach 12in/30cm tall.

Tolerant of a wide range of soils, mache or corn salad is invaluable during fall and winter for providing tasty fresh greens for the kitchen table.

Mustard (Brassica juncea) Grown for its spicy seedling leaves and beautiful yellow flowers. This cool season crop bolts quickly in warm weather. Sow seeds 1in/2.5cm apart and harvest in as little as three weeks. Mustard makes a wonderful cover crop, adding green manure to the soil quickly. Be sure to turn it under before it goes to seed or there will be more mustard than one can eat.

Arugula/Rocket (Eruca vesicaria var. sativa) Also known as rucola or roquette, this plant is of Mediterranean origin. The spicy leaves are used in salads. Arugula prefers cool climates and grows well in a cold frame or greenhouse in winter.

Shungiku (Glebionis coronaria) Also known as edible chrysanthemum. Delicious in salads, this green is sown ½in/1cm apart. Harvest when the leaves are 4–8in (10–18cm) tall.

Cress (Lepidium sativum) A fast-growing plant that runs to seed quickly in hot weather. Its seedling leaves are harvested for salads. Grow it in a cold frame in winter and use it to fill spaces between larger vegetables like beans or tomatoes before they mature. Harvest ten days after sowing by cutting the leaves. The roots will regrow for additional cuttings.

Miner's Lettuce (Montia perfoliata) A cold hardy plant with heart-shaped leaves that can be eaten fresh in salads or cooked like spinach. Can be grown all winter in mild climates or in cold frames. Direct seed 2in/5cm apart and harvest leaves continually. Miner's lettuce can self-seed. Harvest leaves after forty days.

Minutina/Erba Stella (Plantago coronopus) This is the most cold hardy salad plant for winter.

Flowerbuds are also edible. Sow ½in/1cm apart and begin harvesting in fifty days. Leave roots to regrow another crop.

Purslane *(Portulaca oleracea)* The yellowish green leaves are used fresh in salads or cooked. Sow 1in/2.5cm, apart during spring after any risk of frost has passed, and begin harvesting in fifty days. Always leave a few leaves in the ground when harvesting so that the plant can grow and produce another crop. Check regularly for slugs which can cause severe damage.

Watercress *(Rorippa nasturtium-aquaticum)* A spicy leaved perennial used in salads and soups. Prefers a moist well-watered part of the garden. Place stems of leaves in water to root, then plant outside. May be grown in a pot sitting in a dish of water. Harvest leaves as needed.

Sorrel *(Rumex acetosa)* Early spring greens that add a lemon flavor to salads or soups. Direct seed in the garden in early spring.

Dandelion *(Taraxacum officinale)* The tender young leaves are used raw in salads. Blanching can prevent bitterness. The flowers and roots are also edible. Harvest from your lawn.

New Zealand Spinach *(Tetragonia tetragonioides)* A 2ft/60cm high, spreading plant with pointed leaves that may be cooked or used raw in salads. It tolerates heat but is sensitive to frost. To assist germination, soak in warm water for twenty-four hours before planting. Harvest after fifty days.

Mache/Corn salad *(Valerianella locusta)* This hardy annual grows in a wide range of soils to provide greens in fall and winter. Sow in the garden 1in/2.5cm apart and keep moist. Harvest leaves in twelve weeks and the roots will produce a second crop. Grows well indoors in winter.

SALSIFY AND SCORZONERA

Salsify *(Tragopogon porrifolius)* A hardy biennial grown for its roots which are similar to scorzonera. The roots, young leaves, and flowerbuds are eaten cooked. The purple flowers are attractive in a flower garden. Cultivation is the same as for carrots; however, salsify roots are best stored at high humidity.

Scorzonera *(Scorzonera hispanica)* A hardy biennial with black-skinned, slender roots. They have yellow or white flowerheads. The cultivation is the same as for carrots, but store roots at high humidity. Scorzonera also needs a longer season to produce good-sized roots. They may be overwintered in the ground in mild climates.

The dark-fleshed roots of scorzonera are prepared in the same way as potatoes. Their edible yellow flowers can also be used to decorate dishes.

Figs *Ficus carica*

Plant type Deciduous bush

Nutrition Good source of calcium. Significant source of iron, phosphorus. Source of vitamins A and C, potassium, and fiber.

Uses Fruits are often made into jams and jellies as well as having many uses fresh in the kitchen.

SITE AND SOIL

Choose a protected site and be prepared for the tops to die back. In cold climates, figs can be grown under glass or against a protected sunny wall. They dislike soil that is high in nitrogen, as fruiting will be poor. Mulch the roots heavily or dig up and bury entire plants in a trench (known as laying down) during winter.

CARE AND MAINTENANCE

Remove heavy mulches in the spring. Thin fruits to encourage a crop of good-sized fruits. Prune dead wood in spring just before growth begins. Figs are one of the rare fruits that do not need pollination to set fruit.

Pests and diseases Figs are rarely affected by pests and diseases. Cover ripening fruits with close-woven netting to keep birds away. In areas prone to gopher damage, plant the roots in protective underground cages.

HARVEST

In warm climates figs can bear two crops in a growing season. Hand-pick the fruits just as they start to droop on the stem. Preserve figs by drying.

VARIETIES

Brown Turkey Tolerates cold climates but will produce two crops a year in warm areas.

Desert King Suitable for areas with cool winters.

Lattarula Produces good-quality fruits and will grow in varying climates and soils.

The large, sweet fruits of the fig are a good source of calcium. Except where the climate is very warm, fig trees need to be grown under glass or trained against a protected sunny wall.

Quinces *Cydonia oblonga*

Plant type Deciduous tree or bush

Nutrition Reliable scientific data unavailable.

Uses Raw quinces are usually unpalatable. Jellies and jams are often made from the fruits and the juice can be added to apple cider.

SITE AND SOIL

Quinces are hardy in a wide range of climates and soil types. They grow particularly well on the bank of a pond or stream. Plant quinces in a spot that is protected from cold winds.

CARE AND MAINTENANCE

Mulch well to conserve moisture. A seaweed solution may be used as a foliar feed. Prune dead wood in winter. Many varieties sucker from the roots creating a bush; quince may be pruned to maintain a tree shape. The fruits are self-fertile.

Pests and diseases Quinces are rarely affected by pests and diseases. If you notice fireblight, prune off the affected branches.

HARVEST

Harvest in the fall and store separate from other fruits. They prefer to be stored in a cool place with good air circulation.

VARIETIES

Aromatnaya A variety that can be eaten fresh.

Contorted Valued for its beautiful pink flowers in the spring and unusual twisted form.

Harvan Bears sweet fruits with white flesh.

Smyrna An old variety with tender yellow fruits.

Valued in the flower garden as ornamental small bushes or trees, quinces are delicious when cooked. The raw fruits are usually unpalatable.

ROSE
ROSACEAE

Apples *Malus domestica*

Plant type Deciduous tree
Nutrition Excellent source of phytochemicals
Significant source of vitamin C. Source of vitamin
A, iron, and fiber.
Uses Some apples are best eaten fresh; others are
best cooked or pressed for cider or juice.

SITE AND SOIL

Apples will grow in a wide range of soils and
climates. Be sure to choose a variety that is hardy
in your climate and a rootstock that is compatible
with your soil type. Apples need to experience cold
weather in winter or they will not bear fruit. Some
dwarf varieties may be grown in containers. There
are hundreds if not thousands of varieties and two
are needed for cross-pollination. In the small
garden it may be wise to have only one tree and
graft several varieties onto different branches. In
this way they can cross-pollinate each other and
the gardener can have several varieties without
taking up a large amount of space in the garden.

CARE AND MAINTENANCE

Weed in the early spring, apply organic fertilizers
if necessary, and then mulch around the base of
the tree. During the first four years after
transplanting, supplemental water may be

*Apple trees are easy to grow and their fruits offer a
wonderful source of nutrition. The blossoms provide
floral interest in spring.*

necessary. Consistent moisture during the four years after transplanting will result in an earlier crop by up to three years. Water is usually the limiting growth factor in fruit trees. Protect the trunks from rodent damage before winter. Prune trees during winter or early spring (see pp. 164–7).

Pests and diseases Apple maggots or codling moths bore holes in the fruits. Aphids and mildews, canker, and scab may affect the trees.

HARVEST

Early varieties do not generally keep well and should be used immediately. Mid-season and late varieties can be stored in a root cellar or eaten fresh. Leave late varieties on the tree as long as possible before storing and take great care not to bruise them.

CIDER-MAKING VARIETIES

Baldwin Traditional tasty variety.

Herefordshire Redstreak Produces strong ciders and liquors.

Westfield Seek No Further Ideal for eating fresh, for cider-making, or for cooking.

COOKING VARIETIES

Cortland Good in pies and apple sauce.

Macintosh One of the most popular apples for cooking, eating fresh, or for cider-making.

EARLY VARIETIES

Chenango Strawberry Beautifully colored.

Duchess of Oldenburg Popular for cooking or for making cider.

Lowland Raspberry Hardy variety that is best eaten fresh.

LATE VARIETIES

Cornish Gilliflower Produces one of the finest tasting apples.

Cox's Orange Pippin An excellent keeper with a good flavor.

Heirloom apple varieties like the cooking variety 'Westfield Seek No Further', above, are being reintroduced because of their unique flavor.

ROOTSTOCK VARIETIES

Antanovka Full-sized tree that suits heavy soils.

Budagovski 9 (Bud-9) Produces a 9ft/2.75m tree. Bud-9 on Bud-118 produces a superb semi-dwarf tree of approximately 12ft/3.6m.

Budagovski 118 (Bud-118) A semi-standard tree (about 22ft/7m), depending on the variety grafted.

Poland 22 Mini-dwarf that requires staking but may be used as an interstem on 'Antanovka' for a mini-dwarf without staking.

Ranetka Full-sized tree that suits light soils.

OTHER VARIETIES

Almata Pink-tinted variety that can be used to make an unusual-colored apple sauce.

Maiden's Blush Produces a yellow apple that is suitable for drying.

Winter Red Flesh Produces fruits with attractive pink flesh.

ROSE
ROSACEAE

251

Apricots *Prunus armeniaca*

Plant type Deciduous tree

Nutrition Excellent source of vitamin A. Significant source of vitamin C. Source of potassium, calcium, and iron.

Uses Apricots are wonderful eaten fresh; they also taste good when dried. They make delicious jam.

SITE AND SOIL

This early season fruit usually grows on small trees, which are suitable for compact city gardens. Apricots need to be well-protected from frost because they flower early, from late winter onward. Consider fan-training the tree against a wall for added protection against spring frosts. Some varieties are very cold hardy while others can tolerate very warm conditions. Choose a variety that best suits your climate. Plant in a sheltered site with good drainage and a light loam soil. Heavy soils will need to have plenty of compost incorporated.

CARE AND MAINTENANCE

Weed the site in the early spring, and feed with an organic fertilizer if necessary. Apply a thick layer of mulch around the base of the tree. It may be necessary to thin fruits to produce a better crop. Prune any dead wood in winter. Apricots are generally self-fertile but will bear more heavily with cross-pollination.

Pests and diseases Birds are the worst pest, attacking fruit as it ripens. Protect the fruits from birds and wasps with nets. Aphids and scale may be a problem. Canker and borers affect apricots.

HARVEST

Apricots are enjoyed at their best when picked ripe and eaten immediately. They may be dried for delicious treats that can be stored all year.

VARIETIES

Blenheim Produces large sweet fruits and is suitable for drying.

Harglow A late-blooming variety which shows some resistance to diseases.

Manchurian Apricot A seedling that produces wonderful fruit.

Apricots are an excellent source of vitamin A. The compact size of many apricot trees makes them ideal for growing in small city gardens.

ROSE
ROSACEAE

Cherries *Prunus avium/Prunus cerasus*

Plant type Deciduous tree
Nutrition Excellent source of phytochemicals.
Good source of vitamin C and fiber.
Source of vitamins A and B2, iron, and calcium.
Uses Sweet cherries are for eating fresh. Sour
cherries are most often used in cooking.

SITE AND SOIL

Cherries need well-drained soil that is high in
nutrients and has good moisture retention, as the
fruits need plenty of water. Open up heavy soils by
incorporating plenty of compost before planting.
It is easiest to grow cherries in warm dry climates;
however they need to experience cold weather in
winter otherwise they will not bear fruit. Sour
cherries tend to be more cold hardy. Some cherry
trees have a large spread (up to 30ft/9m). If your
garden cannot accomodate a fully grown tree, opt
for a dwarf variety.

CARE AND MAINTENANCE

Weed in the early spring and apply organic
fertilizers if necessary. Mulch around the base of
the tree. Prune in winter or early spring to remove
any dead or diseased wood. Use netting to protect
the fruits from birds. Cherries are not self-fertile,
therefore two varieties are needed to set fruit.
Pests and diseases Birds can plunder the fruits a
few days before harvest. Bacterial canker and
viruses may also affect trees.

HARVEST

Ensure that the tree has consistent moisture in the
last few weeks before harvest. Too much moisture
can result in fruit that splits from swelling, while
too little moisture may result in shriveled fruit and
reduced storage time. Harvest the cherry clusters
by hand, detaching them by the stalks.

Cherries are much loved by birds, so protect them with nets or bird scarers to make sure that you get to enjoy the crop of juicy, glossy cherries when they are ripe.

ROOTSTOCK VARIETIES

Mazzard The most common rootstock for
standard-sized trees.
Nanking Dwarf tree, up to 10ft/3m tall.

SWEET CHERRY VARIETIES

Bing Established favorite with a great flavor.
Royal Ann Bears juicy light-yellow fruit.

TART CHERRY VARIETIES

Montmorency Suitable for pie-making.
Morello An English variety of tart cherry that is
sweet enough when ripe to eat fresh.

Plums *Prunus domestica*

Plant type Deciduous tree

Nutrition Significant source of vitamin C. Source of vitamin A, potassium, and fiber.

Uses Plums are eaten fresh or dried, made into jams and jellies, and used in cooking. Prunes are the dried plums, in which the nutrients and flavor are concentrated.

SITE AND SOIL

Plums are hardy in a wide range of climates. Some varieties are able to withstand very cold winters. They grow well in heavy soils and can tolerate damp, clay soils. Plums should be planted in a sheltered site that will protect the spring blossoms from damage by frost. Alternatively, fan-train the tree against a warm wall.

CARE AND MAINTENANCE

Plums require little care yet produce a large crop. Weed in the early spring, fertilize if needed, then mulch around the base of the tree. Prune in winter as necessary. Most plums are not self-fertile; two varieties are required for cross-pollination.

Pests and diseases Plums are affected by many diseases and the best defense is to supply optimal growing conditions and to practice good hygiene. Practice good sanitation by removing any windfalls during the fall and by harvesting all remaining fruits on the tree before winter. This helps to keep brown rot and gray mold at bay. Bacterial leafspot and apple maggots may be a problem. Hang up a sticky red ball, which looks like an apple, to attract and trap the pests.

HARVEST

Plums do not store well. Pick them when ripe and use immediately. Or, if your climate is dry, you can leave late-maturing plums to dry on the tree.

ROOTSTOCK VARIETIES

American Plum A hardy full-sized tree.

Manchurian Plum May be used without grafting to produce fruit for wildlife.

PLUM VARIETIES

Assiniboine Extremely hardy variety.

Early Italian Excellent self-fertile fruit.

Greengage Self-fertile, small green fruits.

Stanley Grown for its large, dark blue fruits.

Superior Matures quickly and is a good pollinator to other varieties.

There are many varieties of plum and they come in a wide range of sizes and colors. The late dark-skinned plums are the sweetest.

ROSE
ROSACEAE

Peaches *Prunus persica*

Plant type Deciduous tree
Nutrition Significant source of vitamin C.
Source of vitamin A and fiber.
Uses Fruits are eaten fresh, or made into jam.

SITE AND SOIL

Peaches need well-drained yet moist soil that is high in nutrients. Heavy soils should be opened up by incorporating lots of compost. Be sure to grow a variety that is hardy in your climate. Choose a sheltered site that will protect the delicate blossoms from damage by late spring frosts.

CARE AND MAINTENANCE

Weed in the early spring and apply an organic fertilizer if necessary. Apply a layer of mulch around the base of the tree. Some varieties are self-fertile, others require cross-pollination. Hand pollination may be required with peaches. Thin the peaches to encourage a crop of good-sized fruits. Protect trunks from rodent damage before winter. Prune trees during winter.

Pests and diseases Peach leaf curl is the most common problem. It defoliates and kills trees. Small trees can be covered with a net to protect from birds and wasps; protect individual fruits on large trees in the same way. Earwigs may also attack fruit.

HARVEST

Let the fruit ripen completely before harvesting. Peaches do not keep well and should be used immediately. The fruit may be canned in a light syrup for later use.

ROOTSTOCK VARIETIES

Montclair Very hardy rootstock.
Siberian C Cold-hardy rootstock that itself

Nectarines are very closely related to peaches and require the same growing conditions. Unlike peaches, nectarines are always fuzzless.

produces good fruits. Because it is a seedling, the fruit will not be as uniform as cultivated varieties.

CULTIVATED PEACH VARIETIES

Frost Curl-resistant variety.
MP1 Curl-resistant variety.
Red Haven Grows well in short seasons if there is sufficient warmth.
Reliance The most cold-hardy cultivated peach.

NECTARINE VARIETIES

Close relatives of peaches, nectarines have the same cultural requirements, but are less hardy.
June Glo Tolerates mild wet climates.
Merricrest Self-fertile, cold-hardy variety.
Red Gold Produces a good crop of medium-sized fruits but may require shelter in cold winters.

Pears *Pyrus communis*

Plant type Deciduous tree
Nutrition Significant source of vitamin C.
Source of calcium, potassium, and fiber.
Uses Eaten fresh or used in pies and desserts.

SITE AND SOIL

Pears are easy to grow and will tolerate a wide range of soils. The European type tends to be more hardy than Asian types *(Pyrus pyrifolia)* and matures in a shorter season. Look for a variety that is hardy in your climate. Plant trees in a location that protects the early blossoms from frost. The graft unions may be planted below the soil level for a full-sized tree; some European pears grow best with the graft below the soil level.

There are two basic types of pear – European, such as 'Williams' Bon Chrétien' (above), and the rounded Asian, which generally requires warmer climates.

CARE AND MAINTENANCE

Weed in the early spring, apply organic fertilizers if necessary and then mulch around the base of the tree. For a crop of good-size fruits, thin the shoots in spring. Prune dead branches during winter. Pears can be pruned in summer if necessary, but late season pruning can result in lots of vegetative growth that may die back in a harsh winter. Pears usually require cross-pollination but some varieties are self-fertile.

Pests and diseases Mealy fruit arises when fruits ripen in very warm or cold weather. Open-center pruning can help to avoid fireblight and scab. Pear decline is a disease that causes the leaves to wilt; trees dry out and can die within a season. Protect trees from rodent damage before winter.

HARVEST

Handpick the fruits before they are fully ripe, just as soon as they will easily detach from the tree. If left on the tree to ripen the flavor becomes unpalatable. Pears keep well in a root cellar, often until late winter. Store them apart from apples.

ROOTSTOCK VARIETIES

European Pear The most common rootstock, resulting in a full-sized tree.
OH Shortens a tree by one-half to three-quarters. It is resistant to fire blight and pear decline.

PEAR VARIETIES

Beurré Giffard A cold-hardy variety.
Kosui Produces small yellow fruits. Grows better in cool damp climates than other Asian varieties.
Singo A very sweet Asian pear with yellow skin and white flesh.
Williams' Bon Chrétien An early to mid-season variety. The fruit is excellent eaten fresh or canned.

Walnuts *Juglans* spp. **and Hickories** *Carya* spp.

Plant type Deciduous tree

Nutrition Walnuts are an excellent source of phytochemicals and a significant source of vitamin E. Source of vitamin C, folic acid, iron, copper, potassium, phosphorus, and fiber. Hickories are a source of vitamins B3, B6, folic acid, potassium, copper, iron, magnesium, phosphorous, and fiber.

Uses Nuts are eaten fresh, baked in cakes, or as crunchy toppings. They are also ground for flour.

SITE AND SOIL

Walnut trees may reach maturity at 60–150ft/18–45m depending on variety. They grow best in heavy soils. Light soils should be amended with lots of compost. Keep the soil moist but not waterlogged. Walnuts usually require cross-pollination to produce well.

CARE AND MAINTENANCE

Walnut trees require very little care. Prune any dead branches in winter.

Pests and diseases Watch for squirrels stealing nuts at harvest time.

HARVEST

Collect the nuts promptly as they drop in the fall. The green covering over the nut is sticky and stains; remove it before drying the nuts.

VARIETIES

Heartnut (Juglans ailanthifolia var. cordiformis) A good nut producer, with tropical-looking leaves.

Butternut (Juglans cinerea) Produces sweet nuts. Prone to disease in North and South America.

Black Walnut (Juglans nigra) A hardy tree, but its roots produce a harmful chemical (see p. 119).

Carpathian Walnut (Juglans regia) Noted for the beautiful shape of the tree.

HICKORIES

The pecan, shagbark, and shellbark are all long-lived varieties of hickory *(Carya* spp.), which produce tasty nuts. Pecans grow better in dry locations than shagbarks and shellbarks, which thrive in humid conditions.

Northern Pecan (Carya illinoenis) Able to withstand the cold winters of the north. It requires about 130 days to ripen nuts. Produces small nuts with good flavor.

Shagbark (Carya ovata) A beautiful tree reaching 90ft/27.5m. It takes many years from planting until the first harvest, perhaps as long as twenty years, but is well worth the wait.

Shellbark (Carya laciniosa) A very hardy and fast-growing tree that produces large nuts.

When stored in a dry place, walnuts will keep for more than a year, ensuring that you have a steady supply to enjoy at the table.

WALNUT
JUGLANDACEAE

Hazelnuts *Corylus* spp. **and Chestnuts** *Castanea* spp.

Plant type Deciduous tree or bush

Nutrition Source of vitamins A, C, and E, folic acid, potassium, calcium, magnesium, and phosphorous.

Uses The nuts can be eaten fresh, dried or ground.

SITE AND SOIL

The term hazelnuts refers to hazels and filberts. Hazelnuts tolerate poor soil conditions and will grow in most climates. They suit hedgerows and wet areas. Hazels are smaller than other nut trees, forming bushes with a height/spread of 15–20ft/4.5m–6m, and produce nuts within 3–4 years.

CARE AND MAINTENANCE

Many hazels have bush form unless they are kept pruned to tree shape. Remove any dead branches. Hazels require cross-pollination.

Pests and diseases Filbert blight may affect trees in some areas, so choose a resistant variety.

HARVEST

When nuts are ready for harvest they drop from the tree. If squirrels or other pests start to steal nuts, harvest the nuts early.

HAZEL VARIETIES

American Hazelnut (Corylus americana) A hardy bush that produces small fine-tasting nuts.

Barcelona (Corylus avellana) A reliable producer that is resistant to filbert blight.

FILBERT VARIETIES

Filazels (Corylus cornuta x C. avellana) Earliest-ripening type of filbert.

Giant Filbert (Corylus maxima) Produces wonderful tasting nuts on a 20ft/6m high tree.

CHESTNUTS

Chestnut trees produce tasty nuts that are good roasted, or made into soup. Try to plant only varieties resistant to chestnut blight.

American Chestnut (Castanea dentata) May be susceptible to blight.

Chinese Chestnut (Castanea mollissima) Reaching to 25ft/7.6m and is resistant to blight.

Sweet Chestnut/European Chestnut (Castanea dentata) This variety has been in cultivation for over 2000 years.

Grown as an informal hedge or small tree, hazelnuts produce a reliable harvest. Their catkins provide welcome color and decoration in late winter.

Blueberries *Vaccinium* spp.

Plant type Deciduous bush

Nutrition Excellent source of phytochemicals. Good source of vitamin C. Source of iron and fiber.

Uses Berries are used fresh or frozen, made into jellies, jams, or preserves. They are a fine addition to many baked goods.

SITE AND SOIL

Blueberries prefer acidic soils (pH 4.0–5.0) that are very moist. They are often found growing wild along the edges of rivers or lakes. Although they are self-fertile, blueberries produce better when more than one variety is grown. They are very cold hardy and will tolerate a wide range of climates. Highbush varieties range in height from 18in/45cm to 6ft/1.8m. Lowbush varieties are 6in/15cm to 18in/45cm.

CARE AND MAINTENANCE

During the first year after planting, remove all flowers to encourage bushes to establish quickly. Do not overfertilize blueberries. Prune bushes when planting. Remove any dead wood in winter. Highbush blueberries should be pruned to remove older wood and branches that intertwine. Bushes that are crowded produce a smaller crop. Mulch well to conserve water. If you irrigate blueberries, be aware that they tolerate lime-free water only.

Pests and diseases Yellow leaves are often caused by iron deficiency or a soil pH that is too high. Use floating row covers over lowbush varieties and nets over taller varieties to protect the fruits from attack by birds.

HARVEST

Pick the berries when they are fully ripe and use or preserve them immediately.

'Northland' blueberries are high in sugar, making them excellent for jellies, jams, and baking. The berries are ready for harvest when they turn dark blue.

EARLY VARIETIES

Patriot Cold hardy variety that bears large fruits.

St. Cloud Bush of about 24in/60cm.

MID-SEASON VARIETIES

Blue Ray Hardy variety with large berries.

Northland Fairly hardy with medium berries.

LATE VARIETIES

Jersey Easy-to-grow variety.

OTHER VARIETIES

Lingonberries (Vaccinium vitis-idaea)

Low-growing type of blueberry. The small red berries taste deliciously tart and may be eaten fresh or used to make a jam or a sauce for venison.

Cranberries *Vaccinium macrocarpon*

Plant type Evergreen bush

Nutrition Significant source of vitamin C.
Source of fiber.

Uses Berries used in desserts and for sauces.

SITE AND SOIL

Cranberries prefer wet and boggy acidic soils, so choose a wet site that is enriched with plenty of acidic compost. Cranberries are self-fertile and range in size from 6in/15cm to 24in/60cm.

CARE AND MAINTENANCE

Weed cranberries well in the spring. Apply a heavy mulch to preserve moisture. If you live in a dry climate, set up a drip irrigation system fitted with a timer for good results. Like blueberries, cranberries dislike alkaline tap water.

PESTS AND DISEASES

Pests and diseases A high pH causes most problems with cranberries.

HARVEST

Pick berries before the first frost or their flavor will be affected. Cranberries store extremely well by freezing or making into jams and jellies.

VARIETIES

Edible cranberries should not be confused with American (highbush) cranberries *(Viburnum trilobum)* which are good for ornamental purposes or as wildlife feed.

Pilgrim A fast-growing bush with tasty berries – a reliable producer.

Stevens Tolerates almost any high acid site with sufficient irrigation.

True Bog Cranberries A tasty, hardy species.

A close relative of blueberries, cranberries are grown for their firm red berries, which are a significant source of vitamin C.

HEATH
ERICACEAE

Strawberries *Fragaria* spp.

Plant type Perennial

Nutrition Excellent source of phytochemicals and vitamin C. Source of calcium, iron, fiber, and potassium.

Uses Eaten fresh and used in desserts.

SITE AND SOIL

Strawberries will grow in a wide variety of climates and can be grown under glass (with heat) in winter. They need a very rich soil to fruit well. Cultivated types are significantly larger and produce many runners. The cultivated varieties are purchased as plants, not seeds, and are asexually propagated by collecting and replanting runners.

CARE AND MAINTENANCE

The plants have shallow roots which makes weeding difficult. Mulch them with a thick layer of straw to suppress weeds and space the plants widely to ease weeding. Reapply straw mulch as necessary throughout the season. It may be helpful to run over the straw with a lawnmower before mulching. Runners will drain the plant's energy away from producing fruits. Root some runners for future use in other beds and remove the rest. Remove debris from the bed in the fall to discourage diseases.

Pests and diseases Use floating row covers to protect the crop from birds. Molds can be a problem, so remove any rotting fruit immediately.

HARVEST

Some varieties bear early, others bear late, and alpine and everbearing strawberries bear from early summer through to early fall. Handpick the fruits as they ripen and use immediately. They do not store well unless made into jams, jellies, preserves, or syrups.

One of the most nutritious fruits, packed with beneficial phytochemicals, strawberries can be grown in containers where space is limited.

ALPINE STRAWBERRY VARIETIES

The dainty-looking Alpine strawberries are grown from seed. Their small, delicious fruits look similar to wild strawberries.

Alexandria The best red alpine strawberry.

Rügen Produces large berries.

Yellow Fruited Produces a fruit with good taste. Does not attract birds like red varieties.

SEASONAL VARIETIES

Allstar Mid-season variety with very large sweet berries. Disease resistant.

Earlyglow Early disease-resistant variety.

Sparkle Late variety that is ideal for jam-making and freezing.

Tristar A tasty, everbearing strawberry, that starts fruits in early summer (or earlier in warm climates) and continues to produce fruit into fall.

ROSE
ROSACEAE

261

Raspberries *Rubus idaeus*

Plant type Deciduous bush

Nutrition Excellent source of vitamin C and phytochemicals. Source of calcium, iron, fiber, and potassium.

Uses Eaten fresh or used in desserts.

SITE AND SOIL

Raspberries will grow well in any moist soil that is neutral to slightly acidic in pH. Raspberries are very hardy and tolerate a wide range of climates. They are self-fertile and grow on canes that reach up to 4ft/1.2m in height.

CARE AND MAINTENANCE

Weeding and mulching in the spring will help to produce a large crop. Generally raspberries need little care except for pruning. There are two basic types: red (which includes yellow) and black. Summer-bearing raspberries produce fruit on two-year-old canes. Canes that are three years and older should be removed. Everbearing raspberries fruit in spring on two-year-old canes and bear fruits again in fall on the tips of canes grown during that summer.

Pests and diseases Birds are the only major pest affecting raspberries. If they are a problem, cover the plants with nets. Remove mulch in winter to discourage infestation by pests. If a virus affects your plants, replace them with a resistant variety in a new location.

HARVEST

If the fruit does not come off easily, it is not ready to be picked. Handpick the raspberries carefully and gently, as any pressure will damage the fruit. Harvest when it is cool and not wet. Raspberries freeze well, but are at their best when freshly picked.

To prolong the soft fruit season, plant a variety such as 'Heritage' (above) which produces two crops of fruit, one in early summer and another in the fall.

VARIETIES

Fall Gold Everbearing variety with yellow fruits.

Heritage Produces an early summer crop and a heavier crop from early to late fall.

Latham A winter hardy variety.

Taylor A late season variety grown for its taste.

HYBRID BERRIES

Black Caps/Munger Black Raspberry Large berries held on purple canes. Very hardy.

Boysenberry Similar to blackberry in flavor.

Loganberry A raspberry–blackberry cross.

Tayberry This is a cross between a raspberry and the blackberry 'Aurora'.

Thimbleberry Also known as a wild raspberry. Very hardy with a delicate flavor.

Blackberries *Rubus fruticosus*

Plant type Deciduous bush or vine

Nutrition Excellent source of phytochemicals. Source of calcium, iron, and fiber.

Uses Eaten fresh or cooked with apples for flavor and color.

SITE AND SOIL

Blackberries prefer very rich moist soils. They are hardy in all but the coldest locations. Check that the variety you choose is hardy in your climate; those that grow best in very cold climates often do not fruit well. They are self-fertile. Choose a site with care because some varieties can be invasive.

CARE AND MAINTENANCE

In spring, weed and mulch the plants. Generally blackberries need little care except for pruning. Bush and vine types should be pruned like black raspberries. Blackberries bear on two-year old canes, just like raspberries. Head back canes (to about 5in/13cm) the first summer after planting to encourage formation of laterals.

Pests and diseases Blackberries are not generally affected by pests or diseases. Birds do not usually attack the crop.

HARVEST

Blackberries should only be harvested when they are so ripe that they fall off the plant at the gentlest touch. The fruits spoil quickly and should be used immediately.

THORNLESS VARIETIES

These are not as hardy as thorned varieties.

Hull Blackberry Bears large sweet fruits.

Kiowa Produces huge fruit and needs no support.

Oregon Thornless Noted for its decorative foliage.

Blackberries can be very thorny (as is 'Loch Ness', right), and this makes their cultivation a prickly and often painful task. Instead, opt for a thornless variety to make harvesting easier.

ROSE
ROSACEAE

Gooseberries *Ribes uva-crispa* var. *reclinatum*

Plant type Deciduous bush
Nutrition Source of vitamins A and C, calcium, phosphorus, and iron.
Uses The dessert varieties are wonderful fresh; the small green varieties are most often made into jam and preserves.

SITE AND SOIL

Gooseberries are very cold hardy and tolerate a wide range of soils, except for sandy dry soils. They thrive in cool climates. Gooseberry bushes reach up to 4ft/1.2m; they are self-fertile.

CARE AND MAINTENANCE

Weed and mulch in spring; prune the bushes in winter. Although gooseberries are often grown as multi-stemmed bushes, they produce better when pruned to a single stem. They can also be trained as a cordon. Stems will bear for about five years, after which they should be removed. New shoots will quickly replace them. Pruning can also be used to open up the bush; this makes it easier to pick the fruits from between the thorns.

Pests and diseases Birds may attack ripe fruit. Gooseberries are prone to molds and mildews in humid areas. Prune to ensure good air circulation. White pine blister rust may affect plants.

HARVEST

Handpick as the fruits approach ripeness for use in jams and preserves; harvest ripe fruits for eating fresh. Protect your hands with lightweight gloves.

VARIETIES

Achilles Noted for its delicious red fruits.
Oregon Champion Medium to large pale berries.
Pickswell Has large light green berries that turn pink when fully ripe.
Poorman An old American variety.

'Oregon Champion' gooseberries (left) are grown for their sweet, juicy fruits, which are eaten fresh and can also be cooked in pies or made into jams, jellies, and preserves.

SAXIFRAGE
SAXIFRAGACEAE

Currants *Ribes* spp.

Plant type Deciduous bush

Nutrition Source of vitamins A, B1, B2, B3, and C, calcium, phosphorus, and iron.

Uses The fruits are tart and so are often not eaten fresh. They are usually made into jelly, jam, preserves, and juices, or used in cooking.

SITE AND SOIL

Currants are very cold tolerant and grow best in cool soils. Blackcurrants like rich soil with plenty of compost worked in. Currants generally do not require rich soil. Currants are self-fertile and form a 4–7ft/1.2–2m tall bush.

CARE AND MAINTENANCE

Weed and mulch in spring. Use a mulch around the plant to keep the soil cool too. Prune in winter. Although it is only necessary to prune out dead wood, currants are often growns as cordons.

Pests and diseases Birds are a major pest, eating the redcurrants as soon as they are ripe. Molds and mildews may affect plants that have not been kept well pruned. Rust may also affect plants.

HARVEST

Handpick currants beginning in summer as they turn the appropriate color for that variety. The harvest season extends well into fall. Juicing is easy and a great way to store currants.

BLACKCURRANT VARIETIES

Consort Bears extra-sweet black fruits.

Coronet Resistant to white pine blister rust.

Crusader Exceptionally high in vitamin C.

RED- AND WHITE-CURRANT VARIETIES

Cherry Red Cold-hardy variety.

Red Lake Can be eaten fresh.

Whitecurrant Produces translucent fruits.

Blackcurrants demand a rich soil with plenty of compost worked in, but they will reward you with a heavy crop of fruits in late summer. 'Consort' is shown right.

Kiwi Fruits *Actinidia deliciosa*

Plant type Deciduous vine
Nutrition Excellent source of vitamin C. Significant source of vitamin E. Source of vitamin A, calcium, iron, potassium, and fiber.
Uses Eaten raw and used in desserts.

SITE AND SOIL

Kiwi fruits, also known as Chinese gooseberries, are only hardy in warm winter areas. Most varieties are not self-fertile; one male plant must be planted along with as many females as are desired. They require full sun and fertile soil to

Hairy outer skins protect the tasty lime-green flesh and slender black seeds of kiwi fruits. The fruits are ripe if they dent slightly when pressed gently.

crop heavily. The vines reach about 25ft/7.5m in length and need to be supported with trellis.

CARE AND MAINTENANCE

Kiwis grow quickly and need to be pruned back hard in late winter or early spring. It may be necessary to tie the vines to the trellis. Head back the sideshoots in summer and fall, to control the size of the vine and to encourage the plant to devote energy to ripening fruit. Kiwi fruits will probably need watering during dry periods in the summer months.
Pests and diseases Kiwi fruits are generally not affected by pests or diseases.

HARVEST

In fall, harvest the fruits before first frost. If picked before fully ripe, they will keep for two to three months in the refrigerator or any cool dry location – put them on the counter to soften before use.

ARGUTA/TARA VINE VARIETIES

Arguta kiwis have hairless skins; they are hardy in moderately cold climates.
Ananasnaja May produce up to 100lbs/45kg of fruit on each vine under optimal conditions.

KIWI FRUIT VARIETIES

Hayward A popular variety.
Saanichton A slightly more hardy variety.

KOLOMIKTA VARIETIES

Kolomikta kiwis are quite cold hardy and the males have foliage tinted from green to pink to white. Kolomiktas grow better in partial shade than in direct sunlight in warmer climates.
September Sun A female variety that has attractive colored foliage similar to that of male kolomiktas.

Grapes *Vitis vinifera*

Plant type Deciduous vine

Nutrition Grapes are a significant source of vitamin C. Souce of vitamin A, calcium, and iron. Raisins are a significant source of vitamin B6, iron, phosphorus, magnesium, copper. Source of calcium, potassium, and fiber.

Uses Wine grapes are mostly used for wine. Table grapes are eaten fresh, juiced or used in cooking. Species grapes are generally sour and are made into jellies, jams, and preserves.

'Flame' (left) and 'Thompson Seedless' (right) are both good table grapes. Grapes can be eaten fresh, made into wine, or dried for use as raisins.

SITE AND SOIL

Grapes will grow in a wide variety of soils. Table and species grapes produce juicier grapes in rich soils; wine grapes dislike rich soils. The vines need to be pruned and trained on a support or wall. If not pruned, grape vines tend to grow very long and produce small hard berries that never ripen. Species grapes often bear small edible grapes but production is better with pruning.

CARE AND MAINTENANCE

Train vines to ensure good air circulation, which discourages molds and diseases, and to keep the fruits off the ground. Grapes are produced on two-year-old sideshoots. Prune back the shoots to about eight buds in the spring. After fruiting the sideshoot is pruned back (in the next spring) leaving a stub with a bud to produce a shoot for the following year's crop.

Pests and diseases Viruses have no cure. Molds and mildews may be a problem in humid areas. Watch for Japanese beetles, and bird, gopher, and deer damage.

HARVEST

Using pruners, cut the bunches of fruit when ripe. Most varieties ripen all at once.

WINE GRAPE VARIETIES

In warm locations, grow Chardonnay, Cabernet, or Pinot Noir. In cool climates, choose Frontenac.

TABLE GRAPE VARIETIES

Edelweiss A cold-hardy variety that makes excellent juice, and even a decent white wine.

Flame A seedless variety. Good for home gardens.

King of the North One of the most hardy grapes.

Thompson Seedless A grape for warmer areas.

SPECIES GRAPE VARIETIES

Many species grapes do not produce edible fruit but these recommendations produce useful grapes. They usually produce fruit over a long period.

Concord (Vitis labrusca) Tasty and easy to grow.

GRAPE
VITACEAE

Herb Selection

Dill (Anethum graveolens) Annual, full sun, 36in/90cm tall. Sow directly with 4in/10cm spacing, in spring. An herb used in cooking and for flavoring foods. Use both seeds and greens.

Tarragon (Artemisia dracunculus) Perennial, full sun, 18in/45cm tall, hardy to 15°F/–9°C. Transplant (6in/15cm spacing) in spring. The dried leaves are used in sauces or to flavor meat.

Caraway (Carum carvi) Biennial, full sun, 24in/60cm tall, hardy to 20°F/–7°C. Transplant (1in/2.5cm spacing) in spring. The seeds (which only form in the second year) are used in baking and to flavor stews. The leaves may be added to salads or chopped into soups.

Cilantro/Coriander (Coriandrum sativum) Annual, full sun (partial sun in very warm climates), 12–18in/30–45cm tall. Sow directly with 3in/8cm spacing in spring. The greens are called cilantro and are very often used in Mexican cuisine. The seeds, which are both sweet and spicy, are used in sausages, chutneys, and baking.

Florence fennel/Sweet fennel (Foeniculum vulgare var. dulce) Perennial, full sun, 24–36in/60–90cm tall, hardy to 10°F/–12°C. Sow directly or transplant (5in/13cm spacing), in spring. Fennel is often grown as an annual in cold climates for its feathery leaves, which are used for flavoring. Florence fennel is grown as a herb and as a vegetable. The leaf stems (bulb) can be eaten raw or cooked.

Bay (Laurus nobilis) Tree, full sun, hardy to 10°F/–12°C. Bay trees may be grown in pots and brought indoors in winter in cold climates. The leaves are used to flavor soups and sauces.

Lavender (Lavandula angustifolia) Perennial, full sun to partial shade, 18in/45cm tall, transplant (1in/2.5cm spacing) in late spring, hardy to –5°F/–20°C. Lavender flowers are added to jams, breads, and vinegars. The scent is popular in soaps and potpourri sachets.

German chamomile/Scented mayweed (Matricaria recutita) Annual, full sun, 6–30in/15–75cm tall, transplant (6in/15cm spacing) in spring. Chamomile is generally used as an infusion to aid insomnia and digestion. Leaves have antiseptic qualities.

Mint (Mentha spp.) Perennial, full sun, 12–36in/30–90cm tall, hardy to 0°F/–18°C. Transplant seedlings (12in/30cm spacing) in spring or fall. Mints are best propagated by cuttings that are rooted in the spring or fall, or by division of an

The aromatic leaves of sweet green basil make them a valuable addition in cooking. Basil is ideal for growing in pots on a kitchen windowsill.

existing plant. Mint can be invasive, so consider growing it in a pot. Mint leaves are used as flavoring in the kitchen. Be sure to pick leaves before the plant goes to flower.

Basil (Ocimum basilicum) Annual, full sun, 6–24in/15–60cm tall. Sow directly or transplant with 4–8in/10–20cm spacing, after last frost. Basil is used for flavoring vegetables and other foods in the kitchen. Pesto is a sauce made from basil and other ingredients and is used in Italian cuisine.

Marjoram (Origanum majorana) Perennial grown as annual, full sun, 12–24in/30–60cm tall. Sow directly or transplant with 6in/15cm spacing, in late spring. The flavor of marjoram is similar to oregano, and is used for flavoring in the kitchen.

Greek Oregano (Origanum vulgare var. hirtum)/Mexican Oregano (Lippia graveolens) Perennial, full sun, 1–6in/2.5–15cm tall, cold hardy to 9°F/–13°C (Greek), 10°F/–12°C (Mexican). Mexican can be grown as an annual. Transplant seedlings with 1–2in/2.5–5cm spacing, in late spring. Greens used in Italian cooking.

Parsley (Petroselinum crispum) Biennial, full sun, 15–24in/35–60cm. Parsley takes four to six weeks to germinate. Soak parsley seeds in warm water for several hours before sowing indoors in late winter. Transplant (6in/15cm spacing) in spring. Pinch out flowers on parsley overwintered outside. Grow in pots indoors during the winter for a fresh supply. Parsley is also decorative in the ornamental bed. The flat leaf variety has more nutrition and flavor than the curly leaf variety.

Rosemary (Rosmarinus officinalis) Perennial, full sun, 1–4ft/12–1.2m tall, the tender sorts hardy only to 20°F/–7°C, hardier ones to 10°F/–12°C. Transplant with 18in/45cm spacing, after last frost. The evergreen foliage is used to flavor meat.

A vigorous grower that can overtake a bed if not restrained, Moroccan spearmint produces lilac, white, or pink flowers in summer.

Its upright or trailing spikes of pale blue or pink flowers are a valuable addition to flowerbeds.

Sage (Salvia officinalis) Perennial, full sun or part shade, 12–36in/30–90cm tall, hardy to 5°F/–15°C. Transplant (12in/30cm spacing) in spring. Sage is used to flavor meats and sauces, and is popular in stuffing.

Stevia (Stevia rebaudiana) Shrub, partial shade in warm climates, 1–2in/2.5–5cm tall, transplant (1in/2.5cm spacing) in spring, hardy to 32°F/0°C. Stevia is propagated by root cuttings. Its leaves are extremely sweet yet contain almost no calories. Dry the leaves and grind them for use as a sugar replacement.

Thyme (Thymus vulgaris) Perennial, full sun to partial shade, 12in/30cm tall, hardy to 20°F/–7°C. Transplant (6in/15cm spacing) after last frost. Greens used in French and Italian cooking to flavor soups and sauces.

APPENDIX I: TOOLS

BASIC TOOLCARE

It is important to keep your gardening tools and equipment in the best possible condition, so that they perform the task required and remain serviceable for a long time. Tools should be cleaned immediately after use and put away in a clean, dry storage area. More gardening tools are damaged by rain than by usage.

Use a stiff brush to remove any dirt and residue that has become attached, then wipe the tool dry with a soft cloth or rag. Store the tool away from moisture to reduce any chance of it rusting. Try to hang your tools on wall hooks, especially if your shed is prone to damp during the winter. Have a place for every tool and put each one away after use. Tools with wooden handles benefit from a seasonal coating of preserving oil, such as linseed oil. This prevents the wood from becoming too dry and brittle.

Any tools that have come into contact with diseased plant material need to be cleaned thoroughly to avoid spreading infection to other plants. A dip in a bleach/water solution will usually suffice. Sterilize your seed-starting trays and supplies before use in spring by washing them in hot, soapy water.

SHARPENING

Many tools have cutting blades which need to be sharpened regularly for them to make good,

Grasscare tools Rakes and scythes are useful for harvesting grains and hay.

clean cuts (see pruning advice on pp. 164–7). Blunt or rusted blades can tear or snag a plant stem, leaving a wound that will be prone to infection.

If you sharpen your cutting tools regularly with a file or whetstone, they will always be a joy to use. However, if you let the blades become hopelessly dull, they will probably need to be sent to a professional sharpening service.

Gardener's basics A spade, fork, rake, hoe, and shovel form the backbone of a gardener's tool kit.

LONG-HANDLED TOOLS

Spade For digging, chopping roots, prying out rocks, dividing perennials, and cutting straight edges. You are likely to use a spade more than any other garden tool, so be sure to choose one that suits your height and strength. The standard size for

Hoeing tools *These long-handled tools are used to dislodge weeds easily when standing.*

spades is about 38in/95cm, but tall gardeners should opt for a 43in/107cm long model. Shorter or less strong gardeners may consider a "border" spade, which has a small head. A companion border fork is also available.

Many gardeners prefer a stainless steel head over traditional hand forged steel because wet soil does not stick to the surface. Although their price may be tempting, avoid buying cheap ones as they are made of thin steel that bends and breaks easily.

Fork For loosening subsoil and lifting root crops, such as potatoes and parsnips. A companion to the spade, a fork cuts into soil more easily. The strong tines can be used to mix compost and additives into the soil. The North American variety has broad, flat tines and is better for lifting potatoes. The English version has thin, square tines and is a general-purpose tool. Choose a fork that suits your height and strength; see the sizes recommended above for spades. A fork made of hand forged steel is best because it is strong and unlikely to bend in normal usage.

Broadfork For single digging and aerating the soil. The broadfork is a two-handled, deep cultivation tool. It is used to renovate existing beds that are starting to show signs of compaction. Working from the edges of the bed, the long tines are driven deep into the soil, right through the surface of the bed. The long handles enable even small gardeners to use their weight to loosen the soil. The purpose is not to turn the soil, but just

to loosen it. Work your way across the bed, then finish it as described in Chapter 4 (see Renovating existing beds, pp. 132–3).

Garden rake For smoothing the soil, working in compost, and removing rocks and debris from beds. The rake is also useful for covering seeds with soil and for working broadcast seeds into the top layer of the bed. Using the back of the rake, you can create a fine, level tilth. Choose a forged steel rake with twelve tines.

Lawn rake For removing leaves from the lawn. A spring-tine rake has

flexible metal tines; a fan rake has stiff bamboo tines.

Round nose long-handled shovel For digging in heavy or rocky soil. This shovel is quite well suited to digging deep round holes for transplanted trees and bushes. Choose a model with a heavy steel head and a long handle. The typical overall length is about 5ft/1.5m.

Shovel For scooping up compost or other material and transferring them to another location. It is not used for digging. A shovel is larger than a garden spade and has angled sides that contain the material on the blade.

Three-tine cultivator or claw hoe For dislodging large weeds and loosening the surface of the soil.

Collinear hoe For cutting off weeds just below the surface (as illustrated on p. 146). It is used by holding its long handle in both hands with your thumbs pointing upward. Your back should be comfortably straight and the blade of the hoe should be parallel to the ground.

HANDTOOLS

Trowel/hand fork For working in garden beds. These are simply smaller versions of shovels and forks.

Three-tine cultivator For delicate weeding in beds.

Bricklayer's trowel For transplanting seedlings into the soil. Hold the tool with the blade facing down and your thumb facing up. Drive the trowel into the soil and pull it towards you, leaving a hole for a soil block. Use the trowel to lift a soil block out of the tray and lower it into the hole.

CUTTING TOOLS

Pruning shears For cutting back woody growth and removing dead, diseased, or damaged branches. Do not skimp on getting good pruners; left-handed versions are available. Do not try to cut branches that are too large for the bite of the tool, as it will damage the pruners.

Pruning saw For removing branches and cutting down trees. A "turbo saw" is an indispensable cutting tool.

Garden knife A simple pocket knife is very useful if kept sharp. Use a budding knife for grafting. The hooked end of an asparagus knife is used for cutting off asparagus spears below the soil level.

Hedge trimmers For trimming and shaping hedges. Manual trimmers are safer and easier to use than the electric models. Be sure to sharpen them regularly.

Half-moon edger For cutting a straight edge where the bed meets the sod.

Long-handled edger For cutting grass that grows over the edge of a bed. These look like hedge trimmers with long handles. Keeping the edges of the beds trimmed makes the beds look tidy.

OTHER EQUIPMENT

Wheelbarrow For mixing soil with compost when planting trees, and transporting soil and sundries around the garden. The garden cart suits large gardens and plots, and should be fitted with inflatable tires. It does not tip like a wheelbarrow when carrying very heavy loads.

Still going strong *Old farming tools will last a lifetime if they receive proper care.*

Handtools Keep cutting tools sharp and sterilize them after cutting diseased material.

Buckets and baskets For collecting produce in your garden. Choose rubber buckets, as metal ones tend to rust and plastic ones break easily. Baskets that attach to your belt are useful when picking small fruits.

String trimmer For edging grass around beds and paving, and for removing weeds between pavers and around tree trunks. Take care not to girdle trees by hitting their bark with the string trimmer; keep the exposed nylon line facing away from the tree. Wear protective goggles to shield your eyes from debris thrown up by the trimmer.

WATERING EQUIPMENT

Watering can A well-balanced watering can is indispensable in the garden. A removable brass rose allows you to water newly planted seedlings without causing erosion.

Garden hose Choose a good quality hose that is resistant to kinks and has heavy brass fittings. The most useful lengths of hose are 50ft/15m and 100ft/30m.

Sprinkler For irrigating newly seeded lawns or large green manure beds. Both racheting types and oscillating ones are common.

Watering wand For watering container plants, hanging baskets, window troughs, and beds. The wand attaches to a hose and has a shut-off control fitted on the handle.

It allows you to water plants in a bed without wetting the foliage.

Soaker hose For delivering water to the roots of plants without wetting the foliage. Water is released slowly so that it seeps into the ground instead of forming puddles on the surface of the soil. Choose a high-quality soaker model as cheap ones form kinks and clog up easily. Drip irrigation tape is a flattened tube with precise, evenly spaced holes. It works like a soaker hose, but without clogging. Since dirt particles can ruin a soaker hose, filter the water with a 20 micron filter beforehand. (See pp. 144–5.)

Watering tools Choose the method of applying water that best suits the site and the plants' needs.

APPENDIX II: PRESERVING

PRESERVING PRODUCE

Many fruits and vegetables are only available for a short time during the growing season, but with proper storage and harvest extension techniques, they can be made available throughout the year. It is best to store food by methods that retain the maximum amount of vitamins, minerals, phytochemicals, and other nutrients. Canning and freezing are the most common methods of preservation used today, although traditional techniques are experiencing a revival because they preserve nutrients more efficiently and generally use less energy to preserve.

WHY FOOD SPOILS

Fruits and vegetables spoil because of bacterial action. Bacteria, yeast, and molds are everywhere. Unlike canning and freezing, traditional preserving methods, such as lactic fermentation, do not necessarily kill bacteria; they simply prevent them from multiplying by slowing down or stopping their growth. For example, pickling creates an acidic environment that prevents the growth and spread of microorganisms.

CHOOSING A STORAGE METHOD

First consider the fruit or vegetable that you wish to store and your intended use of the food. Before the invention of canning and freezing, root cellaring, drying, and lactic fermentation were the most common

Capturing the taste Glass jars with tightly sealed lids are ideal for pickling and preserving foods.

methods of storage. Everything that could be kept fresh in a cool, moist place, such as a root cellar, was stored that way. However, some fruits and vegetables do not store for long periods of time by this method. Fruits keep particularly well by drying and vegetables tend to store well by lactic fermentation. Other methods of live storage are less useful because they alter the flavor significantly.

CANNING AND FREEZING

Both canning and freezing are forms of dead storage (see *Keeping Food Fresh* by The Gardeners and Farmers of Terre Vivante). Canning requires lots of heat to process foods over long periods of time, killing bacteria and molds that cause food to spoil.

During the heating process, many vitamins are destroyed and phytochemicals are often broken down. Freezing, like canning, kills or slows the growth of bacteria and molds. It requires significant energy too, from the time of storage until the time of usage. With most fruits and vegetables, the vitamin content decreases the longer the food is frozen. However, canning and freezing remain good methods of preservation for some fruits and vegetables. Frozen peas, for example, retain almost all their nutritive value.

LIVE STORAGE

Preserving by methods of live storage is generally preferred

Clear effect *Flavored oils make attractive ornaments when stored in colored or shaped glass bottles.*

because more phytochemicals and vitamins are retained. One method of live storage is to leave the vegetable in the garden and harvest it when needed. Some vegetables can be harvested throughout the winter by practicing forms of harvest extension (see pp. 90–2).

There are many traditional forms of live storage. Very often the method of preservation affects the flavor of the food; for example, cabbage is made into *sauerkraut*. Sometimes the nutritional value of crops actually increases during live storage, such as winter squash and pumpkins, stored in a root cellar.

ROOT CELLARING

This is the process of keeping fruits and vegetables fresh in a cool, moist place. In areas where winter temperatures are near or below freezing, a root cellar can be built to preserve food. The cellar can be as simple as a container of vegetables partially buried in the ground, that can be covered with soil and insulating hay or straw, or it can be a protected basement window well. A more formal root cellar resembles a small room below ground level. It is built inside or outside the home and fitted with insulation and ventilation.

The goal of a root cellar is to keep food between 32°F/0°C and 40°F/5°C with very high humidity (80–90 per cent). Failure to achieve high humidity can result in evaporation that causes food to shrivel and spoil. Molds can be a problem in high humidity, so make

sure there is good ventilation in the cellar. The old adage about one rotten apple spoiling the barrel holds true. Remove immediately any foods that start to spoil. Vegetables and fruits should be stored apart, as should different fruits. Generally, different vegetables can be stored in the same container without causing any problems.

BUILDING A ROOT CELLAR

A basement window well can become a simple, small root cellar. Place a heavy screen over the top of the window well – ¼in/0.5cm wire mesh works well. The screen will keep out mice and other pests. On top of the screen, place a few boards for support and a hay bale.

The bale can be adjusted to let in cold air or to cover the window well completely in extremely cold weather. Place the food to be preserved in the window well from inside the house, and add a thermometer to monitor temperature. The window can be opened and closed as necessary to keep the food from freezing.

If your home has an outdoor basement entrance with steps and a hatch, you have the makings of an inexpensive root cellar that preserves food extremely well. The steps even provide different temperature zones. You will probably need additional moisture in a root cellar of this size, so keep water-filled pans at the base of the steps to ensure proper humidity. The top steps are coolest

Layering beans For decorative effect, store dried beans in alternating layers of color.

because they are furthest from the warmth of the house and closest to the cold outdoors. The bottom steps are warmest because of heat leakage from the basement into the root cellar. Store root crops and other cold storage vegetables on the top steps, fruits on the middle steps, and squashes and melons on the bottom steps. Keep onions, garlic, and other vegetables that prefer dry conditions, in an unheated room.

A small room can be built against the north wall of the basement. The room should be well insulated and have a tight-fitting door. Make the floor from gravel, which should be moistened from time to time to keep humidity levels at 80–90 per cent. The room should have ventilation; a shaded window works well.

LACTIC FERMENTATION

The process of lactic fermentation has fallen out of favor; *sauerkraut* remains the only notable exception. Lactic fermentation preserves vegetables without heat or cold and retains their nutritional value. The process is simple but only works on vegetables.

Grate or slice vegetables into small pieces and season them with herbs before adding salt or a mild salt water solution. Without salt, the process will not work. The amount of salt added depends on the quantity of vegetables. Weigh the vegetables and add the salt at a rate of 1.5–2.0 per cent of the weight. Let the vegetables soak in their own juices (or brine solution if salt water was added). Microorganisms develop in the solution and convert the sugars in the vegetables into lactic acid. When the vegetables and solution become acidic enough, the bacteria that cause food to rot and spoil will be unable to survive. All the vegetables' nutrients are retained. If the preserved food is eaten without being cooked, the nutritional content will be close to that in fresh vegetables.

Canning jars can be used for this process. Allow 1–3 tablespoons of salt per 1qt/l jar. Leave the jars without their lids on in the kitchen for a week or so, covered with a cloth to keep out contaminants. Be sure the liquid stays above the level of the vegetables – evaporation may lower the level. Then cover the jars loosely with the lids and move them to a cool place like a root cellar. Tighten the lids after five weeks, when the gas given off during the fermentation process will have died down. Some cooks prefer to loosely fasten the lids for the first week of fermentation.

Vegetables preserved in this way are acidic and tend to be only palatable in small quantities unless they are prepared by cooking. They are a good supplement to vegetables stored in a root cellar. Many people choose to cook vegetables preserved in this way to reduce their acidity, but this destroys nutrients and affects texture. You can rinse the vegetables to reduce the salt content and acidity before eating. If water is added, be sure that it is not chlorinated, as this will prevent fermentation.

DRYING

Fruits and herbs can be stored effectively by drying, but most vegetables lose their flavor and vitamins when dried. Sun-dried tomatoes, dried beans, corn, and popcorn are notable exceptions. Drying in the kitchen can be easily accomplished in any climate. Fruits are simply placed on trays or non-metallic screens and left in a warm oven or a hot dry place until 80–90 per cent of the moisture is removed from the food. The lack of moisture stops the growth of bacteria that spoil food. As the fruit dries, the sugar becomes concentrated and the flavor is much sweeter. If the food is not dried in excessive heat, most of the nutrients are preserved. Food stored in this way can be kept for long periods of time without spoiling.

Some fruits may lose their color and nutrient content when dried. This is caused by the action of certain enzymes. In some fruits, blanching for a few minutes before drying destroys these enzymes and prevents color and vitamin loss. For specific details on drying fruits, consult a cookery book. Slice the fruit thinly, and peel the fruit if desired, before oven or sun drying.

SUN DRYING

Make a drying rack from a simple wooden frame covered with a non-metallic or fiberglass screen, or a very thin non-absorbent cloth. Allow plenty of air space between the sliced fruit when it is placed on the screen. Low humidity, air circulation, and hot days are the key to success when drying outdoors. Set up the screen on a stand that allows air to flow over and under the fruit. Make sure it cannot be upset by the wind or attacked by pests. Cover the tray with another screen or thin cloth to protect from insects.

OVEN DRYING

Preheat the oven to 150°F/66°C and use a good quality kitchen thermometer to ensure accuracy. Place the fruit on cookie sheets in a single layer, spaced widely apart and position them several rows apart on the oven shelves. Open the door to lower the oven temperature to 120°F/49°C. Rearrange the cookie sheets from

Drying onions Before storing onions, they must be cured for a few days after they are harvested.

top to bottom, turning them so that fruit dries evenly. Return the heat to about 140°F/60°C for half of the drying time. The overall drying time varies from 6 to 48 hours, depending on the size of the pieces and the fruit being dried.

Test the fruit for dryness by squeezing it to see whether any moisture is released. Fruit should appear leathery and vegetables should be dry and brittle. The weight of each piece will be reduced by one-half to two-thirds.

OTHER METHODS OF LIVE STORAGE

There are many other methods of preserving food that do not destroy nutrients. Most produce food that has distinctive flavor for specialized uses. An example of this is making grapes, blueberries, or apples into wine.

Preserving in vinegar or pickling
This is similar to lactic fermentation. Vegetables, such as cucumbers and beets, are stored in a vinegar/water solution to create an acidic environment to prevent food spoilage.

Preserving with sugar Jellies and jams are typical examples. Avoid adding more sugar than is necessary to preserve the food – this makes the jam sweeter and adds calories.

Preserving in oil Used to preserve garlic and other flavorful vegetables, the oil that remains is almost as valuable as the vegetable itself because of its flavor. Many vegetables and fruits can be kept in oil for a long time and used as needed in the kitchen. They make attractive ornaments when stored in colored or shaped glass bottles.

Preserving in alcohol A traditional method of preserving medicinal plants. Fruits are often made into wine or simply placed in alcohol to prevent them from spoiling.

SUPPLIERS

UNITED STATES

A. M. Leonard
241 Fox Drive
PO Box 816 Piqua
OH 45356
Tel: 800-433-0633
The best source of tools and
supplies for the gardener.

Bear Creek Nursery
PO Box 310 Northport
WA 99157
Tel: 509-732-6219
Suppliers of high-quality fruit trees
bushes, and brambles.

Bountiful Gardens
Ecology Action
5798 Ridgewood Road Willits
CA 95490
Tel: 707-459-6410
Promotes biointensive gardening.
Supplier of vegetable seeds.

DripCo Irrigation
4335 Eastlake Blvd Washoe Valley
NV 89704
Tel: 800-332-1570
Suppliers of inexpensive, easy-to-
assemble drip irrigation.

Fedco
PO Box 520 Waterville
ME 04903
Tel: 207-873-7333
Suppliers of a range of seeds,
bushes, and trees.

Gardeners' Supply Co.
128 Intervale Road Burlington
VT 05401
Tel: 800-863-1700
Suppliers of tools, greenhouses,
worm composters, and some
indoor seed-starting supplies.

Johnny's Selected Seeds
1 Foss Hill Road
RR1 Box 2580 Albion
ME 04910
Tel: 207-437-4301
Supplies seed and tools, including
seed blockers and collinear hoes.

Lehmans Hardware
One Lehman Circle
PO Box 41 Kidron
OH 44636
Tel: 888-438-5346
A good source of tools.

Nourse Farms
41 River Road South Deerfield
MA 01373
Tel: 413-665-2658
www.noursefarms.com
Source of quality fruit bushes.

Oikos Tree Crops
PO Box 19425 Kalamazoo
MI 49019
Tel: 616-624-6233
Extensive plant list.

Peaceful Valley Farm Supply
PO Box 2209 Grass Valley
CA 95945
Tel: 530-272-4769/888-894-1722
Stocks tools and soil amendments.

Prairie Nursery
PO Box 306 Westfield
WI 53964
Tel: 800-476-9453
www.prairienursery.com
Specialists in ecological gardening.

Raintree Nursery
391 Butts Road Morton
WA 98356
Tel: 360-496-6400
Source of fruit trees, berries, and
unusual edible plants.

Seed Savers Exchange
3076 North Winn Road Decorah
IA 52101
Tel: 319-382-5990
Extensive collection of heirloom
seeds. Seed Savers preserves rare
varieties of seeds.

Seeds of Change
PO Box 15700 Santa Fe
NM 87506
Tel: 800-762-7333
www.seedsofchange.com
Fully certified organic seed.

Seeds Blum
27 Idaho City Stage Road Boise
ID 83716
Tel: 800-528-3658
www.seedsblum.com

R. H. Shumways
PO Box 1 Graniteville
SC 29829
Tel: 803-663-9771
Supplier of open-pollinated seeds.

St. Lawrence Nurseries
325 State Hwy 345 Potsdam
NY 13676
Tel: 315-265-6739
A good source for fruit trees.

White Flower Farm
The Bulb Book
PO Box 50 Litchfield
CT 06759
Tel: 800-255-2852
www.whiteflowerfarm.com
Supplies bulbs, premium annuals,
perennials, shrubs, and bushes.

CANADA

Canadian Organic Growers, Inc.
Box 6408, Station J
Ottawa, ON K2A 2Y6
Tel: (705) 444-0923
Fax: (705) 444-0380
National organic organization.

Richters Herb Specialists
Goodwood, ON L0C 1A0
Tel: (905) 640-6677
e-mail: orderdesk@richters.com
www.richters.com
Major seed supplier.

Seeds of Diversity Canada
Box 36
Toronto, ON M4T 2L7
Tel: (905) 623-0353
Supplies organic seeds.

Attracting beneficials Leaving an
area unmowed provides a habitat
for beneficial insects and animals.

INDEX

ACKNOWLEDGMENTS

Many thanks to my family – especially David, Helen, Charlie, Stella and William – for their inspiration and support. I also wish to thank everyone at Frances Lincoln, especially Jo Christian, Jo Grey, and Carey Smith. Special thanks to my friends Stella, John, Lavinia, and Francis. For her work on the organization of the book in the early days, I'm indebted to Susan Berry. There is no way to express my gratitude to Steven Wooster for his spectacular photography. I also thank John Ferguson for introducing me to Frances Lincoln. David deserves so much appreciation for being my own personal horticultural expert in his proofreading of the 110,000 word manuscript. And finally I'd like to thank everyone who allowed photos to be taken in their gardens.

Hardiness Across Canada

Plants that survive winters are called hardy, while those that succumb to cold weather are called tender. The nine Canadian hardiness zones define the areas in which a plant is likely to be hardy based partly on minimum winter temperatures. Each zone can grow plants from lower numbered zones. For example, if you live in zone 4 you can include plants from zones 3, 2, and 1 in your garden. The zones are only a guide, however. Within each zone are microclimates, individual pockets that may be warmer or colder than the surrounding region. To find out which zone your garden is in, talk to experts at local garden centers.